THE DEVELOPMENT OF TRAFFIC LIABILITY

Rail and road accidents are examples of new sources of harm, particularly personal injury, which arose almost simultaneously across Western Europe. The area of rail accidents provides early examples of a move away from fault liability in certain countries, but not in others. Although statutory regulation and extra-statutory standards form part of the context of liability, private law actions for damages and the plasticity of fault ideas remain central to the law's response. Insurance determines the relative importance of private law actions. Traffic liability is a field in which different solutions have been developed by different legal systems. For example, France developed strict liability in the 1920s and 1930s, and no-fault liability in 1985, English law has remained wedded to fault. The stability of each legal solution suggests that the background insurance position has been settled in the different countries, albeit in differing ways.

WOLFGANG ERNST is Chair of Roman Law and Private Law at the University of Zurich Faculty of Law.

COMPARATIVE STUDIES IN THE DEVELOPMENT OF THE LAW OF TORTS IN EUROPE

Series editors
John Bell and David Ibbetson

THE DEVELOPMENT OF TRAFFIC LIABILITY

Volume 5

Edited by
WOLFGANG ERNST

CAMBRIDGE
UNIVERSITY PRESS

CAMBRIDGE
UNIVERSITY PRESS

University Printing House, Cambridge CB2 8BS, United Kingdom

Cambridge University Press is part of the University of Cambridge.

It furthers the University's mission by disseminating knowledge in the pursuit of education, learning and research at the highest international levels of excellence.

www.cambridge.org
Information on this title: www.cambridge.org/9780521199537

First published 2010
First paperback edition 2014

A catalogue record for this publication is available from the British Library

Library of Congress Cataloguing in Publication data
Ernst, Wolfgang.
The development of traffic liability / Wolfgang Ernst.
p. cm.
Includes index.
ISBN 978-0-521-19208-8 (hardback)
1. Liability for traffic accidents–Europe. I. Title.
KJC1706.E76 2010
346.40322–dc22 2009042809

ISBN 978-0-521-19208-8 Hardback
ISBN 978-1-107-47575-5 Paperback

Hardback only available as:
ISBN 978-0-521-19953-7 6-volume set

CONTENTS

SERIES EDITORS' PREFACE

The European Legal Development series has arisen from a project funded by the Arts & Humanities Research Council (AHRC) from January 2005 until February 2008.

The aim of the project as a whole was to examine the nature of legal development in Western Europe since 1850, focusing sharply on liability for fault. Behind this, there is a more abstract purpose: to attempt to cast some light on the factors that have influenced the way in which the law has changed over this period. Legal historians have looked at the general question, usually focusing on the rather facile distinction between the English Common law and continental European legal systems. Though rooted in the sources, these works have been marred by a somewhat unsophisticated methodology and an inevitably selective use of evidence. Comparative lawyers have developed far more sophisticated methodologies, but their theoretical perspectives have too often borne little relation to empirical data. Over the last twenty years, tort lawyers have looked at the same types of question, but their analysis has invariably been at a high level of generality and has rarely looked at the historical component. By bringing together experts with different disciplinary backgrounds – comparative lawyers and legal historians, all with an understanding of modern tort law in their own systems – and getting them to work collaboratively, we have aimed to produce a more nuanced comparative legal history, and one that is theoretically better informed.

The topic of legal development is broad; to make it manageable, we have undertaken a programme of work that has been built up from a number of case studies and has moved towards a more general analysis and conclusions. Although we have been concerned with the development of the law, and although many of those involved in the project have been lawyers, we have also been concerned to include and benefit from the insights of historians and scholars in other disciplines.

Liability for fault between 1850 to 2000 has been our major area of study. Around 1850, there were many similarities in approaches to liability for fault across the legal systems of Western Europe. But since then, there has been significant divergence. Our method has been first to chart the changes and then to seek the explanations for what happened. Although there have been many changes in tort and delict laws over the period, the idea of liability for fault remains central to private law approaches to the compensation of victims of harms caused by the actions of others.

As a first stage, the project worked on six case studies, which illustrate the general theme of liability for fault and its development within the period:

- legal doctrine
- medical liability
- product liability
- relations between neighbours
- technological change
- traffic and railways.

This research involved scholars from a range of countries, in particular England and Scotland, Spain, the Netherlands, Germany, France, Sweden, Austria and Italy. Each working group drew on the expertise of both senior and more junior scholars familiar with different European legal systems, and contained a mixture of comparative lawyers and legal historians.

A second stage has involved further groups examining a number of salient factors in legal development. The topics covered in this stage are:

- institutions and professions
- social and political ideas
- the economy (including the impact of insurance).

A final strand to the work is an overview book.

This book, edited by Wolfgang Ernst, provides us with a good example of the benefits of this approach. We gain a clear insight into the way in which established principles of tort engaged with the problems thrown up by new technologies in transportation, first in railways and then in relation to roads. Alongside these, we see the way in which regulatory law, private insurance and state-run compensation schemes developed to deal with the issues the law now confronted. Regulatory law and the requirements of private insurers dealt with many of the issues of preventing accidents. Improving the working conditions of railway employees or the conditions of the roads had very rapid and important impacts on the number of deaths and personal injuries. After some time, compensation systems outside tort offered remedies to many of the victims of accidents, whether these be the employees of railway companies (through workmen's compensation) or non-driver victims of road accidents. In this matrix of legal interventions, we can see that the place of tort law and of fault in particular changes. We become aware of its limitations. There is the question of how far the law of tort or delict changed in the period, and how far it was simply bypassed in order to prevent accidents and provide compensation. In addition, we see the very important place of insurance as a context for measuring whether tort law needed to change and whether it was adequate in channelling compensation. The factors for legal development identified in this book are ones that will be developed in later volumes.

Particularly in relation to this book, the editors are grateful for the contribution of Matthew Dyson, a PhD student on the AHRC project, who made a significant contribution to the formulation, discussion and execution of this part of the project, as well as reviewing the text of several contributions. His own work on the relationship of criminal and civil fault will be published separately and will complement significantly the understanding of the topics presented in this book.

John Bell and David Ibbetson

ABBREVIATIONS

AAMN	*Anales de la Academia Mattritense del Notariado*
AC	Aranzadi civil
AcP	*Archiv für die civilistische Praxis*
ADHGB	Allgemeines Deutsches Handelsgesetzbuch (General German Commercial Code)
ALR	Allgemeines Landrecht (Prussian Civil Code 1794)
BGB	Bürgerliches Gesetzbuch (German Civil Code)
BGH	Bundesgerichtshof
BGHZ	Entscheidungen des Bundesgerichtshofs in Zivilsachen
BOE	Boletín Oficial del Estado (Spain)
BW	Burgerlijk Wetboek (Dutch Civil Code)
CA	Court of Appeal
Cass. ch.	Cour de cassation, chambres réunies
Cass. civ.	Cour de cassation, chambre civile
Cass. com.	Cour de cassation, chambre commerciale
CC	Código Civil 1889 (Spanish Civil Code)
CCJC	Cuadernos Cívitas de Jurisprudencia Civil
CCm	Código de comercio
chr.	Chronique
CIV	Additional Convention to the International Convention on the Carriage of Passengers and Luggage by Rail (1973)
CJ	Chief Justice
concl.	Conclusions
COTIF	International Convention on Transport by Rail
CP	Código Penal
D.	Receuil Dalloz (France) / Decreto (Spain) / Digest of Justinian
DA	Damages Act (Sweden)
DAR	*Deutsches Autorecht*
DC	Recueil Dalloz critique
DP	Recueil Dalloz Périodique
Ds	Departementsserien
EC	European Community

EGBGB	Einführungsgesetz zum BGB
Engelhard and Van Maanen	E.F.D. Engelhard and G.E. van Maanen, *Aansprakelijkheid voor verkeersongevallen* (Nijmegen: Ars Aequi, 1998)
EVO	Eisenbahnverkehrsordnung (Railway Traffic Regulations)
EWCA Civ	England and Wales Court of Appeal, Civil Division
FED	Forsikrings- og Erstatningsretlig Domsamling (Denmark)
F. Reglero Campos, *Accidentes*	F. Reglero Campos, *Accidentes de Circulación. Responsabilidad Civil y Seguro*(Cizur Menor, Aranzadi, 2004)
HGB	Handelsgesetzbuch
HR	Hoge Raad
JC	*Jurisprudencia Criminal*
JCP	Juris-Classeur Périodique, la Semaine Juridique
JFT	*Tidskrift uitgiven av Juridske föreningen i Finland*
JUR	Jurisprudencia
JW	*Juristische Wochenschrift*
JZ	*Juristenzeitung*
KB	Koninklijk Besluit
LGDJ	Librarie générale de droit et de jurisprudence
LJ	Law Journal; Lord Justice
LOPJ	*Ley Orgánica della Procedura Judicial*
LOV	Lover (Norwegian laws)
LRCSCVM	*Ley de responsabilidad civil y seguro en la circulación de vehículos de motor*
MLR	Modern Law Review
MP	Member of Parliament
MRW	Motor- en Rijwielwet 1924
MvH	Magazijn van Handelsrecht
NJ	*Nederlandse Jurisprudentie*
NJA	*Nytt Juridiskt Arkiv*
NJB	*Nederlands Juristenblad*
NJF	*Nederlandse Jurisprudentie Feitenrechtspraak*
NJW	*Neue Juristische Wochenschrift*
NS	Nederlandse Spoorwegen
NTBR	*Nederlands Tijdschrift voor Burgerlijk Recht*
obs.	Observations
OLG	Oberlandesgerichtshof
PRA	Prussian Railway Act 1838
RD	Real Decreto
RDCirculación	*Revista de Derecho de la Circulación*
RDN	*Revista de Derecho Notarial*
RDP	*Revista de Derecho Privado*
RG	Rettens Gang (Norway)

RGAT	*Revue générale des assurances terrestres*
RGLJ	*Revista General de Legislación y Jurisprudencia*
RGZ	Reichsgerichts in Zivilsachen
RHPFIG	Reichshaftpflichtgesetz (Imperial Law on Liability)
RJ	Repertorio de Jurisprudencia
RJCA	Repertorio de Jurisprudencia Comunidades Autonomas
RRCSCVM	Reglamento sobre la Responsabilidad Civil y Seguro en la Circulación de Vehículos a Motor
Rt.	Norsk Rettstidende
RTD civ.	*Revue trimestrielle de droit civile*
S.	Recueil Sirey
SAN	Sentencia Audiencia Nationales
SAP	Sentencia Audiencia Provinciales
SOU	Statens Offentliga Utredningar
SOV	*seguro obligatorio de viajeros*
SSTS	Sentencias del Tribunal Supremo
Stb.	Staatsblad
STC	Sentenzias Tribunal Constituzional
STS	Sentencia del Tribunal Supremo
STSJ	Sentencias Tribunales Superiores de Justicia
StVG	Straßenverkehrsgesetz (Road Traffic Act) 1952
TC	Tribunal des Conflits
TDA	Traffic Damage Act (Sweden)
TPR	Tijdschrift voor privaatrecht
Trb.	Tractatenblad Trema
TS	Tribunal Supremo
VR	*Verkeersrecht*
W.	Weekblad van het Recht
WAM	Act on Liability Insurance of Motor Vehicles
wp	Working Paper
WPNR	*Weekblad voor Privaatrecht, Notariaat en Registratie*
WVW	Wegenverkeerswet 1994 (Road Traffic Act)
ZAkDR	Zeitschrift der Akademie für Deutsches Recht

1

General introduction: legal change? Railway and car accidents and how the law coped with them

WOLFGANG ERNST

1 Railways

The development of railways is one of the defining features of 'the Long Revolution' which introduced the industrial age. The possibility of transporting goods and persons cheaply and in very large numbers was crucial for the whole process. The constant expansion of railways, which made distances 'shrink' as never before, posed enormous challenges to the social, economic and legal fabric. Huge amounts of capital were needed, and this need was met by forming corporations and adopting novel techniques of corporate financing. Railway projects became a prime object of speculation. Again, when railway lines had to cross several territories in a single country, the need for trans-border agreements boosted trends towards economic and political unification. Clashes of political and financial power, local and national interests, made for high drama. Railways were also to become giant, nationwide employers. All in all, the sheer amount of capital needed, the size of areas and territories affected and the number of people employed made railways a very special case. In short, the 'railway-ization' of western societies was part and parcel of the Industrial Revolution, which restructured these societies throughout the nineteenth and twentieth centuries.

Like all new technologies, railways entailed new risks. The success story of railways was accompanied by a sad tale of numerous railway accidents, many on a terrifying scale. The personal injuries resulting from this aspect forms the topic that this book considers. How did the legal system react to the occurrence of so many railway accidents? In this volume, the contributors have tried to answer this question by looking at a number of selected countries, namely England, France, Germany, the Netherlands, Spain and Sweden. Do the legal developments in these countries show similar patterns? Can we determine what drove legal change?

In what respects were railway accidents 'new'? Why could the law not handle them in just the same way as all other accidents had been? After all, carriages or stagecoaches had been involved in collisions for centuries, and the law had reacted appropriately. Two issues, neither entirely new, seem to predominate. The first issue was that liability for 'ordinary' accidents depended on fault, or *culpa*, and this fault requirement was inappropriate where the state of the (new) technology made (some) accidents unavoidable. If the accident was unavoidable, how could an individual be at fault? The second issue was one of scale: the running of a railway was no longer a local matter, but rather called for large-scale organizations. This made it difficult for victims to single out any particular individual who could perhaps be blamed, and even if a culpable individual could be identified, it was more likely than not that he would be personally unable to meet the liability arising from the accident. Could one then sue the railway company? This was an issue of 'vicarious liability' (*respondeat superior*), and it was an issue because, in general, at least within certain systems, an employer was liable for a delict caused by an employee only if the employer had been careless in choosing or supervizing him.

A caveat must be inserted here: there were many different types of railway accidents. Damage might be caused to the goods being carried or to property with which trains collided. Victims of personal injuries could be passengers or bystanders, some on platforms, others on crossings. Railway employees themselves formed another major group of victims.[1] The classic instance of a grain field going up in smoke due to a spark from a train's chimney was but one case of many, and is dealt with at length in another volume in this series.[2] The legal issues could be very different depending on the type of accident. Most notably, passengers and persons who had handed over their goods to be transported by rail could rely on

1 For example, the 1877 British Royal Commission on Railway Accidents reported that from 1872 to 1875, on average, 1,308 people were killed each year on the railways, and a further 4,236 were injured. More than half of these were employees of the railways (on average, 741 deaths each year and 2,252 injuries). In 1875, 3 employees were killed for every 1,000 people working on the railways. German studies also show that injuries to employees of the railway companies from 1851 to 1879 on average accounted for 76% of all injuries suffered from railway accidents. By various means, employees were excluded from the compensation offered to passengers. Furthermore, it was shown that about 90% of accidents were caused through their own fault. See the English and German reports below, pp. 13 and 86 n.42.

2 See M. Martin-Casals, *The Development of Liability in Relation to Technological Change* (Cambridge University Press, 2009).

contract, whereas all other victims had to rely on the regime of liability in tort. This, in turn, could be different depending on whether personal injury or damage to personal property was at stake, and quite different laws again might apply where the damage was to landed property (the *actio negatoria* of the civil law systems was available even in the absence of fault). In some systems, the liability regime could also depend on whether the railway was state-run or operated by private enterprise. These categorizations were not all drawn along the same lines in all countries. Hence, there was no single issue of 'the' railway accident. Rather, there was a multitude of issues arising from incidents involving trains – varying from country to country – that in retrospect we see as merely facets of the challenge to the legal system brought about by technological progress and its various consequences. This book has deliberately focused on personal injuries. The parallel volume on *The Development of Liability in relation to Technological Change* includes a discussion on property damage caused by sparks emitted from steam trains.[3]

Turning to the outcomes of the particular research undertaken for this volume, the first finding is the most surprising: in responding to the issues arising from railway accidents, the legal systems did not 'change' at all – the requirement of fault and the structure of vicarious liability remained very much as they had been before the issues relating to railways ever presented themselves or had been more or less resolved.

The legal system had been challenged, but it met the challenge not by changing, but rather by 'branching out'. New instruments, developed ad hoc, adjusted the traditional system to the specifics of the railway agenda. In short, instead of 'changing', the law evolved by using some traditional instruments, adapted slightly for the specific area where the needs were novel. The basic rules were not altered. Over time, there was a shift in the balance between the traditional rules and their special 'offspring' with the result that the 'newer' rules came to seem the more 'natural'. In the long run, indeed, this may amount to a complete replacement of the old rules by the new ones. To begin with, however, legal change does not seem to take the form of altering the existing law, let us say, of delict, so as to make the rules look any different.

For this 'branching out' of new solutions designed to respond to the novel issues that presented themselves, the law used already well-established instruments. Nothing was created *ex nihilo*. The instruments employed varied from country to country, depending on the different

[3] See Martin-Casals, *The Development of Liability in Relation to Technological Change*.

legal cultures. France mainly relied on the tightening of public safety regulations, whose breach entailed liability to make compensation. In Germany, railway victims benefited from alterations made by the courts and legislator in the rules regarding the burden of proof. Legislators in some countries (Sweden among them) introduced laws to overcome the problem of an underdeveloped vicarious liability. The statutory introduction of strict liability was another response, but by no means a universal one.[4] A common feature of all these measures was their falling back on well-established legal instruments. None of these measures as such were 'new': reversals of burden of proof, regulations as the basis of a tortfeasor's liability and even strict liabilities were not unfamiliar. The handling of railway accidents was improved by the use of established legal concepts. Even the provision of better compensation for railway employees through the workmen's compensation schemes used a newly created but general set of concepts. The challenges of the railway sector provoked nothing that could rate as a distinct legal 'invention'.

Much is commonly made of the introduction of strict liability. Some see it as a turning point, a radical departure from the traditional structures of tort law, and the foundation of an alternative, more 'modern' system of liability in tort. Nothing could be further from the historical truth. Strict liability had been around for a long time before it was invoked to help railway victims pursue their claims more effectively. The civil law systems knew a number of actions based on strict liability rather than fault. All that legislators needed to do was to take the concept of strict liability and employ it for the statutory regulation of railway accidents. The theoretical confrontation of fault and strict liability has been overrated, by both the champions of fault as the alleged sole basis of all tort liability and the champions of strict liability as the allegedly better way of dealing with accidents. Fault and strict liability can both be subjected to qualifications and exceptions (reversals of burden of proof on one hand, defences of *force majeure* and contributory negligence on the other) so as to permit liability to be fine-tuned depending on the circumstances. It is interesting to note that the efforts of theorists, from the mid twentieth century onwards, to promote strict liability as a general new model for a more progressive 'tort' law failed to persuade the legislators to follow them.

[4] Compare, in particular, Germany with England or Spain: see below, pp. 80–90, 15–17 and 153–70.

2 Motor cars

The story of the motor car, likewise seen from a legal perspective, is different and much more dramatic. The advent of the automobile, though likewise a technological invention and a social novelty, was much less conspicuous than the invention of the railway. For locomotives, a completely new grid of railway lines had to be laid out, whereas cars initially ran on existing roads long used by carriages, horsemen and pedestrians. Cars called for no expensive and extensive infrastructure, so there was no need for large-scale financing operations. No giant corporations sprang up to invest in and operate motorized traffic, and there were none of the speculative bubbles that had accompanied many railway projects. The beginnings may have been quite humble – the first cars were used by individuals rich and adventurous enough to engage in an expensive, avant-garde hobby – but the imprint that automobiles were to leave on the development of societies throughout the twentieth century was absolutely indelible. Railways certainly contributed crucially to the overall transformation of economies and societies from the mid nineteenth century onwards, but the long-term impact of the automobile on the lives of individuals and also on societies as a whole was probably greater. As the automobile became ubiquitous, society had to respond in new, unprecedented ways, for instance, to give just one example, in town planning and building. All in all, the motor car cut deeper into the social fabric than the train.

Just as the growth in automobile traffic was gradual, so the development of the applicable law took much longer than the process of responding to railways. The outcome, however, is truly remarkable. Nowadays, road accidents seem to be handled almost everywhere in a sort of 'systemic', quasi-bureaucratic way. This is largely because the issue of liability has become entwined with insurance. Insurance companies, active internationally as well as nationally, are at the core of today's system. The actual participants of an accident rarely confront each other on the question of compensation; their insurers take these issues in hand and apply very efficient standard procedures which they have reciprocally agreed, 'knock-for-knock' agreements between insurance companies being the most striking feature of this system. Insurers are in constant contact with car manufacturers (who are also involved by their possible product liability), drivers' associations and legislators, and their role in the handling of road accidents has long had to be taken into account whenever changes in the law are to be made. In many countries, social security systems are also involved in the 'systemic' handling of accidents, especially those involving personal injuries.

One sign of the increasingly bureaucratic approach is the way that, in many countries, the role of contributory negligence has changed. To begin with, contributory negligence was an 'all or nothing' defence, consonant with the aim of early civil procedure to establish which of the litigants was in the wrong. Nowadays, contributory negligence has become just another factor in assessing the compensation due to the victim, a development in line with the tendency of bureaucratic procedures to introduce mitigation and proportionality.

The system of differential insurance premiums depending on drivers' accident records, and other factors did introduce some novel elements of incentive and deterrence. Indeed, the 'behavioural control' of car drivers may today rest as much on the premium system as on the traditional imperatives of tort law. The system is complex, and the private-law liability regime is but one element in it – a crucial element, admittedly, but one embedded in an elaborate insurance system.[5]

The legal change we can observe here is not, or not mainly, the gradual erosion of the fault requirement. Those focusing on this element alone could rightly conclude that there was little or no 'change' at all. What is new, indeed, is the institutional framework, the expert bureaucracies that handle road accidents by applying standard procedures, operating in the light of the macro economic effects of road accidents and an unrelenting interest in increasing road safety. This 'institutionalization', the emergence of this complex 'collective' or quasi-bureaucratic system for road accident compensation, is a true innovation of the twentieth century.

How did we arrive at the present position? Let us first try to discover what must have been the primary stimulus for legal change, and then look at the actual process. The systems devised by all the countries considered here are remarkably similar, despite the numerous differences in the legal detail of their respective tort laws and the resulting 'path dependencies'. The systemic interplay of insurance companies seems to work well, even if the liability laws are quite different. This leads to the conclusion that the driving factor has been a common sociological feature rather than this or that legal rule.

The main force driving this process, it seems, was not so much the 'injustice' of the tort laws as they stood at the beginning of the twentieth century (indeed, one could argue that in most countries the changes in driver's tort liability have been quite modest) but rather that the massive number of road accidents made it imperative to adopt a swifter, more

[5] On insurance systems, see esp. below, pp. 43–8, 61–3, 104–9, 204 and 211–14.

efficient way of handling the compensation issue. It takes a great deal of time and money to resolve accidents in court, where disputed issues of causation, fault and the quantum of damages often call for expert evidence. The growing number of accidents made it very difficult for the legal systems to handle each and every case on an individual basis. The need for enhanced efficiency in dealing with these large numbers was obviously very influential in the production and selection of possible solutions. There comes a point where mass matters, as Clausewitz observed.[6] In the case of road accidents, it was not technology as such that called for legal innovation, but rather the sheer mass of occurrences that needed to be resolved every day. (It is true that road traffic became much safer, thanks to constant efforts, but this effect was more or less outweighed by the steady increase in the number of cars on the roads.) It may well be that the strongest argument for non-fault (strict) liabilities is not so much that they produce a more just result (although a case can well be made that they do), as that by eliminating fault (a matter of controversy in almost all cases), they make it easier to settle claims for compensation. It was surely the urgent need for efficiency, in the face of an ever-increasing number of cases, that caused the gradual adoption of more schematic, bureaucratic and standard procedures for handling road accidents.

While bureaucratization, relying on the insurance industry, is a common feature of all legal systems we have looked into, the traditional peculiarities of the different tort systems have proved to be astonishingly resistant to change. The requirements for compensation claims still differ considerably from country to country. This is true even after several interventions of the European Union. We take this not only as signifying a strong path dependency, but also assume that, for the overall functioning of the bureaucratic system, the delicate details of the rules on tortious liability may be of limited importance only.

While the various legal systems all moved in much the same general direction, one country stands out: all along, Sweden seems to have reacted more swiftly to the new challenges. In 1975, it also took what is perhaps the next logical step in the development, namely to remove the relationship between car driver or owner and the victim from the issue of compensation altogether and to establish a state fund from which victims claim compensation. It is tempting to ask why Sweden has been readier than both a common law country like England and all the civil law countries to discard doctrinal concerns. Courts and legislators, car manufacturers

[6] C. von Clausewitz, *On War*, trans. J. Graham (London: Trübner, 1873), Vol. VI, Ch. 27.

and insurers (and their respective pressure groups), and drivers and their associations.

If the need for greater efficiency was the driving force for development, how did the legal systems 'react' to this exigency? The evolution of our very elaborate, complex systems for compensation, involving the interaction of a multitude of institutional actors, has been a slow process in which courts, doctrinal writers and legislators, as well as insurance companies, have contributed to the emergence of ever-more refined settlement techniques. 'Grand schemes' to reform the field of road accident compensation, not so very different from the sort of no-fault systems now in place in a number of the systems studied here, were occasionally advanced (mostly by doctrinal writers). But there was never any serious attempt to enact such schemes.[7] Perhaps it was too much to expect legislators to create, in one stroke, a complex system that calls for the delicate interaction of a multitude of 'players': insurers, drivers and pedestrians.

If the changes in the handling of road accidents occurred in a piecemeal way, the overall effect has proved momentous. Most of the legal techniques involved were already familiar in the early twentieth century, but no one then could have conceived or planned the elaborate interplay of insurances which today takes care of road accidents. The territory was uncharted, but the legal systems ended up by navigating it with remarkable success. Gradualism is a characteristic of legal developments, but it does not stand in the way of very considerable changes, changes brought about by a prolonged series of ad hoc solutions without any prior master plan setting out the overall direction. One is put in mind of the concept of evolution, a powerful process characterized by many slight alterations, taking place without any clear idea of what is to follow.

[7] For example, there were debates in the 1930s proposing a no-fault insurance scheme for motor-vehicle accident victims in France (Picard 1930), Germany (Trendel 1935), Spain (1934) and Sweden (a Bill in 1938): see below, pp. 61–2, 107, 177 and 205–6. By contrast, some leading academics were particularly important in promoting ideas. This was more true of legislation on roads than the development of railway legislation (mainly because universities were so small in the nineteenth century); see, for example, Ivar Strahl (below, pp. 206–7) in Sweden in the 1940s and 1950s, influential mainly because he chaired a number of committees that led to legislative proposals. André Tunc was also important in France, strongly influenced by his stay in the United States in the early 1950s (see below, p. 65). Early proposals in Sweden (1957) and France (1965) failed because the insurers were not happy (see below, pp. 208–9 and 64–5). But the Swedish reforms of 1975 were supported by insurers, and the French reforms of 1985 were not opposed by them (see below, pp. 210 and 67–9).

The main development just described has taken place in the field of private law at large. Insurance contracts are instruments of private law, and most insurance companies are private law entities. The legislator has fine-tuned the role of insurers in the handling of car accidents, most notably by making insurance against liability compulsory and by granting the victim an *action directe* against the insurance company. If one refrains from unduly emphasizing such interventions, one could say that the private law systems have proven of enormous vitality in progressing towards efficient solutions. Seen from a traditional point of view, the result is somewhat paradoxical: whilst still operating with private law instruments, the overall system now has a decidedly bureaucratic character.

Public law, however, has also played its part. When we consider the responses of the different legal systems, we can see the importance of the interplay of public law regulation with private-law liability regimes. Sensible safety regulations can diminish the number of accidents and reduce the amount of damage caused. Drivers, required by statute to obtain a licence, found their conduct at the wheel increasingly regulated in ways that restricted their previous liberties. For example, drink-driving rules imposed standards of conduct on drivers, and the compulsory use of seat belts constrained the freedom of passengers as well. Legislators have increasingly required manufacturers to make their vehicles safer or incur liability for defects, and the safety of roads was increased (with the introduction of traffic lights, pedestrian crossings, speed limits and speed bumps). Such preventive measures are obviously preferable to tinkering with liability regimes, which mostly come into operation when the damage has been done. It is true that the risk of incurring liability constitutes an incentive to careful driving, but it remains doubtful how effective such mechanisms may be.[8] Though legislators obviously preferred to adopt 'direct' measures as a means for 'behaviour control' rather than rely on the untested effectiveness of tort law, regulatory and liability regimes do interact, and private law has always been shaped, to some degree, by public law regulations. The Edicts of the Aediles provide the best-known examples: those Roman public law regulations, designed to repress unfair practices in the Roman slave and cattle markets, eventually had a great effect on the private law relating to

[8] See P. Cane, *Atiyah's Accidents, Compensation and the Law* (7th edn, Cambridge University Press, 2006), 426–8.

the seller's liability for latent defects.[9] In the case of road accidents, the violation of safety regulations became a new and increasingly important basis of liability in tort, as well as for the defence of contributory negligence.[10]

What were the respective contributions of courts, legislators and doctrinal writers to this process? The answer varies from country to country. Doctrinal writers, being able to 'think outside the box', often came up with grand schemes, and if they appeared too far-reaching for immediate implementation, quite a few of them were vindicated by later developments, sometimes with a considerable time lag. Two writers whose names cannot be ignored in any European history of car accident law are Strahl (in Sweden) and Tunc (in France).[11]

Courts can only naturally make improvements step by step, and supreme courts (which alone can effectively move the law forward) can do so only if the 'right' case comes up by way of appeal. Even landmark cases usually turn only on narrow points, the French *Jand'heur* decision (1927/1930) perhaps being an outstanding exception.[12]

As to legislators, they also seem to be, in general, reluctant to endorse any of the grand schemes proposed, though their 'reaction time' is not usually so long as to justify a charge of legislative inertia.

3 International influences on legal development

Another interesting feature emerged from a comparison of the law of different countries. Even though developments generally took place within the framework of legal systems set up by the 'nation state', there has been a constant exchange of ideas between various jurisdictions. Technological novelties occurred at different times in different countries, so the late comers could conveniently profit from the experiences of the 'early adopters'. Legal developments in England, where railways originated, were taken up by the Prussian legislator, whose statute in turn became a model for the Netherlands and Italy.[13] The European Community has, of course, greatly intensified the reciprocal knowledge of events in other member states, but there were fruitful exchanges even before the European Community tried to harmonize our legal developments. No 'national' story would be complete if it failed to recognize such infusions from other countries. In this

[9] See W. Buckland, *A Textbook of Roman Law* (3rd edn, Cambridge University Press, 1963), 491.

[10] See below, pp. 92, 153–8 and 192.

[11] See below, pp. 206–9 and 95.

[12] See below, p. 61.

[13] See below, p. 129.

respect, we are indeed dealing with a 'European' – and not just national – legal history.

Furthermore, throughout the twentieth century, doctrinal writers and legislators increasingly looked to legal developments in the United States, so that in addition to studying developments from a European perspective, we must look across the Atlantic Ocean and note the influence of American legal developments on the European scene (and vice versa). As a society especially shaped by the automobile, the United States was clearly going to have a pivotal role in any study of the relevant law. Our present law is the legacy not just of European legal history in the twentieth century, but also of Western legal history as a whole.

2

The development of traffic liability in England and Wales

RODERICK BAGSHAW

1 Railway accidents

1.a What is a railway accident?

A wide range of events leading to personal injuries have some claim to be referred to as 'railway accidents'. Whilst the most obvious, and dramatic, paradigms involve a moving train colliding with another train or with some stationary object (such as a landslip), or a moving train becoming derailed as a result of a defect in the locomotive, the rolling stock or the permanent way, or a moving train running someone down (an intending passenger, an employee, a highway user, a trespasser on the railway, etc.), other common patterns are also frequently encountered, for instance: injuries suffered by passengers in carriages when trains start too jerkily or stop too suddenly; injuries suffered by passengers descending from trains (often because there is a gap between carriage and platform, or because the train has over-shot or stopped short); injuries suffered by passengers whilst embarking (often involving doors and hands); and injuries suffered whilst on the platform (a wide range, from tripping over a weighing machine to being struck by the open door of a moving train or getting a spark in the eye).

An essential variable factor in a legally significant typology of such railway accidents is the relationship between the injured party and the defendant railway company. R. W. Kostal structures his important study around a contrast between the treatment of railway employees and of passengers.[1] Cutting across both categories (employees and passengers), however, are complexities caused by the existence of a multiplicity of railway

[1] R. W. Kostal, ' "The Instrumentality of Others": Railway Accidents and the Courts, 1840–1875', Ch. 7 in R. W. Kostal (ed.), *Law and English Railway Capitalism 1825–1875* (Oxford: Clarendon Press, 1994). The contrast was not a special 'railway' phenomenon: the

companies.[2] Thus, whilst an injury to a passenger might be due to the carelessness of the employees of the company from which he had taken a ticket, it might instead be due to the carelessness of another company, perhaps because that other company was responsible for the permanent way, or was responsible for another train sharing the line, or even because the ticket entitled the passenger to transfer to that other company's train. One might also add to the contrast between the treatment of employees and passengers the further contrast between trespassers on railway facilities and lawful visitors. English tort law subjected trespassers to a special (non-protective) regime before *Herrington* v. *British Railways Board*[3] (though some devices were used to mitigate this)[4] and still differentiates between lawful visitors and others.[5]

The relative frequency of these different types of incident on the Victorian railways can be seen in statistics reported by the 1877 Royal Commission on Railway Accidents.[6] Returns from the railway companies indicated that from 1872 to 1875, on average, 1,308 people were killed each year on the railways, and a further 4,236 were injured. More than half of these were servants of the railways (on average, 741 fatalities per year and 2,252 injuries). Of those killed or injured who were not servants, approximately half were non-passengers: in the relevant four years, there were 131 suicides and 1,010 trespassers were killed. With regard to passengers, an average of 39 were killed each year (1,388 injured) in accidents involving collisions or derailments, whilst 119 were killed by collateral causes (362 injured), probably principally as a result of being run down. The Board of Trade's figures derived from their investigations of railway accidents in the same period record that forty-two passengers were killed on average each year 'by causes beyond their control'.[7]

legal treatment of railway passengers represented continuity with stagecoach precedents, whilst the unfavourable treatment of railway employees flowed largely from the generally applicable 'common employment' rule.

[2] In 1850, there were fifteen large railway companies, controlling 75% of the United Kingdom's gross traffic revenues between them. By 1870, the same companies controlled 83% of the revenues, though the 'big four' between them accounted for more than half of this (44% of the total): T. R. Gourvish, *Railways and the British Economy 1830–1914* (London: Macmillan, 1980), 10. The concentration was similar at the outbreak of war in 1914, by when there were 178 railways companies in Great Britain and Ireland.

[3] [1972] AC 877. [4] See below, text from note 95.

[5] Occupiers Liability Act 1984.

[6] By 1875, approximately 11,800 miles of railway line were open in Great Britain and Ireland (6,100 miles in 1851, 19,500 in 1907 and 10,000 in the United Kingdom in 2006).

[7] The figures for 1851 demonstrate a similar pattern (113 deaths, of which one was a suicide, 33 were trespassers and 62 were employees, with 32 of them blamed for their own demise,

The amount paid by the railway companies in compensation for personal injuries in 1875 was £381,038. To put that figure in context, a member of the middle class would have annual earnings of between £100 and £1,000, a jury's award for the killing of a family breadwinner would often exceed £1,000[8] and a single serious accident involving a passenger train could cost a company in excess of £50,000.[9] The gross receipts of the railway industry for the same year were £61.2 million, and 507 million passenger journeys were taken, not including those made by the holders of season tickets. But it seems likely that most of those injured on the railways, and most of the dependents of those who were killed, did not receive compensation through tort law.[10] A claimant who was demonstrated to have been 'contributorily negligent' could not succeed, and additional obstacles were faced by trespassers on the tracks and by employees who were injured by accidents caused by the negligence of their co-workers. The position of employees attracted particular legislative and judicial attention, but it is a story that has been told elsewhere,[11] and discussion below will concentrate on the law affecting passengers.

and, of the 17 passenger fatalities, only 8 were recorded as killed by causes beyond their own control).

[8] See, for example, *Rowley* v. *London and North Western Railway Co.* (1873) 8 Ex. 221, where the jury had awarded £6,200 to the family of a forty-year-old attorney practising in Manchester (though the decision was overturned because of a minor misdirection); *Dublin, Wicklow, and Wexford Railway Co.* v. *Slattery* (1878) 3 App Cas 1155, where the jury had awarded £1,205 to a widow with children.

[9] The London, Brighton and South Coast Railway Company informed the Board of Trade that the accident at New Cross in 1869 had cost it in excess of £70,000 (though the Directors had reported to shareholders [according to *The Guardian*, 2 February 1871] that they had charged £45,000 against revenue to cover claims). The accident involved a goods train running into the back of a special train carrying licensed victuallers back from a social event.

[10] Many apparently took out insurance against suffering injury. Frederick S. Williams, in the first edition of his popular book, *Our Iron Roads: Their History, Construction and Social Influences* (London: Ingram Cooke & Co., 1852), 370, recorded that at most railway stations it was possible to buy a single-journey assurance ticket, which on death as a result of an accident would pay a third-class passenger £100 for 1 penny, a second-class passenger £500 for 2 pence and a first-class passenger £1,000 for 3 pence. He also recorded that the Railway Passengers' Assurance Company sold approximately 240,000 such assurance tickets in the second half of 1851 but complained that this meant that they were bought by only one in every 183 passengers. He demonstrated by calculation that if every passenger had paid 1 pence per journey into a relief fund during the second half of 1851, this would have enabled a payment of £1,000 to be made to each person killed and £250 to each person injured.

[11] See, for example, P. W. J. Bartrip and S. B. Burman, *The Wounded Soldiers of Industry: Industrial Compensation Policy 1833–1897* (Oxford: Clarendon Press, 1983).

1.b Negligence or the stricter liability of a common carrier?

The Railway Clauses Consolidation Act 1845, which was intended to consolidate the provisions usually inserted in private Acts authorizing the making of particular railways, provided that the Act was not intended to make a railway company liable further than they would be if they were a stagecoach proprietor.[12] This was significant since the English courts had already considered whether the liability of a stagecoach proprietor to its passengers ought to mirror the strict liability[13] of a common carrier of goods to their owner. In *Aston* v. *Heaven*,[14] where the claimant was injured when the defendant's stagecoach overturned, apparently after the horses were startled by a bright reflection, Eyre CJ emphatically distinguished the obligations of a common carrier of goods and a carrier of passengers ('totally unlike') on the basis of the special need to provide a prophylactic against the temptation to steal goods. He directed the jury that they had to consider whether the stagecoach driver was negligent, albeit that the 'smallest negligence' would be sufficient.[15]

Sir James Mansfield CJ maintained this distinction between common carriers of goods and of passengers in *Christie* v. *Griggs*.[16] In that case, however, the accident was caused by the snapping of the axle-tree on the stagecoach, and the question arose whether, even if fault was the relevant criteria in establishing liability for 'driving', proprietors ought to be treated as having warranted the 'fitness of the vehicle'. Sir James Mansfield CJ's opinion was that proprietors warranted that any coach was 'as good a coach as could be made'. The effect was to make proprietors liable for 'careless' construction of coaches, even if they did not construct them. Some later stagecoach cases suggested an even sterner warranty with regard to the vehicle: for instance, in *Bremner* v. *Williams*,[17] Best CJ stated that 'every coach-proprietor warrants to the public that his stage-coach is equal to the journey it undertakes'. But liability for 'driving' remained resolutely fault-based. So, for instance, in *Crofts* v. *Waterhouse*,[18] the Court

[12] Railway Clauses Consolidation Act 1845, s. 89. The first edition of W. Hodges, *The Law Relating to Railways and Railway Companies* (London: S. Sweet, 1847), 463–7, relies almost entirely on stagecoach cases for its brief description of liability to passengers.

[13] Following *Coggs* v. *Bernard* (1703) 2 Ld Raym 909 at 918, the common carrier was liable to the owner for any loss or damage other than that caused by acts of God or enemies of the king. At common law, it was possible to contract out of such liability (*Riley* v. *Horne* (1828) 5 Bing 217), but Parliament attempted to regulate such practices in the Carriers Act 1830 and the Railway and Canal Traffic Act 1854.

[14] (1797) 2 Esp. 533, Common Pleas.

[15] The jury found a verdict for the defendants.

[16] (1809) 2 Camp. 79.

[17] (1824) 1 Car. & P. 414.

[18] (1825) 3 Bing. 319.

of Common Pleas ruled that there must be a new trial where Littledale J had directed a jury that if a coach had overturned because it strayed beyond the limits of the road, then the defendant proprietor was liable. Best CJ offered a clear formulation of the proprietor's obligations:

> The coachman must have competent skill, and must use that skill with diligence; he must be well acquainted with the road he undertakes to drive; he must be provided with steady horses; a coach and harness of sufficient strength, and properly made; and also with lights by night. If there be the least failure in any one of these things, the duty of the coach proprietors is not fulfilled, and they are answerable for any injury or damage that happens. But with all these things, and when every thing has been done that human prudence can suggest for the security of the passengers, an accident may happen. The lights may, in a dark night, be obscured by fog; the horses frightened, or, as it happened in the present case, the coachman may be deceived by a sudden alteration in objects near the road, by which he had used to be directed on former journeys.[19]

The question of whether a carrier of passengers owed the same obligation to them that a common carrier of goods owed to their owner was reopened and directly addressed in the railway context in the case of *Readhead* v. *Midland Railway Co.*[20] In this case, the claimant had been injured when the carriage he was travelling in overturned after a tyre broke because of a flaw in the welding. Witnesses stated that such flaws could not be detected during the process of manufacture and would not be revealed by either a visual inspection or a ringing of the metal afterwards. A majority in the Court of Queen's Bench upheld Lush J's direction to the jury that the claimant was not entitled to recover unless 'they were of opinion that the defendants were guilty of negligence'. This decision was in turn upheld by the Exchequer Chamber.[21] Although Blackburn J dissented in the Queen's Bench, he did not equate a carrier's obligation to its passengers with a common carrier's responsibility for the goods that it carried, but instead argued that a carrier of passengers was bound 'at his peril to supply a vehicle in fact reasonably sufficient for the purpose'.[22] He

[19] (1825) 3 Bing. 321. The coachman claimed to have been deceived during a journey on a moonlit night by the fact that one of two cottages that had stood at a corner in the road when he passed the spot twelve hours previously had subsequently been demolished.

[20] (1867) 2 QB 412 (Queen's Bench); (1869) 4 QB 379 (Exchequer Chamber).

[21] Importantly, whilst the Exchequer Chamber held that a railway company did not warrant that its carriages were free from dangerous defects, it left open the question of whether a railway company might be liable for a dangerous defect resulting from the manufacturer's *negligence*. See below, p. 27.

[22] (1867) 2 QB 412, at 432.

was apparently attracted by an analogy with the obligation of a 'supplier' of goods for a particular purpose to supply goods reasonably sufficient for that purpose. By contrast, the Exchequer Chamber preferred to draw an analogy with the obligation of an occupier with regard to the state of its premises.[23]

The basic distinction between the strict liability of the common carrier of goods and the fault liability of a carrier of passengers was still familiar in the second half of the twentieth century.[24]

1.c *Tort or contract?*

The question of whether a duty owed to a passenger was solely contractual was, naturally, most likely to arise where a claimant was not in privity with the railway company who he wished to sue. One group of cases involved passengers who had not purchased tickets. As early as 1851, in *Marshall* v. *The York, Newcastle, and Berwick Railway Co.*,[25] it was accepted that an injured passenger whose ticket had been bought by another could claim on a 'duty implied by law to carry him safely'. Consistently with these dicta, personal injury claims were also successfully brought by, for instance, an infant[26] and a newspaper reporter using a free pass.[27]

A more complicated group of cases involved passengers who had taken a ticket from one company, which entitled them to travel on a train operated by another company, and that other company was responsible for the accident. These cases were complicated largely because in goods cases there was an understandable reluctance to allow the consignor to

23 In *Francis* v. *Cockrell* (1870) LR 5 QB 184 and 501, a case arising out of the collapse of part of a temporary grandstand at Cheltenham racecourse, the Court of Queen's Bench treated their decision (that an occupier could be liable for a builder's negligence) as one that would apply in railway cases. When the duties of occupiers to their lawful visitors were amended by statute in 1957, the changes were made to expressly apply to any corresponding duties of the controllers of railway carriages: Occupiers Liability Act 1957, s. 1(3)(a).

24 O. Kahn-Freund, *The Law of Carriage by Inland Transport* (4th edn, London: Stevens, 1965), 452.

25 (1851) 11 CB 655, at 662 *per* Jervis CJ. The case actually involved loss of the luggage of a valet, his ticket having been purchased by his master, Lord Adolphus Vane (the third son of the first Earl Vane and Viscount Seaham).

26 *Austin* v. *Great Western Railway Co.* (1867) LR 2 QB 442. Only Blackburn J expressly adopted a non-contractual explanation. The other members of the court suggested that the infant could claim on the contract made by his mother.

27 *Great Northern Railway Co.* v. *Harrison* (1854) 10 Ex 376. Awkwardly for the claimant, the free pass was in the name of another reporter, but the court held that there was

circumvent a limitation on liability in his contract with the first carrying company by claiming against some other company involved in carrying the goods further down the track.[28] When the point was directly raised in a personal injury case (in *Foulkes* v. *Metropolitan District Railway Co.*),[29] Thesiger LJ held that the company responsible for the train in which the passenger travelled 'so far as concerns its own line, in which term I include a line over which running powers are exercised, and its own acts and omissions, is under the same obligations in reference to the security of the passenger, as it would have been if it had directly contracted with him'.[30] Indeed, this decision was immediately treated as having impliedly overruled the previous luggage cases, at least in cases of misfeasance.[31] In John Lely's 1888 edition of Hodges' *Treatise on the Law of Railways*, he bluntly asserts that the action is 'of tort'.[32]

A third group of cases involved passengers who were injured in collisions caused by the negligence of railway companies other than the one that they had contracted with and which was carrying them. In these cases, the question of whether the passenger could sue the negligent company with which they had no contract was often masked by the fact

sufficient evidence to leave to the jury the question of whether the claimant was lawfully in the carriage. In *Collett* v. *London and North Western Railway Co.* (1851) 20 LJ QB 411, the injured claimant was a post office official who the railway was bound by statute to carry without charge. The Court found, rather brusquely, that the statute imposed a duty to carry with reasonable skill and care, and the injured person could claim damages for breach of that duty.

28 *Bristol and Exeter Railway* v. *Collins* (1859) 7 HLC 194, HL. *Mytton* v. *Midland Railway Co* (1859) 4 H & N 615 was to similar effect, though here the immunity of the ticket-issuing company was statutory. P. S. Atiyah is probably too generous to the claimants in suggesting that their trouble was a result of them being 'held to have sued the wrong railway company': *The Rise and Fall of Freedom of Contract* (Oxford: Clarendon Press, 1979), 504.

29 (1880) LR 5 CP 157, CA.

30 Ibid., at 170. Bramwell LJ agreed that there could be a duty without a need to establish a contract, but held that such a duty could not make a defendant liable for nonfeasance (at 159). Baggallay LJ, like Thesiger LJ, seems to have found that when the defendant company accepted the claimant as a passenger they came to owe him the 'same duty' as would have been owed to a passenger they contracted with (at 164).

31 *Hooper* v. *London & North Western Railway Co.* (1880) 50 LJ QB 103. The classification of this case as one of misfeasance is not straightforward; the damage was caused by a brace of pheasants in the claimant's portmanteau decaying during an unexplained three month delay in its arrival. In *Meux* v. *Great Eastern Railway Co.* [1895] 2 QB 387, the Court of Appeal confirmed that when a railway porter negligently allowed a portmanteau to fall onto the track, the owner of the goods in it that were damaged could sue in tort even if she was not a passenger, and hence had no contract with the railway company.

32 In *Kelly* v. *Metropolitan Railway Co.* [1895] 1 QB 944, the Court of Appeal confirmed that railway accident cases were 'founded upon tort' for the purposes of a statute regulating

that they could sue the carrying company for breach of its non-delegable duty.[33] But by 1873 it seems to have become accepted that a claim in tort against the negligent company would be possible.[34]

Although it seems to have become firmly established before the last quarter of the nineteenth century that claims for injuries caused by the negligence of railway companies could be brought in tort, there remained some situations where a contractual claim might be advantageous. For instance, in *Hobbs* v. *The London and South Western Railway Co.*,[35] it was held that passengers could claim compensation in contract for the physical inconvenience of having to walk home on a wet night when they were not taken to the destination to which they had bought tickets, whilst it must be doubtful if this would have been recognized as actionable damage by the law of torts.

1.d Exclusion of liability

The fact that most passengers had a contractual relationship with their carriers might have provided the opportunity to negotiate for exclusions or limitations on liability. However, Kostal, writing of the period up to 1875, suggests that few attempts were made to exclude or limit liability vis-à-vis passengers (in contrast to the position relating to goods) because of anticipated judicial hostility.[36] And whilst arguing the case

recovery of costs. Lord Esher MR stated (at 946). 'At the present time a plaintiff may frame his claim in either way [contract or tort], but he is not bound by the pleadings, and if he puts his claim on one ground and proves it on another he is not now embarrassed by any rules as to departure. The question to be tried is the same in either case. The plaintiff must rely on and prove negligence, and whether that negligence is active or passive seems to me to be immaterial.' The significance of the last sentence quoted was to clarify the recent decision in *Taylor* v. *Manchester, Sheffield, and Lincolnshire Railway Co.* [1895] 1 QB 134, which had suggested that railway negligence cases were only 'founded on tort' when they involved 'misfeasance'.

[33] See below, pp. 25–29.

[34] *Wright* v. *Midland Railway Co.* (1873) LR 8 Exch 137, discussed below, pp. 28–29.

[35] (1875) LR 10 QB 111. The claimants had sought £300 for the inconvenience of having to walk approximately 5 miles with their two young children; the defendants had paid £2 into court and the jury awarded £8.

[36] It is not clear what form this 'hostility' would have taken. In *Burke* v. *South Eastern Railway* (1879) 5 CPD 1, the Court held that the defendant, which had sold the claimant a ticket from London to Paris, could rely on a special contractual term excluding its liability for any injury he suffered whilst on French railways. In *Richardson, Spence and the 'Lord Gough' Steamship Co.* v. *Rowntree* [1894] AC 217, the House of Lords did not condemn a contractual provision limiting a steerage passenger to a maximum claim of US$100 for any personal injury, but held that it had been correct to leave to the jury the question of whether the passenger had been given 'reasonable notice' of the term.

of *Ludditt* v. *Ginger Coote Airways Ltd*[37] in 1946, Diplock reported that 'there appears to have been no decision of the English courts in which it has been held that a railway company can limit its liability for negligence to passengers except when they are travelling at less than the maximum fare'. The exception, however, was of considerable practical importance. It seems that by the early twentieth century, railway companies were seeking to exclude or limit their liability to passengers on excursion trains[38] and those using special workers' tickets.[39] The Privy Council expressed the opinion in *Ludditt* that there was no common law restriction on the liberty of a carrier of passengers to make a special contract excluding or restricting its liability,[40] but it is not clear if this led to more attempts to exclude liability. Exclusion against non-passengers may have been more widespread; for instance, J. Charlesworth in 1938 suggests that railway companies demanded that licensees took platform tickets so as to allow them to exclude all liability.[41] Exclusion and restriction of liability to fare-paying passengers was prohibited by the Transport Act 1962, s. 43(7).

1.e Standard of care

Although several cases suggest that railways were expected to reach a high standard in order to avoid being found negligent, it seems clear that the judges of the 1860s did not direct juries to demand perfection. The direction to the jury of Erle CJ in *Ford* v. *The London and South Western Railway Co.*[42] is of particular interest in this regard: 'The railway company is bound to take reasonable care; to use the best precautions in known practical use, for securing the safety and convenience of their passengers … They are entrusted with most important interests, with human lives, and a jury may reasonably require an amount of care proportioned

[37] [1947] AC 233, at 237.

[38] *Thompson* v. *London, Midland and Scottish Railway Co.* [1930] 1 KB 41.

[39] *Great Western Railway Co. of Canada* v. *Braid* (1863) 1 Moo PC (NS) 101, PC (employee's free pass; train); *Grand Trunk Railway Co. of Canada* v. *Robinson* [1915] AC 740, PC (half-fare special contract whilst accompanying livestock; train); *Wilkie* v. *London Passenger Transport Board* [1947] 1 All ER 258, CA (employee's free pass; omnibus). In *Nunan* v. *Southern Railway Co.* [1923] 2 KB 703, Swift J held that a passenger using a special worker's ticket had intended to agree to a limit on the amount he could recover if he survived, but not to limit what his dependents could recover if he was killed.

[40] [1947] AC 233, at 242. This followed dicta of Lord Haldane LC in *Grand Trunk Railway Co. of Canada* v. *Robinson* [1915] AC 740, at 747.

[41] J. Charlesworth, *The Law of Negligence* (1st edn, London: Butterworths, 1938), 104.

[42] (1862) 2 F & F 730.

to those interests. At the same time a jury would not be entitled to expect the utmost care that could possibly be conceived, or the highest possible degree of skill.' He elaborated this by distinguishing between precautions 'in known practical use' and other innovations: 'It is not to be expected that the directors shall at once have in use every invention or discovery of science.' Moreover, he expressly urged the jury to consider a balance between safety and convenience: 'It is easy to conceive a precaution, for example, a slower rate of speed, which would add a very small degree of security, while it would entail a very great degree of inconvenience. And a company ought not to be found guilty merely because they possibly might have done something more for safety, at a far greater sacrifice of convenience.'[43]

At the end of the same decade, in *Hart* v. *Lancashire and Yorkshire Railway Co.*,[44] the Court of Exchequer had to decide whether any evidence of negligence had been adduced in a case where a driver had a fit whilst operating a train.[45] In explaining why the company was not negligent for not having had a second driver on board, Bramwell B referred both to the fact that fares would have had to increase to accommodate such a change and to the supposed views of the 'man on the Clapham omnibus'.[46] The case also established the proposition that taking steps in the aftermath of an accident to prevent a recurrence could not be admitted as evidence of negligence.

Twentieth century treatise writers[47] have made use of the summary of the standard of care offered by Cozens-Hardy MR in *Newberry* v. *Bristol Tramways and Carriage Co. Ltd*,[48] where the trolley arm on an electric tram came away from the overhead wire, became entangled, was plucked from its socket and fell onto a passenger's head. Such arms had been plucked from their sockets four times in 30 million miles of tram journeys over five years, without previous injury, and experts testified that the design

[43] (1862) 2 F&F 733. The jury found that the claimant's injuries were caused by negligence with regard to both the speed of the train and the brake power.

[44] (1869) 21 LT 261.

[45] To avoid the out-of-control train colliding with a full-speed express train on the main line, a pointsman deliberately diverted it onto a branch line where a local train, on which the claimant was a passenger, was stationary. The judges expressed conflicting views as to whether a claim against the pointsman would have succeeded.

[46] 21 LT 261, at 263. This legal usage of the phrase 'man on the Clapham Omnibus' predates that offered in the *OED* (2nd edn) by more than thirty years.

[47] H. W. Disney, *The Law of Carriage by Railway* (8th edn by H. M. Paul, London: Stevens, 1929). Similarly, Kahn-Freund, *The Law of Carriage by Inland Transport*, 456.

[48] (1912) 107 LT 801, at 803 CA.

used was the best known because the detachable arm reduced the risk of the electrical cables being pulled down. After the jury found a verdict in favour of the injured passenger, Channel J asked them to specify the precaution that they thought the defendant ought to have adopted: they were not able to do so. A majority in the Court of Appeal quashed the verdict because, in the words of Cozen-Hardy MR, the jury had departed from the law that 'it is sufficient that the carrier should adopt the best known apparatus, kept in perfect order, and worked without negligence by the men employed. If he does that, he ought not to be responsible for the consequences of an extremely rare and obscure accident which cannot, in a business sense, be prevented by any known means.'

It is not easy to discern any significant change in the formulation of the standard of care across the period surveyed. If anything, there are some hints that the economic strictures faced by the railways in the second half of the twentieth century were reflected in a generous approach to defendants vis-à-vis imperfections in rolling stock. Thus, in *O'Connor* v. *British Transport Commission*,[49] a three year old fell onto the tracks after opening the door in a guard's van. Evidence was given that the door handle was of a type deliberately introduced into guards' vans in 1930 because it was easier to open from the inside, that such handles were not used in passenger compartments and that whilst new rolling stock since 1946 had used a different design, more than 20 vans of the old style were in use on mainline trains. The Court of Appeal upheld the trial judge's decision in favour of the defendants. After quoting Erle CJ's direction to the jury in *Ford's* case, Sellers LJ added: 'His words must be read, I think, in relation to the circumstances then existing, for I do not understand it to be universal law that every railway or omnibus or taxi-cab or passenger aircraft undertaking which trades for reward must have the latest standard of design in the way submitted by counsel. Economically and practically it would be impossible.'[50] Even Lord Evershed MR, who was inclined to favour the claimant, accepted that the 'actual operation of the railway services must to some extent be subject to the exigencies of ordinary and prudent management'.[51]

[49] [1958] 1 WLR 346.

[50] Ibid., at 351.

[51] Ibid., at 356. See, similarly, with regard to staffing levels, *Tomlinson* v. *Railway Executive* [1953] 1 All ER 1, where the Court of Appeal held that it was not negligent for the sole porter at a station to delay clearing compressed snow from the platform in order to light emergency lamps.

1.f Proof of fault

Whether a railway defendant had acted negligently was regarded as a question of fact, and hence one for the jury.[52] But it was widely acknowledged that juries were inclined to treat railway companies harshly,[53] so the issue of judicial control of the jury was heavily litigated in railway cases during the second half of the nineteenth century. The basic position, confirmed by the House of Lords in *Metropolitan Railway Co.* v. *Jackson*,[54] was that it was a question of law for the judge whether the claimant had adduced evidence of negligence fit to be considered by the jury. *Jackson*, like other cases, pointed to a distinction drawn by Willes J[55] between the former rule that a case should not be withdrawn from the jury 'if there was any evidence, even a scintilla, in support of the case' and the new rule that a case should be withdrawn by the judge if there was no evidence 'that ought reasonably to satisfy the jury that the fact sought to be proved is established'. Although this 'new' approach was slightly more generous to railway defendants, it still meant that a case should go to the jury if evidence had been given that, if it was accepted by them, might be sufficient to establish negligence, even if such a weight of contrary evidence was introduced as to make a verdict for the defendant appear irresistible.[56] In such a case, the defendant would have to rely on the post-trial power to overturn a verdict if it was against the weight of the evidence, in the sense of there being 'such a preponderance of evidence … as to make

[52] The Common Law Procedure Act 1854 made trial by judge alone possible if the parties agreed. Since 1933, jury trial has only been available at the discretion of the court in an ordinary negligence case. See, now, Supreme Court Act 1981, s. 69(3).

[53] When giving examples of cases where juries might go astray, Baron Bramwell immediately suggested actions against railway companies (and running down actions): (1869) 47 LT 337, quoted in A. H. Manchester, *A Modern Legal History of England and Wales 1750–1950* (London: Butterworths, 1980), 98. Similarly, *Dublin, Wicklow and Wexford Ry. Co.* v. *Slattery* (1878) 3 App Cas 1155, at 1205 *per* Lord Blackburn: 'The Plaintiff in this case may, I am afraid, not without some grounds, think that she being a widow with orphans, and the Defendants a railway company, she had a chance that jury after jury would find for her, whatever were the directions given.'

[54] (1877) 3 App Cas 193.

[55] Giving the judgment of the Court of Exchequer Chamber in *Ryder* v. *Wombwell* (1868) LR 4 Exch 32, at 39. This case did not involve a railway defendant, but rather a young aristocrat pleading the defence of infancy. In such cases it seems that juries demonstrated a ready tendency to find that the items purchased were 'necessaries' so as to defeat the defence. In the particular case, the jury had found an antique goblet and a pair of jewelled cufflinks to be 'necessaries'.

[56] *Dublin, Wicklow, and Wexford Railway Co.* v. *Slattery* (1878) 3 App Cas 1155, in particular *per* Lord Hatherley at 1168, *per* Lord Penzance at 1176 and *per* Lord Gordon at 1217.

it unreasonable, and almost perverse, that the jury when instructed and assisted properly by the judge should return such a verdict'.[57]

Clearly a claimant might sometimes find it difficult to demonstrate what caused an accident, especially if the witnesses who were most likely to know had perished. Consequently, although claimants bore the burden of presenting evidence to establish that it was more likely than not that the defendant or its servants had been negligent, and this negligence had caused their injuries, in particular circumstances they could rely on the doctrine of *res ipsa loquitur*. Where this doctrine applied its effect was to indicate that the defendant's negligence would be treated as established if no further explanation of the events was provided by the defendant. It could be argued that the doctrine achieved no more for the claimant than what the facts triggering its application might have achieved without it: for instance, in the words of Kennedy LJ, the doctrine applied where 'there is, in the circumstances of the particular case, some evidence which, viewed not as a matter of conjecture, but of reasonable argument, makes it more probable that there was some negligence, upon the facts as shown and undisputed, than that the occurrence took place without negligence'.[58] But the doctrine seems to have played a useful role in distinguishing those cases where the allegation of negligence was unacceptably conjectural from those where, in order to avoid losing, the defendant would be obliged to provide a convincing exculpatory explanation for the incident. The doctrine was invoked in railway cases where there was a derailment[59] or a collision with another train[60] or with buffers.[61] But in other situations, as might be expected, its availability fluctuated with experience. Thus, whilst in 1873[62] the Exchequer Chamber was willing to conclude that a carriage door flying open whilst a train was in motion was sufficient evidence of negligence on the part of the defendant's employees in the absence of an explanation, by 1944[63] the Court of Appeal thought

[57] *Metropolitan Railway Co.* v. *Wright* (1886) 11 App Cas 152. The quotation comes from the judgment of Lord Selborne LC in the Court of Appeal (at 153). The House of Lords dismissed the appeal, expressing a preference for a test in terms of unreasonableness rather than near perversity.

[58] *Russell* v. *London and South Western Railway Co.* (1908) 24 TLR 548, at 551.

[59] *Dawson* v. *Manchester, Sheffield and Lincolnshire Railway Co.* (1862) 5 LT 682.

[60] *Skinner* v. *London, Brighton and South Coast Railway Co.* (1850) 5 Ex 787; *Ayles* v. *South Eastern Railway* (1868) LR 3 Ex 146.

[61] *Burke* v. *Manchester, Sheffield and Lincolnshire Railway Co.* (1870) 22 LT 442.

[62] *Gee* v. *The Metropolitan Railway Co.* (1873) LR 8 QB 161, Exch Ch.

[63] *Easson* v. *London and North Eastern Railway Co.* [1944] 1 KB 421, CA.

that where a door was shown not to have been defective, such an incident was more likely to be a result of meddling by a third party.[64]

1.g A non-delegable duty

Whilst the cases discussed above suggest that a railway company's liability to injured passengers depended on negligence, it must be noted that the defendant company did not have to act carelessly itself. For instance, the ordinary rule of vicarious liability for the acts of employees in the course of employment applied so as to make railway companies whose employees performed their tasks carelessly – tasks such as driving, signalling or shutting carriage doors – liable to passengers injured as a result.[65] (The employer's position vis-à-vis other injured employees was different during the lifetime of the 'common employment' doctrine.)

From an early stage in the development of railway liability, however, it became clear that a railway company could be liable to its passengers even if it *and* its employees had acted carefully and only some person *other* than its employees had acted negligently.[66] The basis for such liability was that a railway company undertook to its passengers that they 'should be carried throughout the journey for which the ticket was issued with reasonable care'.[67] Thus, if a train belonging to one company ran over permanent way

[64] The *Gee* case seems to have involved a type of door that could not be opened from the inside, *per* Grove J., LR 8 QB at 180: 'if you arranged a door so that the passengers could open it from the inside, it would be an extremely perilous system'. By contrast, the *Easson* case involved a type of door that an adult passenger, but not the victim who was a small child, could open by leaning through the window and using the outside handle.

[65] In practice, focusing on the negligence of individual employees tended to distract from the systemic faults of railway companies. For instance, where a train hit the back of the train running in front of it on the same line, there was a tendency to blame the driver for failing to keep a proper look out, rather than to blame the company for continuing to use a time interval system for separating trains or allowing the train in front to be pulled by an insufficiently powerful locomotive. Similarly, focusing on the negligence of individual signalmen was more common than reference to the fact that they were often expected to work long days in atrocious conditions.

[66] It is sometimes said that such a rule makes railway companies 'vicariously liable for the acts of an independent contractor', but this is a misleading way of describing the law: under the doctrine of vicarious liability for the negligent acts of employees, it is generally thought that the employer is made liable for the tort of the employee, whilst in the cases described in the remainder of this section, the railway company is held liable 'for its own failure' to ensure that the journey of the passenger is as safe as reasonable care could make it.

[67] *John* v. *Bacon* (1870) LR 5 CP 437, at 441 *per* Bovill CJ, describing the basis of the decision of the Exchequer Chamber in *Great Western Railway Co.* v. *Blake* (1862) 7 H & N 987, in which he had appeared on behalf of the unsuccessful railway company. Keating J, who took part in both decisions, agreed with Bovill's recollection (at 442).

belonging to another company, then the train-owning company could be liable to its passengers for a defect in the permanent way attributable to the other company's carelessness: for instance, in *Buxton* v. *North Eastern Railway Co.*,[68] the defendant's train collided with a bullock whilst running over line owned by the Midland Railway. It was conceded that if the bullock had strayed onto the track because of the Midland's fault in maintaining its fencing, then the North Eastern would be liable.

One problem raised by this line of cases was the question of how far the ticket-issuing company's liability might extend. It was quickly held that it could cover negligence in the management of the line. Thus, in *Thomas* v. *Rhymney Railway Co.*[69] the claimant, a passenger in a train belonging to the defendant, was injured when it ran into the back of a train belonging to the Taff Vale Railway Company on a section of track owned by the latter. The collision was caused by employees of the Taff Vale Railway Company allowing its train to run without a proper tail light and allowing the defendant's train to follow too closely behind it.[70] The Exchequer Chamber held that the defendant company was nonetheless liable since its undertaking to its passenger was 'not only that they will not themselves be guilty of negligence, but that the passenger shall be carried with due and reasonable care along the whole line from one end of the journey to the other'.[71]

It seems that the non-delegable duty could also be relied on to make the owner of a line liable for the negligence of those who designed and built it. Thus, in *Grote* v. *Chester and Holyhead Railway Co.*,[72] the claimant had been a passenger in a train operated by the Shrewsbury and Chester Railway Co. on a line belonging to the defendants, and was injured when a cast-iron bridge over the River Dee collapsed. After the claimant obtained a favourable verdict, the defendants objected that there had been a misdirection and sought a new trial, arguing that they had not been negligent because they had engaged the eminent engineer, Robert Stephenson, to design the bridge. Parke B intervened in this argument to suggest that even if they had engaged a competent engineer, they would remain liable 'unless *he* also used due and reasonable care, and employed proper materials in the work'.[73] Pollock CB's judgment, which stated that the jury

[68] (1868) LR 3 QB 549. [69] (1871) LR 6 QB 266.

[70] The line was clearly using the notoriously dangerous time interval approach to separating trains.

[71] (1871) LR 6 QB 266, at 273. [72] (1848) 2 Ex 251.

[73] Emphasis added. The reference to 'proper materials' may suggest that Parke B was aware that the jury at the Coroner's Inquest into the fatalities resulting from the accident had expressed grave concern about the use of *cast* iron in such structures. Indeed, in response

ought to have been directed that the defendants would avoid liability if 'the best method is adopted, and the best materials are used', is also consistent with the view that a defendant might be liable for the fault of an independent engineer.[74]

The Exchequer Chamber in *Readhead* v. *Midland Railway Co.*[75] left open the question of the carrier's liability in the event of fault by the manufacturer of a carriage wheel. But the question was confronted by the Queen's Bench the next year in *Francis* v. *Cockrell.*[76] Although this case involved the partial collapse of a temporary grandstand at the Cheltenham race course, the judgment concentrated on the railway cases.[77] The Court put forward two reasons of principle why a railway defendant should be liable for the negligence of an independent manufacturer. Firstly, this should be the case because a passenger has no control over the selection of the manufacturer, whilst the carrier makes the selection and can introduce requirements as to quality and safety checks into its contract with the manufacturer. Secondly, the Court noted that the passenger would not have a direct action against a negligent manufacturer, so it was just to allow the passenger to sue the carrier and leave the carrier to then sue the manufacturer.[78] Subsequent railway cases seem to have assumed that it was settled that the non-delegable duty covered the care with which

to the jury's concern, a Royal Commission had been appointed in August 1847 to inquire into 'the application of iron to railway structures'. (The Commission did not report until July 1848.)

74 The claimant's verdict was upheld since Williams J confirmed that he had, in fact, directed the jury in line with these principles.

75 (1869) LR 4 QB 369, at 393. Some previous cases assumed that the carrier was not liable: in *Stokes* v. *Eastern Counties Railway Co.* (1860) 2 F & F 691, Cockburn CJ directed the jury that one of the questions it had to consider was whether the defendant company had itself welded the tyre that was defective (at 693).

76 (1870) LR 5 QB 184. The judgments referred to *Readhead's* case despite the fact that that case had not been decided in the Exchequer Chamber when the *Francis* case was argued.

77 Hannen J, delivering the judgment of the Court, stated that 'the same reasoning which is applicable to the case of a carrier of passengers is applicable to the case of a person who … provides places for spectators at races or other exhibitions' (at 194).

78 (1870) LR 5 QB 184, at 193–4. *Winterbottom* v. *Wright* (1842) 10 M & W 109 was generally cited in support of the proposition that there would be no direct claim against a negligent manufacturer, though the report suggests that in this case the defendant may have only contracted to supply the mail coach and keep it in good repair, rather than having manufactured it. That said, the defendant's counsel, Byles, argued against liability by raising the alarming consequence that if his client lost, then 'every one of the sufferers by such an accident as that which recently happened on the Versailles railway might have his action against the manufacturer of the defective axle'. The Versailles accident, in which a train derailed and caught fire because of a broken axle, had occurred less than a month before *Winterbottom* v. *Wright* was argued.

the manufacture of the locomotive and carriages had been undertaken.[79] Writing in 1965, Kahn-Freund described the non-delegable duty as 'a fundamental principle of the law of carriage at common law. It is submitted that it is still the law today.'[80]

The non-delegable duty could not, however, be stretched to cover every mishap causing an accident on the railway. For instance, in *Daniel* v. *Metropolitan Railway Co.*,[81] the House of Lords considered a case where contractors engaged in building the Smithfield Meat Market over the railway line negligently knocked a girder onto a passing train. The House of Lords unanimously held that the defendant railway company was not liable. In considering the scope of the non-delegable duty the Lord Chancellor, Lord Hatherley, distinguished between negligence in the maintenance and management of any portion of line over which a passenger was carried by the defendant and 'any mischief occasioned by any matter extraneous altogether to the work in which they were engaged'.[82] In *Wright* v. *Midland Railway Co.*[83] two years later, the Court of Exchequer confronted a case where the claimant had been a passenger in a Midland Railway train (which was on a line belonging to the Midland Railway Co.) when it was struck by a train operated by the London and North Western Railway, whose driver had negligently ignored the signals. The claimant's counsel conceded that the defendant could not be liable for the act of a trespasser who blocked the rails, but maintained that if a carrier could be liable when another company left a locomotive on the line, as in the

[79] See, for example, *John* v. *Bacon* (1870) LR 5 QB 437, at 443 *per* Montague Smith J; *Wright* v. *Midland Railway Co.* (1873) LR 8 QB 137, at 147 *per* Pollock B. The non-delegable duty did not extend, however, to wagons belonging to third parties being used on the defendant's lines: in such cases, the defendant's duty was merely to take reasonable care to examine them for defects: *Richardson* v. *Great Eastern Railway Co.* (1873) 1 CPD 342, CA.

[80] Kahn-Freund, *The Law of Carriage by Inland Transport*, 502–3. He felt the need to reassert the principle because of doubts created by the Occupiers Liability Act 1957. This statute expressly allows an occupier to fulfil his duty to a lawful visitor by reasonably relying on an independent contractor: s. 2(4)(a). The statute applies to moveable structures, but was expressly stated not to affect the obligations imposed by a contract to carry for reward: s. 5(3). This suggested that, at the very least, the statute might have altered the duty that a carrier owes to a non-contractual passenger with regard to the safety of a carriage.

[81] (1871) LR 5 HL 45.

[82] Ibid., at 55. Later in the same paragraph of his speech, he seemed to phrase the non-delegable obligation more narrowly: 'I apprehend that all that is to be done by those who carry passengers for hire is that they are bound to see that everything under their own control is in full and complete and proper order.' Perhaps he assumed that a railway company had some measure of control over the track that it had power to use, and how it was managed.

[83] (1873) LR 8 Exch 137.

leading case of *Great Western Railway Co.* v. *Blake*,[84] there should similarly be liability when the other company's locomotive ran into the carrier's train. The Court unanimously rejected this claim. Bramwell B held that a carrier would be liable for the state of the permanent way (track, switches, etc.) over which its train travelled, if it was not in such a state as reasonable care by its owner[85] ought to have made it, and would be liable for the carelessness of those who it relied on, almost as agents, to manage the safety of the journey (even if they were not employees of the carrier),[86] but distinguished these situations from others involving the careless behaviour of third parties. The Court regarded the analogy with the non-liability of a cab proprietor to it passengers for the negligent driving of another highway user as compelling.[87] But it was also influenced by an increased confidence that the claimant could successfully bring an action against the London and North Western Railway Co., even though he was not in privity with it.[88]

1.h Railway premises

Until 1961,[89] English law held that an occupier owed a less protective duty to licensees than to invitees. Passengers, intending passengers and the senders or consignees of goods were straightforwardly classified as invitees. Those seeing friends off or coming to meet them were regarded as licensees during most of the period surveyed,[90] though this classification was not important in cases of misfeasance. Liability to invitees was based on negligence, and throughout the period surveyed, courts seem to

[84] (1862) 7 H & N 987, Exch Ch.

[85] He expressly raised the hypothetical example of an accident being caused by a bridge over the line being brought down by the London and North Western Railway Co.'s negligence, no doubt echoing the decision in *Daniel* (ibid., at 143).

[86] This was intended to cover *Thomas* v. *Rhymney Railway Co.* (1871) LR 6 QB 266.

[87] Ibid., at 144.

[88] Ibid., at 143. In *Great Western Railway Co.* v. *Blake* (1862) 7 H & N 987, Cockburn CJ and Byles J had both expressed some hesitation as to whether the passenger could have claimed against the company whose employees actually negligently left the locomotive on the track. But the early case of *Grote* v. *Chester and Holyhead Railway Co.* (1848) 2 Ex 251, discussed above at p. 26, seems to have involved a successful claim against a company other than the claimant's carrier.

[89] The Occupiers Liability Act 1957 came into force in 1961.

[90] Charlesworth, *The Law of Negligence*, 104, noting the contrary opinion of Denman J in *Watkins* v. *Great Western Railway Co.* (1877) 37 LT 193. In *Stowell* v. *Railway Executive* [1949] 2 KB 519, Lynskey J applied the dictum of Denman J and held that 'the Railway Executive do invite anybody who desires to go and meet persons coming off trains, particularly to help them with their luggage, to do so'.

have set a realistic standard of fault. Thus in 1866, the Court of Common Pleas thought that there was no evidence of negligence where a passenger had fallen whilst ascending stairs without a handrail at King's Cross station after slipping on the brass edge of a step that had been worn smooth.[91] Although two witnesses had been called to testify that the stairs were dangerous because brass had been used rather than lead, and because of the absence of a handrail, the former point was rejected as mere opinion, and the latter because a handrail was no more than 'might be occasionally found convenient, as, by a man with a wooden leg, or a very infirm person'.[92] In 1952, the courts were equally clear that passengers could demand no more than reasonable efforts to clear snow or oil from platforms, and that injuries caused by failures to remove either immediately might not be actionable.[93]

In railway cases, the rule that only a very limited duty is owed to trespassers – not to inflict injury intentionally or to act 'with reckless disregard of the presence of the trespasser'[94] – was of particular importance. This rule was relevant not only in cases of trespassers on the tracks, but was also invoked against a person who hitched a ride on an out-of-service train.[95] Two doctrines were used with some degree of regularity to mitigate the effects of the trespasser rule, particularly in favour of children. Firstly, a tacit license might be inferred.[96] Alongside this, the concept of

91 *Crafter* v. *Metropolitan Railway Co.* (1866) LR 1 CP 300.

92 Ibid., at 303 *per* Erle CJ. The Court seems to have been particularly influenced by the facts that brass was commonly used on the edge of steps and 43,000 people per month had used the steps concerned without injury.

93 *Tomlinson* v. *Railway Executive* [1953] 1 All ER 1, CA; *Blackman* v. *Railway Executive* [1953] 1 All ER 4; cf. *Stowell* v. *Railway Executive* [1949] 2 KB 519, but in that case the defendants had a routine that, if carried out without negligence, ought to have cleared the slippery residues left after the unloading of the fish train.

94 *Robert Addie & Sons' Collieries Ltd* v. *Dumbreck* [1929] AC 358.

95 *Grand Trunk Railway Co. of Canada* v. *Barnett* [1911] AC 361, PC. Similarly *Lygo* v. *Newbold* (1854) 9 Ex 302, where the claimant rode without authority in a furniture cart that proved defective. A passenger travelling in a first class compartment with a lower class ticket would still be owed a duty of care: *Vosper* v. *Great Western Railway Co.* [1928] 1 KB 340, at 349.

96 In *Dublin, Wicklow and Wexford Railway Co.* v. *Slattery* (1878) 3 App. Cas. 1155, HL, evidence that a railway company's employees assented to a crossing being used defeated the effect of a notice stating 'Beware of the trains: do not cross the road except at the road gates'. In *Cooke* v. *Midland Great Western Railway of Ireland* [1909] AC 229, two members of the House of Lords went further and inferred a licence from the fact that no attempt had been made to keep children away from an unlocked railway turntable, despite the fact that they were known to play on it. But where officials regularly, but ineffectively, chased children away from an escalator, the Court of Appeal treated the situation as one of repeated trespass: *Hardy* v. *Central London Railway Co.* [1920] 3 KB 459.

'allurement' could be relied on, either to assist in establishing the licence or, more often, in establishing that the licensee had been unreasonably endangered. But this doctrine would rarely be of assistance to a child who strayed onto a working line.[97] Secondly, some courts held that the trespasser rule did not apply where the risk was created by the occupier's 'activity' rather than the state of his premises.[98] In *British Railways Board* v. *Herrington*,[99] the House of Lords removed the need to rely on such doctrines by recognizing a duty to take reasonable steps to keep children away from dangers such as electrified rails.[100] In reaching this conclusion, Lord Pearson identified social and physical changes that might be thought to justify it: post-war building had left children with less spaces to play; children tended to be subject to less parental supervision; and they had been exposed to increased dangers by new technology.[101] The decision was reinforced by the legislature passing the Occupiers Liability Act 1984, which imposes a duty of care towards anticipated trespassers with regard to known dangers where 'the risk is one against which, in all the circumstances of the case, he may reasonably be expected to offer the other some protection'.[102]

1.i Psychiatric injuries

Whilst English law adopted a fault liability regime with regard to personal injuries to passengers caused by railway accidents, the same claim cannot be made for wholly psychiatric injuries. From an early stage, railway accidents have been recognized as capable of causing psychiatric injuries to those involved, but concerns about the genuineness of wholly psychiatric

97 *Jenkins* v. *Great Western Railway* [1912] 1 KB 525; *Edwards* v. *Railway Executive* [1952] AC 737; cf. *Gough* v. *National Coal Board* [1954] 1 QB 191, where the child had a licence to cross the line.

98 This doctrine was expressly rejected, however, by the Privy Council in *Commissioner of Railways* v. *Quinlan* [1964] AC 1054, at 1075. It was most clearly expressed by Lord Denning MR in *Videan* v. *British Transport Commission* [1963] 2 QB 650, extending *Excelsior Wire Rope Co Ltd* v. *Callan* [1930] AC 304, HL.

99 [1972] AC 877.

100 Lord Pearson described the change in the law as making clear that an occupier: (i) could be liable to a trespasser for an omission; (ii) might owe a duty to take steps to prevent a person from trespassing; and (iii) could be liable to a trespasser without demonstrating subjective recklessness towards his safety.

101 [1972] AC 877, at 929.

102 Occupiers Liability Act 1984, s. 1(3). The trespasser does not have to be actually anticipated, or the danger actually known about: it is sufficient if there are 'reasonable grounds to believe'.

injuries and the multiplication of claims that might follow if witnesses of traumatic events could recover damages have led to the imposition of special limits on claims.[103] In such cases, English law might hold that the defendant owed no duty of care to the claimant, or, at least, no duty of care with regard to the type of loss suffered.

1.j Contributory negligence

In practice, one of the most important limits on liability for injuries caused in railway accidents was the defence of contributory negligence. Until 1945, this defence prevented a claimant from recovering damages if it could be proved that by an exercise of reasonable care for his own safety he could have avoided his injuries. Thus, if a passenger crossed onto the line in front of a train that he ought to have been able to see,[104] or descended from a train without checking how far beneath him the ground lay,[105] or attempted the hazardous act of closing a carriage door whilst the train was in motion, even though it was only a few minutes from the next stop,[106] then he would be unable to recover for any injuries suffered even if the defendant admitted negligence. It seems, however, that juries had a tendency not to find contributory negligence when a claimant excited sympathy. Consequently, the question arose whether a judge could withdraw a case from the jury if there was an unanswerable case of contributory negligence. The conclusion eventually reached was that although a claimant did not have to prove an absence of contributory negligence in order to succeed, if he admitted contributory negligence in the course of presenting his case, or *his* witnesses conclusively proved it, then the judge could withdraw the case from the jury.[107] The possibility of contributory

103 An important early case, involving an unsuccessful claim for psychiatric injury caused by a near miss on a level crossing, was *Victorian Railways Commissioner* v. *Coultas* (1888) 13 App Cas 222, PC.

104 *Davey* v. *London and South Western Railway Co.* (1883) 11 QBD 213. A contrary decision might be reached where the claimant had been invited onto the line, for instance by an open gate at a level crossing: *North Eastern Railway Co.* v. *Wanless* (1874) LR 7 HL 12.

105 *Sharpe* v. *Southern Railway* [1925] 2 KB 311, CA. A contrary decision might be reached if the claimant knew the platform well but the train stopped at a point opposite which the platform was unexpectedly sloping: *London, Tilbury and Southend Railway Co.* v. *Glasscock* (1902) 19 TLR 305, HL.

106 *Adams* v. *Lancashire and Yorkshire Railway Co.* (1869) LR 4 CP 739. A contrary decision might be reached if the claimant merely got up from his seat in order to better look out the window and leaned on the door, which proved not to have been properly shut: *Gee* v. *Metropolitan Railway Co.* (1873) LR 8 QB 161, Exch Ch.

107 This view was clearly expressed by Lord Hatherley LC in *Dublin, Wicklow and Wexford Railway Co.* v. *Slattery* (1878) 3 App Cas 1168, at 1180, and accepted by a majority of the

negligence could also prevent a finding that the defendant's negligence *caused* an injury: for instance, where there was a general absence of evidence as to how a person came by their injuries, as where a dead body was found near an unmanned crossing, then the possibility of contributory negligence might lead a court to hold that there was insufficient evidence to establish that any negligence of the defendant was *probably* the cause of the accident.[108]

One significant doctrine that was altered in the course of the period when contributory negligence was a complete defence was the doctrine of identification. In *Waite* v. *North Eastern Railway Co.*,[109] a five year old was injured when struck by a train whilst being led across the line by his grandmother, and was held to be unable to recover because of *her* contributory negligence. The doctrine of identification was eventually abandoned, but children did not fare much better under the idea that replaced it: a definition of the defendant's duty as only to take such care as would reasonably have prevented injury if the carer had been properly supervising the child.[110]

The Law Reform (Contributory Negligence) Act 1945, which reduced contributory negligence to a partial defence, will be discussed in the section dealing with road traffic accidents.

1.k *Legislative amendments to the rules of liability*

Lord Campbell's Act of 1845 (the direct ancestor of the Fatal Accidents Act 1976), which provided for actions to recover the loss of financial expectation of relatives after the negligent killing of a breadwinner played an important part in railway litigation. (Its passing without strong opposition from railway interests seems to have been linked to the abolition of deodands – the ancient power of Coroners' juries to set a price on an object that had caused a death, with the price to be paid on pain of forfeiture of the object (e.g. a locomotive) to the Crown.) The Act played a significant role in stimulating litigation against railways in the mid Victorian era.

House of Lords in *Wakelin* v. *London and South Western Railway Co.* (1886) 12 App Cas 41, at 48 *per* Lord Watson (with whom Lord Blackburn agreed) and at 52 *per* Lord FitzGerald.

108 *Wakelin* v. *London and South Western Railway Co.* (1886) 12 App Cas 41. A different conclusion was reached where an unwitnessed accident occurred in circumstances where it seemed most probable that the death was caused by the defendant's negligence and improbable that there was contributory negligence: *Jones* v. *Great Western Railway Co.* (1930) 47 TLR 39, HL.

109 (1858) El Bl & El 719, QB; (1859) El Bl & El 728, Exch Ch.

110 *O'Connor* v. *British Transport Commission* [1958] 1 WLR 346, CA.

1.k.i Public ownership

Apart from governmental management of the railway system through the issuing of directives to a Railway Executive Committee comprising the general managers of the twelve leading companies during the First World War, and a similar arrangement during the Second World War, the English railway companies remained private concerns until nationalization by the Transport Act 1947.[111] On nationalization, the railways and their rolling stock were vested in the British Transport Commission and managed, at first, by the Railway Executive. The Transport Act 1962 replaced the Commission with a British Railways Board from 1 January 1963. The Railways Act 1993 structured the privatization of the system, but one element was partially renationalized in 2001. There is no obvious evidence of these changes having a direct or indirect effect on liability rules.[112]

1.k.ii Compulsory and advisory standards of railway safety

The question of whether Parliament ought to legislate to improve railway safety was regularly asked in England between 1840 and 1890. Although the question often received a positive answer, the 'techniques' used by the legislature during this period are worthy of comment. The principal method was to require railway companies to provide information. Thus, companies were obliged to provide information about accidents, and later to report the extent to which they had adopted certain desirable safety measures. On a few occasions, Parliament went further and imposed a duty to adopt a particular measure. A major obstacle in the way of the latter sort of legislation, however, was that different railway companies had often already invested in different forms of technology, and in many cases there was no clear basis for treating one as superior. Those who opposed legislative compulsion were significantly assisted by the history of the Regulation of Railways Act 1868, which obliged companies to provide (on all passenger trains travelling more than 20 miles between stops) a mechanism approved by the Board of Trade by which passengers could communicate with the train staff. Unfortunately, the only mechanism

[111] The Railway Act 1921 had led to the grouping of the railway companies into four new regional companies. But this result was achieved through voluntary amalgamations in the shadow of the Act's provisions, which provided for matters to be referred to an Amalgamation Board.

[112] English law does not have a separate regime of public-law damages liability, but rather applies ordinary tort law to public officials and authorities. A rare exception is the special public tort of misfeasance in public office, but this does not seem to have been used against a nationalized industry.

that the Board of Trade approved was so unreliable that approval had to be withdrawn. Whilst Parliament's response to the Armagh accident,[113] the Regulation of Railways Act 1889, granted the Board of Trade power to order companies to fit automatic brakes to all passenger trains, to complete the interlocking of all points and signals and to use only the telegraph block system, most companies had already adopted these measures.

The power to inspect new railways before they were opened,[114] bolstered two years later by a power to postpone the opening of a new line where such opening was likely to be attended with danger to the public,[115] seems to have been of far greater practical significance. This power was important in ensuring that new lines met modern safety standards even where such standards were not mandatory on existing lines.

2 Traffic accidents

2.a *What is a traffic accident?*

A wide range of events have some claim to be referred to as 'traffic accidents'. The most obvious paradigms may involve collisions between two moving motor vehicles or between a moving motor vehicle and a pedestrian, but other common patterns are frequently encountered, for instance: collisions between moving motor vehicles and stationary objects on the highway (such as a parked lorry) or alongside the highway (such as a wall or a tree); and collisions between moving motor vehicles and animals. Clearly, further variations could involve hybrids, for instance collisions between moving motor vehicles and stationary objects as a result of an attempt to avoid a collision between a moving motor vehicle and another moving vehicle, pedestrian or animal. And each paradigm can be sub-divided further in terms of whether the incident involved negligent conduct by a driver, negligent conduct by a person responsible for some object that the driver collided with (e.g. a pedestrian, an owner of a stationary lorry on the highway, a keeper of an animal, etc.), a mechanical failure that may be traced to a problem with the manufacture or maintenance of the vehicle or a problem with the road surface, with the surrounding architecture

[113] A train carrying mainly children returning from a Sunday School excursion was deliberately split in two after the locomotive failed to pull it up a long gradient. The rear section, which did not have an automatic brake, ran backwards down the gradient and collided with a following train. Eighty-eight people were killed (mostly children) and almost 200 more were injured.

[114] Regulation of Railways Act 1840.

[115] Regulation of Railways Act 1842.

(e.g. street lighting or traffic lights), with signage or with layout. Other overlapping schemes of categorization might reflect different classes of claimants (e.g. drivers, passengers, pedestrians, rescuers and relatives of any of these) or different classes of defendants (e.g. drivers, employers of drivers, owners of vehicles driven by authorized users, owners of vehicles driven by unauthorized users, people responsible for obstructions (e.g. parked vehicles), vehicle manufacturers, highway authorities and social hosts). Whilst a useful sketch of the relevant law can be provided without a perfect typology of 'traffic accidents', an appreciation of the variety within the class is important in understanding the extent to which the sketch that follows falls short of a comprehensive description.[116]

The number of private cars on the road and their distribution across society both changed markedly during the twentieth century. In 1904, there were 8,465 private cars in Great Britain; by 1910 there were 53,169, and the number has continued to grow: 186,801 by 1920; 1,056,216 by 1930; 1,979,000 by 1950; 9,971,000 by 1970; and 26,508,000 by 2006.[117] The 'distribution' of private cars may, however, be more important for understanding the social dynamics involved in traffic accidents. Thus, in 1914, only one person in 232 in Great Britain owned a car, but by 1922 the equivalent figure had changed to one in 78, and by 1938 it was one in 15.[118] In 2006, as a raw figure, the number of road vehicles per head of population stands at a little over 1:2. If, instead, one considers the matter in terms of households, then in 1951, 86% of households did not own a car; by 1961 the figure had fallen to 69%, by 1971 to 48%, by 1981 to 40%, by 1991 to 32% and by 2005 to 25%. Alongside these figures, whilst only 1% of households had two cars in 1951, by 2005 this had risen to 26%, with a further 5% of households having three or more.[119] Thus the typical traffic accident

[116] For instance, the discussion below will not cover accidents caused by wandering livestock (see, e.g., *Searle* v. *Wallbank* [1947] AC 341 and Animals Act 1971, s. 8) or claims by paying passengers on public transport.

[117] These figures do not include all vehicles on the road. So, for instance, in 2004, the total number of road vehicles, including goods vehicles, public service vehicles and motorcycles, stood at 32,259,000. Sources: for years before 1951, see A. H. Halsey and J. Webb (eds), *Twentieth-Century British Social Trends* (3rd edn Basingstoke: Macmillan, 2000), Ch. 13 (by A. Root), and for 1951 and thereafter, see Department of Transport, *Transport Statistics Great Britain 2007* (33rd edn, London: TSO, 2007), section 9.

[118] Halsey and Webb, *Twentieth-Century British Social Trends*, 445.

[119] Department of Transport, *Transport Statistics Great Britain 2007*, table 9.14. Both mean cars per household and the proportion of households having two or more cars were highest in rural areas (1.54; 55%), and lower in London (0.83; 16%) than in other cities with a population over a quarter of a million (1.15; 32%): table 9.15.

of the first quarter of the twentieth century[120] probably tended to involve a pedestrian being injured by a relatively more wealthy private motorist, or by a vehicle owned by a business, such as a goods vehicle or bus. Whilst this pattern was largely dictated by who owned vehicles, it also reflected the fact that urban areas had not been designed to separate pedestrians and motor vehicles.[121] Matters changed during the middle third of the century so that the majority of private motorists were drawn from the middle classes, and collisions between vehicles became more common. Thus, in 1950, there were 167,000 road accidents, which led to the deaths of 2,251 pedestrians and 827 drivers and passengers, but by 1970, whilst the pedestrian fatality figure had risen more slowly than the increase in the number of accidents (to 2,925), the driver and passenger fatality figure had leapt past it (to 3,440). Since peaking in 1972, both figures have fallen, despite the fact that traffic levels have more than doubled (226 billion km of traffic in 1972 to 511 billion km in 2006), but the pedestrian fatality figure has fallen faster than the driver and passenger figure (in 2006, there were 675 pedestrian fatalities and 1,752 driver and passenger fatalities). Indeed, the vast improvements in the protection that cars provide to their occupants in the event of an accident probably masks the extent to which in the final third of the twentieth century collisions between vehicles became the dominant type of road traffic accident.[122] To sketch the change in crude terms, the social dynamic of typical road accidents has moved from relatively rich motorists injuring relatively poor pedestrians to motorists from across the social classes injuring other motorists and their passengers from across the social classes. More significant than this change, however, may be the fact that motor vehicles, more than any other item of technology, exposed a large proportion of the population to the risk of becoming a tortfeasor.[123]

[120] The discussion in this paragraph leaves aside single vehicle accidents where the only casualty is the driver.

[121] The claim is not that early twentieth century roads did not have pavements and curbs (most did), but rather that the designs did not meet the later pattern of building major urban roads so that pedestrians did not have to cross them or could only cross at controlled points.

[122] The figures in the paragraph come from Department of Transport, *Transport Statistics Great Britain 2007*, table 8.1. The quoted figures do not include the number of pedal cyclists or motorcyclists killed.

[123] Similarly, it has been noted that the criminal regulation of motoring was responsible for a substantial increase in the number of encounters between the middle classes, the police and the courts. Between 1900 and 1909, only 6.3% of persons charged with indictable or summary offences were charged with motoring offences. By 1930 to 1933, the

2.b *Were the ordinary principles of fault liability ostensibly applied in road traffic cases?*

If the 'ordinary principles' are taken to be that 'a defendant found to have exhibited less than reasonable care in conducting a particular activity is liable to compensate a claimant for such losses as that carelessness caused, provided such types of losses were not too remote a consequence of the carelessness,[124] subject to the availability of defences', then these were ostensibly applied by the English courts to most categories of road traffic accident throughout the period surveyed.

Several qualifications are necessary, however, in order to provide a more comprehensive answer. Firstly, certain classes of defendants could be held liable, even if they were not personally careless, for instance employers of employees who drove carelessly during the course of employment, or owners of vehicles that were driven carelessly by their authorized agents.[125] Secondly, in particular situations, the ordinary principles would not apply because it would be held that the defendant owed no duty of care to the claimant, or no duty of care with regard to the type of loss suffered. For example, careless drivers might not have to compensate all those who suffered psychiatric injuries[126] or compensate all those who suffered purely economic losses as a result of their carelessness.[127] Thirdly, in particular situations, the law of England and Wales might allow a claimant to rely on a cause of action other than the tort of negligence, and this cause of action might not require proof of carelessness. Thus, for example, cases involving accidents caused by highway obstructions were sometimes presented as involving public nuisance, and some cases have sought to rely on trespass (liability for direct infliction of force). In both situations, the English courts have adapted the causes of action towards consistency with the

comparable figure was 43.2%. Figures from C. Emsley, '"Mother, What Did Policemen Do When There Weren't Any Motors?" The Law, the Police and the Regulation of Motor Traffic in England, 1900–1939' (1993) 36 *Historical Journal* 357.

124 It is well known that the test of remoteness of damage in English law altered during the period under review, but there is no indication that the alteration was specifically linked to considerations raised by road accident cases.

125 See further below, p. 48.

126 A history of recovery for psychiatric injury in road accidents would be almost equivalent to a general history of psychiatric injury in English tort law. Key milestones include *Bourhill* v. *Young* [1943] AC 92; *McLoughlin* v. *O'Brian* [1983] 1 AC 410; *Page* v. *Smith* [1996] AC 155.

127 One of the most commonly invoked examples of an accident causing substantial pure economic losses that will not be compensated in tort involves a motorist negligently causing an accident that blocks a tunnel or a bridge, with the result that hundreds of other motorists suffer pure economic losses through being delayed.

negligence principles, even whilst acknowledging the availability of the different cause of action.[128]

2.c Rejection of strict liability

Fault liability was well established in cases of running down and highway collisions before the age of the motor car.[129] Some of the explanations offered by the late Victorian judges for this are worth noting. Thus, in *Fletcher* v. *Rylands*,[130] the Exchequer Chamber explained:

> Traffic on the highways, whether by land or sea, cannot be conducted without exposing those whose persons or property are near it to some inevitable risk; and that being so, those who go on the highway, or have their property adjacent to it, may well be held to do so subject to their taking upon themselves the risk of injury from that inevitable danger; and persons who by the licence of the owner pass near to warehouses where goods are being raised or lowered, certainly do so subject to the inevitable risk of accident. In neither case, therefore, can they recover without proof of want of care or skill occasioning the accident.

Similarly, in *Holmes* v. *Mather*,[131] holding that a defendant was not liable when his carriage had mounted the pavement and struck the claimant

[128] Thus, in *Letang* v. *Cooper* [1965] 1 QB 232, CA, Lord Denning MR restricted the utility of the tort of trespass to the person in motoring cases by suggesting that it required both intention to apply force and intentional injury. But, in *Dymond* v. *Pearce* [1972] 1 QB 496, CA, both Sachs and Stephenson LJJ accepted that situations could exist in which a claim for personal injury could succeed in public nuisance although a claim in the tort of negligence would fail.

[129] For instance, in *Wakeman* v. *Robinson* (1823) 1 Bing 213, a claim in trespass where the shaft of the defendant's gig had injured the claimant's waggon horse whilst he was attempting to overtake, Dallas CJ stated that 'if the accident happened entirely without default on the part of the Defendant, or blame imputable to him, the action does not lie' (at 215); in *Boss* v. *Litton* (1832) 5 C & P 407, a claim by a pedestrian struck whilst he was walking on the carriageway rather than the footway, which was in a poor condition, it was held that the pedestrian was entitled to walk on the carriageway and was entitled to drivers exerting reasonable care; in *Cotterill* v. *Starkey* (1839) 8 C & P 691, a claim in trespass by a pedestrian run down whilst crossing a highway, Patterson J held that foot passengers had a right to cross, and persons driving would be liable if they did not take care. The reporter helpfully included a direction that Best LCJ had given to a jury in 1827: 'I include within the term negligence, not only careless driving, but exciting the horses to such a rate of speed that they cannot be stopped or properly directed, the knowing driving of unbroken or vicious horses, overloading a coach, or using one that has not sufficient strength or improper harness.'

[130] (1866) LR 1 Ex 265, at 286–7 *per* Blackburn J. The case was unsuccessfully appealed to the House of Lords: (1868) LR 3 HL 330.

[131] (1875) LR 10 Ex 261, at 267.

whilst he was doing his best[132] to control his horse after it had been startled by a dog, Bramwell B stated: 'For the convenience of mankind in carrying on the affairs of life, people as they go along roads must expect, or put up with, such mischief as reasonable care on the part of others cannot avoid.'

In *Wing* v. *London General Omnibus Co.*,[133] the question was raised if it was negligent to send 'motor omnibuses and other vehicles propelled by motor power' onto the streets because they 'had a tendency to skid on slippery roads',[134] even when driven carefully. A majority in the Court of Appeal held that this characteristic did not amount to evidence of negligence, no doubt with a degree of relief since it was acknowledged that 'thousands of motor omnibuses travel in the streets of London in all weathers, and they carry a considerable proportion of the passenger traffic of London'.[135] Fletcher Moulton LJ pointed to the advantages that motor vehicles had over horse-drawn vehicles with regard to safety: motor vehicles were not prone to run away when startled by dogs, or the like, and generally had more efficient braking.[136] He accepted, however, that, as a matter of law, '[i]f a man places on the streets vehicles so wholly unmanageable as necessarily to be a continuing danger to other vehicles, either at all times or under special conditions of weather, I have no doubt that he does it at his peril, and that he is responsible for injuries arising therefrom, even though there has been no negligence in the management of his vehicle'.[137] The significance of this case is that it indicates that reasonably driven and reasonably built motor vehicles had become accepted by 1909 as one of the ordinary risks of metropolitan life that citizens were thought to have accepted.[138]

In *Phillips* v. *Britannic Hygenic Laundry Co. Ltd*,[139] an attempt was made to establish strict liability for accidents caused by 'defective' motor vehicles by using the tort of breach of statutory duty to make actionable a

132 The defendant's servant had actually been driving, but Bramwell B expressly decided the case on the assumption that the defendant was 'as much liable as if he had been driving'.

133 [1909] 2 KB 652, CA.

134 Ibid., at 661.

135 Ibid., at 667.

136 Ibid., at 666. Such advantages must be seen in the context of the omnibus concerned running at five miles per hour.

137 Ibid., at 665.

138 Although the *Wing* case involved a claim by a passenger, Fletcher-Moulton LJ stated that the principles quoted above would have applied had she been a member of the public using the highway.

139 [1923] 1 KB 539, KB; [1923] 2 KB 832, CA. Seven weeks after the defendant's motor lorry had returned from being overhauled by its manufacturer, its axle broke, and a wheel came off and damaged the claimant's vehicle.

regulation providing that 'the motor car and all the fittings thereof shall be in such a condition as not to cause, or to be likely to cause, danger to any person on the motor car or on the highway'.[140] The Court of Appeal upheld the King's Bench's decision that the regulation was not intended to be actionable in this way, but only by means of a criminal penalty.[141] Before the King's Bench, the claimant's lawyer had also argued, unsuccessfully, for strict liability as a matter of common law.[142] McCardie J stated: 'In my humble opinion, such is not, nor ought it to be, the law. The burden would seem unjust.'[143] He cited Bramwell B's explanation for fault liability from *Holmes* v. *Mather*[144] and pointed out that owners of horse-drawn vehicles were not strictly liable to other road users for the defects in their horses.

2.d Standard of care

In *Nettleship* v. *Weston*,[145] Salmon LJ stated that 'in the absence of a special relationship, what is reasonable care and skill is measured by the standard of competence usually achieved by the ordinary driver'. The caselaw dealing with 'proof' of negligence, however, suggests an oscillation between 'the standard *usually* achieved' and 'the standard espoused as appropriate by driving manuals and the Highway Code'. It is clear, however, that the legal obligation is not to drive in as safe a way as is technically possible. The balancing of the safety of pedestrians against the convenience of motorists, which must occur within the fault standard,[146] is illustrated by *Moore* v. *Poyner*.[147] In this case, the defendant was driving through a residential district at about 30 miles per hour on a Sunday afternoon and struck a

[140] Motor Cars (Use and Construction) Order 1904, reg. 6, made under Locomotives on Highways Act 1896, s. 6(1).

[141] English law does not allow injured parties to base a claim for compensation on a defendant's breach of his statutory duty unless the Court finds that Parliament intended the particular statutory duty to give rise to such claims.

[142] A degree of support was derived from *Hutchins* v. *Maunder* (1920) 37 TLR 72, where a motor car owner had been held liable for an accident caused by defective steering gear, even though the defect could not have been discovered by reasonable care. Darling J had stated that it amounted to negligence to put such a car on the road.

[143] [1923] 1 KB 539, at 551. [144] Above, at note 131.

[145] [1971] 2 QB 691, at 703. There is an obvious contrast with the opinion of Lord Denning MR (at 699) that every ordinary driver is expected to 'drive in as good a manner as a driver of skill, experience and care, who is sound in wind and limb, who makes no errors of judgment, has good eyesight and hearing, and is free from any infirmity'.

[146] This is not, of course, to claim that judges perform the balancing themselves. No doubt they generally seek to identify and adopt pre-existing social consensus as to appropriate standards of behaviour.

[147] [1975] RTR 127, CA.

child who ran out from behind a coach that was parked on the curb. The trial judge held that the defendant was negligent in not slowing down or sounding his horn when about to pass the coach, given his awareness that children played in the area. But a majority of the Court of Appeal allowed an appeal because they thought that the standard of care that this implied was too high, and the defendant had not been driving unreasonably.

The main issue in *Nettleship* was whether the standard of care should vary in accordance with the capacity of the defendant, particularly where the claimant had been aware of the unusual lack of capacity (e.g. inexperience) before the accident. The Court of Appeal decided that it should not, with Megaw LJ emphasizing the utility of a 'reasonably certain and reasonably ascertainable' standard.[148] The two exceptions to this that have been widely recognized are where a driver becomes unfit to drive without warning[149] and where a driver responds to the exigencies of an emergency.[150]

2.e *Proof of fault*

As in railway cases, the doctrine of *res ipsa loquitur* was of some use to claimants seeking to prove fault.

2.f *Contributory negligence*

Similarly to its role in railway cases, the defence of contributory negligence played an important role in allocating the losses associated with road traffic accidents.[151] Thus, if in 1928 a motorist approached a cross-roads without due care and struck a motorcyclist travelling across his

148 [1971] 2 QB 691, at 709. More fully (at 708–9), 'I … do not think that our legal process could successfully or satisfactorily cope with the task of fairly assessing or applying to the facts of a particular case such varying standards, depending on such complex and elusive factors, including the assessment by the court, not merely of a person's actual skill or experience, but also of another person's knowledge or assessment of that skill or experience at a particular moment of time.'

149 *Mansfield* v. *Weetabix Ltd* [1998] 1 WLR 1263, CA.

150 *Parkinson* v. *Liverpool Corporation* [1950] 1 All ER 367, CA (sudden braking to save a dog); *Marshall* v. *Osmond* [1983] QB 1034, CA (error of judgment of police driver pursuing a stolen car not negligent).

151 The House of Lords Select Committee on the Prevention of Road Accidents 1937 to 1939 analyzed 100,000 road accidents that took place in 1937, and attributed 64.7% of fatal accidents and 57.4% of non-fatal accidents to the fault of pedestrians. These figures were approximately double the equivalents calculated by the Ministry of Transport in 1936. Both sets of statistics are quoted in S. O'Connell, *The Car in British Society: Class, Gender and Motoring 1896–1939* (Manchester University Press, 1998), 128.

path, the motorcyclist would be disentitled from recovering compensation if he could have avoided the collision by himself driving with reasonable care.[152] Since 1945, the successful invocation of the defence has led to a proportionate reduction in the amount of damages awarded, rather than a judgment for the defendant. The practical effect of the defence, however, is to leave many child pedestrians,[153] other incautious road-crossers[154] and motorists who fail to wear seatbelts[155] without full compensation, even if a driver's fault is established.

2.g *Liability rules and liability insurance*

The strongest link between liability rules and liability insurance can probably be demonstrated through a rhetorical question: is it likely that the present liability rules would exist if no risk distribution device such as third-party motor insurance existed? Richard Lewis[156] has pointed out that, currently in England and Wales, insurance companies are the real defendants in nine out of ten personal injury claims (the others being principally against large 'self-insured' institutions or public bodies) and insurance companies are responsible for paying 94 per cent of tort compensation for personal injury. John Fleming's view was that, without insurance, the tort system 'would long ago have collapsed under the weight of the demands put on it and been replaced by an alternative, and perhaps more efficient system of accident compensation'.[157]

The importance of liability insurance in underpinning road traffic liability can be seen through a sketch of the stages in the introduction of compulsory liability insurance.[158] Liability insurance was first made compulsory by the Road Traffic Act 1930, following the recommendations of a Royal Commission, which had reported the previous year. In 1930, the compulsory policy had to cover 'liability' to third parties (but excluding passengers) for causing death or personal injury, and the cost

152 *Swadling* v. *Cooper* [1931] AC 1.

153 For example *Morales* v. *Ecclestone* [1991] RTR 151 (eleven year old held 75% responsible for his injuries (75% reduction in damages)).

154 For example *Fitzgerald* v. *Lane* [1989] AC 328 (adult held 50% responsible for his injuries (50% reduction in damages for tetraplegia)).

155 For example *Froom* v. *Butcher* [1976] AC 286, CA.

156 R. Lewis, 'Insurers and Personal Injury Litigation: Acknowledging "the Elephant in the Living Room"' [2005] *Journal of Personal Injury Law* 1.

157 J. G. Fleming, *The Law of Torts* (9th edn, Sydney: LBC Information Services, 1998), 13.

158 The following paragraphs draw heavily on J. Stuart-Smith and R. Merkin, *The Law of Motor Insurance* (London: Sweet & Maxwell, 2004), Ch. 1.

of hospital treatment (up to £25). This Act was supplemented soon afterwards by the Third Parties (Rights against Insurers) Act 1930, which sought to prevent insurance proceeds being treated as part of the assets of a defendant who went bankrupt or into liquidation. The Road Traffic Act 1934 made further changes to improve the protection provided to injured third parties by compulsory insurance[159] by giving them a direct action against the insurer in certain additional situations[160] and preventing insurers from relying on specified policy limitations (e.g. as to use of the vehicle) against third-party claims (though the insurer could still seek an indemnity from the assured) and from avoiding policies for non-disclosure unless this was done within three months of a third party's claim being made.

These Acts did not, however, provide any mechanism for compensating victims of motorists who had failed to obtain the compulsory insurance.[161] The Cassel Committee, which reported in 1937, recommended the creation of a central guarantee fund. But the Second World War intervened before legislation was passed. In 1946 the motor insurance industry entered a pre-emptive agreement with the Government which allowed a claimant who had obtained a judgment against an uninsured driver to enforce that judgment against the Motor Insurers Bureau.[162] The problem faced by a victim of a hit-and-run driver (who could not identify a defendant, insured or uninsured, to sue) led to a further agreement – the Untraced Drivers Agreement – between the Motor Insurers Bureau and the government in 1969.[163]

The Motor Vehicle (Passenger Insurance) Act 1971 extended compulsory insurance to injuries suffered by passengers. At the same time, agreements between passengers and drivers to exclude the driver's liability were made ineffective (and the defence of *volenti non fit injuria* (consent to risk) was withdrawn).[164] Since then, most changes have reflected the European

[159] The 1934 Act also extended the requirement to insure against the cost of hospital treatment to the cost of emergency roadside treatment.

[160] Particularly where the assured refused to make a claim against his insurers; the direct action avoided the need to put the assured into bankruptcy.

[161] The courts sought to engineer a partial solution by holding in *Monk* v. *Warbey* [1935] 1 KB 75 that an owner who caused or permitted his vehicle to be driven without compulsory insurance committed the tort of breach of statutory duty to a victim who ought to have been able to benefit from such insurance. This action remains available, despite its significance having been reduced by the MIB agreement: *Norman* v. *Aziz* [2000] Lloyd's Rep IR 52.

[162] New agreements on the same topic were entered in 1972, 1988 and 1999.

[163] Replaced in 1972 and 1996.

[164] The 1960 and 1971 Acts were consolidated in the Road Traffic Act 1972.

Community's Motor Insurance Directives.[165] A significant amendment unconnected to European Community influence has been the introduction of a regime (Road Traffic (NHS Charges) Act 1999) allowing NHS hospitals to recover the true cost of medical treatment from insurers.[166]

The question of the extent to which the existence of third-party motor insurance has influenced the 'form' of the legal rules used in motor accident cases (as opposed to merely ensuring the continued existence of tort liability) is more controversial.[167] The influence of such insurance on statutory changes to liability rules may be easier to demonstrate than its influence on the common law. In this context, Lewis[168] has identified the legislation removing the bar on actions between spouses,[169] allowing actions against the estates of deceased people[170] and dissolved companies[171] and exceptionally allowing a child to sue its mother for injuries suffered *in utero* as a result of her negligent driving.[172]

With regard to the common law, Lord Denning's statements in *Nettleship* v. *Weston*[173] ('[m]orally the learner driver is not at fault; but legally she is liable to be because she is insured and the risk should fall on her') and *Morris* v. *Ford Motor Co. Ltd*[174] ('[t]he damages are expected to be borne by the insurers. The courts recognize this every day. They would not find negligence so readily – or award sums of such increasing magnitude – except on the footing that the damages are to be borne, not by the man himself, but by an insurance company') have been pointed to as important evidence. But the significance of such statements must be measured alongside phenomena such as: (i) a continuing stream of appellate litigation relating to breach of duty in motoring cases, including many where defendants have been successful;[175] and (ii) regular substantial

165 For discussion see, p. 173 (also p. 105).

166 Private hospitals rely on the 1988 Act, consolidating the 1930 provision – though the amounts recoverable have been updated.

167 For example J. Stapleton, 'Tort, Insurance and Ideology' (1995) 58 *Modern Law Review* (MLR) 820; M. Clarke, *Policies and Perceptions of Insurance* (Oxford: Clarendon Press, 1997), Ch. 8; J. Morgan, 'Tort, Insurance and Incoherence' (2004) 67 MLR 384; R. Lewis, 'Insurance and the Tort System' (2005) 25 *Legal Studies* 85.

168 Lewis, 'Insurance and the Tort System'.

169 Law Reform (Husband and Wife) Act 1962.

170 Law Reform (Miscellaneous Provisions) Act 1934.

171 Companies Act 1989, s. 141.

172 Congenital Disabilities (Civil Liability) Act 1976.

173 [1971] 2 QB 691, at 699.

174 [1973] QB 792, at 798.

175 *Mansfield* v. *Weetabix* [1998] 1 WLR 1263, CA, is a prominent example, where the accident was caused by the onset of undetectable illness. More recent, and routine, examples

deductions of damages for contributory negligence even when the consequent uncompensated part of the claimant's loss will not be covered by some other insurance policy (including a deduction of 50 per cent in the *Nettleship* case!).[176]

If the difference between reasonable driving as constructed by the courts and reasonable driving as commonly practised is greater than the difference between reasonable performance of some comparable activity (not covered by insurance) as constructed by the courts and reasonable performance of that activity as commonly practised, then this would provide some evidence of third-party motor insurance influencing the legal standards used in motor accident cases. One risky activity that is commonly uninsured is 'pedestrianism', though here the standards are constructed by courts applying the defence of contributory negligence. Some illuminating comparisons can be drawn: for instance, in driver negligence cases, inexperience is treated as irrelevant when setting the required standard (*Nettleship*), but inexperience (particularly associated with youth) is considered when determining the contributory negligence of pedestrians; similarly, in driver negligence cases, a regular theme is that drivers should anticipate both bad driving by others[177] and careless behaviour by pedestrians,[178] whilst it has been held that pedestrians may assume that drivers will observe red lights and road signs;[179] similarly, non-compliance with a provision of the Highway Code seems to be a more weighty indication of negligence by a driver than of contributory

include *Turner* v. *Arriva North East Ltd* [2006] EWCA Civ 410, CA, where a bus driver was held not liable for driving at a speed close to the speed limit and colliding with a pedestrian who was using a pedestrian crossing whilst the lights were against her, but whilst traffic was stationary in the lanes other than that reserved for use by buses, and *Farley* v. *Buckley* [2007] EWCA Civ 403, CA, where a driver who had turned right at slow speed out of a narrow minor road whilst a refuse truck was waiting to turn left into the minor road was held not to be liable for injuries suffered by the driver of a motor scooter who was overtaking the refuse truck at a reckless speed.

176 Recent cases illustrating the willingness of courts to make substantial deductions for contributory negligence, even in high-value cases, include *Jukes* v. *Etti* [2007] RTR 2 (40% deduction where an adult sought to dash across the road but the driver negligently failed to see him) and *Ehrari* v. *Curry* [2006] EWHC 1319 (QB) (decision on liability upheld on appeal; [2007] RTR 42, CA) (70% deduction where a thirteen year old walked out into traffic from behind a parked car).

177 For example *Wadsworth* v. *Gillespie* [1978] CLY 2534 (held to be negligent to assume that a motorcyclist who is indicating that he is about to make a left turn is about to make a left turn, rather than having accidentally knocked the indicator).

178 *Williams* v. *Needham* [1972] RTR 387.

179 *Tremayne* v. *Hill* [1987] RTR 131. It must be doubted whether pedestrians may assume this in all circumstances.

negligence by a pedestrian.[180] Beyond the points where a direct comparison can be drawn, there are certainly more cases where there is a significant difference between the standard of care as constructed by (appellate) courts and reasonable driving as commonly practiced[181] than there are cases setting an idealized standard for pedestrians. Similarly, cases on reasonable care in inspecting for vehicle defects might be accused of having set an unrealistic standard.[182]

Of course, the form of legal rules is not the only way in which third-party motor insurance may have influenced the 'outcome' of motor accident cases. For instance, insurance may influence which cases are litigated: studies suggest that once a claim has been made, liability is rarely contested, particularly in claims of low value.[183] Where both parties involved in a collision carried (voluntary) loss insurance as well as (compulsory) liability insurance, an agreement between insurance companies might prevent the litigation of 'property damage' claims. The existence of such agreements was judicially recognized in *Morley* v. *Moore*.[184] But Richard Lewis, who wrote the leading legal study on such agreements in England,[185] has more recently written (in 2005) that insurers have become more reluctant to enter such agreements in recent years, and such agreements tend to be confined to insurers having similar risk profiles.

Even where litigation occurs, insurance may have influenced how facts were interpreted, but such an effect would be very difficult to detect.[186]

180 For example *Powell* v. *Phillips* [1972] 3 All ER 864, CA. The case involved an injury to a pedestrian who had stepped into the roadway to avoid slush on the pavement, but with her back to oncoming traffic at night and whilst not wearing or carrying anything white or reflective. It was held that such a breach of Highway Code did not even create a 'presumption of [contributory] negligence calling for an explanation'.

181 For example *Shephard* v. *H. West & Son* (1962) 106 SJ 817 (there was an appeal to the House of Lords on a point relating to the assessment of damages), where it was held to be negligent to overtake a bus at traffic lights as they turned green. A reasonable driver ought to have waited for the bus to move as evidence that no pedestrian was crossing very late in front of it; *Garston Warehousing Co. Ltd* v. *O. F. Smart (Liverpool) Ltd* [1977] RTR 377, where it was held to be negligent to emerge slowly from a side road onto a main road when signalled to do so by a bus driver. The emerging driver then collided with the defendant who was overtaking the bus.

182 *Henderson* v. *Henry E. Jenkins & Sons* [1970] AC 282.

183 Richard Lewis reports that the Compensation Recovery Unit data for 2002–03 suggest that 89 per cent of motor claims are successful.

184 [1936] 2 KB 359.

185 R. Lewis, 'Insurers' Agreements Not to Enforce their Strict Legal Rights' (1985) 48 MLR 275.

186 The phenomenon of insurance influencing interpretation of facts must, of course, be distinguished from the phenomenon that insurers regularly rely on rules-of-thumb that turn on facts which are cheaper to establish in their settlement practices.

When juries were involved in trying motor cases, it was a rule of practice, that they were not to be told that the defendant was insured.[187]

2.h Vicarious liability

Finding a wealthy vehicle owner liable for negligent driving of the vehicle by another could become practically important in cases where the driver was not insured, either because insurance was not compulsory at the time[188] or because compulsory insurance did not cover injuries to passengers[189] or property damage[190] at the time. The courts developed a form of vicarious liability based on a fictional 'agency', where the owner: (i) authorized the driving; (ii) requested it; (iii) delegated a task or duty relating to the vehicle to the agent; or (iv) was in control of the agent's conduct, but not if the agent was driving wholly for his own purposes.[191] In *Launchbury* v. *Morgans*,[192] however, the House of Lords refused to extend the fiction beyond these limits, arguing that even if an extension would help the law to deal with the social difficulties caused by road casualties, such an extension ought to be designed and implemented by the legislature.

2.i Other common classes of defendant

After *Donoghue* v. *Stevenson*,[193] manufacturers could clearly be held liable to those injured by carelessly designed or constructed motor cars. But the author is unaware of a case where a negligent driver has argued for a contribution from a manufacturer on the basis that the manufacturer ought to have designed the vehicle so as to reduce the likelihood of driver error causing an accident.

[187] The jury could be discharged if the rule was breached: *Askew* v. *Grimmer* (1927) 43 TLR 354.

[188] *Samson* v. *Aitchison* [1912] AC 844, PC.

[189] *Hewitt* v. *Bonvin* [1940] 1 KB 188, CA. In the Court of Appeal in *Launchbury* v. *Morgans* [1971] 2 QB 245, at 253, Lord Denning MR speculated that it was in the owner's insurance company's interest to establish that the car was not being driven with the owner's permission, since although the insurance policy would probably have covered injury to passengers (even though that was not compulsory), if the claim fell beyond the policy then the Motor Insurers Bureau would only be liable to cover those losses that it was 'compulsory' to insure against.

[190] *Ormrod* v. *Crossville Motor Services Ltd* [1953] 1 WLR 1120, CA.

[191] *Launchbury* v. *Morgans* [1973] AC 127, at 135 *per* Lord Wilberforce.

[192] [1973] AC 127.

[193] [1932] AC 562. Where a defective motor car causes personal injury, it is now likely to be advantageous to bring a claim based on the Consumer Protection Act 1987, Part I, instead.

Statute (in 1961) imposed a civil liability on highway authorities for damage caused as a result of a (negligent) failure to maintain the road-worthiness of a highway.[194] The history of this liability was traced by Lord Hoffmann in *Goodes* v. *East Sussex County Council*,[195] though the decision of the House of Lords in that case that the duty did not extend to impose liability for accidents caused by a negligent failure to clear snow and ice from the highway was swiftly reversed by Parliament in the Railways and Transport Safety Act 2003, s. 111. But whilst highway authorities are regularly held liable for accidents caused by the dangerous condition of highway surfaces, attempts to claim contributions from highway authorities on the basis that they ought to have exercised other statutory powers (e.g. to remove obstacles to visibility or to erect warning signs) to reduce the likelihood of driver error or to mitigate its effects have generally been unsuccessful at the highest appellate level, with the court concluding that the highway authority owes no duty of care to the injured parties.[196]

2.j Proposals to replace tort liability

The Pearson Commission[197] proposed a special social security benefit, modelled on the industrial injury scheme, to protect road victims, but this was not accepted. In 1991, the Lord Chancellor's Department issued a consultation paper proposing a limited no-fault compensation scheme for road accident victims (claiming between £250 and £2,500 for personal injuries). It was estimated that such a scheme would increase motor insurance prices by between 5% and 7%. This scheme was also not implemented. Consequently, fault-based tort liability, subject to a defence of contributory negligence, remains the primary legal doctrine governing compensation for personal injuries suffered in road accidents.

194 Currently, Highways Act 1980, ss. 41 (duty) and 58 (defence of absence of negligence to claims for damage).

195 [2000] 1 WLR 1356.

196 *Stovin* v. *Wise* [1996] AC 923; *Gorringe* v. *Calderdale* [2004] 1 WLR 1057, HL.

197 Royal Commission on Civil Liability and Compensation for Personal Injury, *Report* (Cmnd. 7054, London: HMSO, 1978), Ch. 18

3

The development of traffic liability in France

GENEVIÈVE VINEY AND ANNE GUÉGAN-LÉCUYER*

1 Introduction

The distinctive character of French delict law is due to the general role that the 1804 Civil Code assigned to fault liability. There the legislator formulated the principle according to which any loss caused to a person through the act of another must be repaired by the person whose fault the loss occurred (article 1382 of the Civil Code). The legislator thus imprinted the notion of fault upon all types of delictual liability: whether it be the liability for the act of things, of others (article 1384 of the Civil Code) or of animals (article 1385 of the Civil Code), the liability of an individual was only envisaged where he was at fault. Marked by the refusal to engage with concrete cases and borne of the will to create general and permanent rules, the rules of liability reflected both the individualism and the moralism of the time. Fault was conceived of as personal, individual and subjective. It concerned the breach of a rule of conduct that regulated a given situation. And, above all, it had to be proved by the victim.

That requirement, which seemed entirely normal in an agrarian, small-scale society, revealed itself rather quickly at the end of the nineteenth century to be unsuitable. The Industrial Revolution marked profound changes indeed. As a result of the exploitation of new techniques, accidents multiplied, affecting notably industrial workers and those who were using modes of transport that were still in expansion, thus bringing to light the disadvantages of a system where liability is individual and subjective. All too often victims found it impossible to prove the precise causes of increasingly 'anonymous' accidents. Unable to satisfy the requirements of proving the individual fault of the employer or transporter, the victims of these accidents were not compensated. When there was no social insurance, this appeared very quickly as an unbearable

* Translation by Sandy Steel, University of Cambridge.

injustice. To combat it, it was imperative to move out of the straitjacket of fault liability.

Thus, the development of French delict law in general, and that of rail and road accidents in particular, has been a move against fault-based liability such as it was conceived by the 1804 legislator. Jurists sought methods of freeing victims from the necessity of proving this moral, individual fault behind the injury, with efforts concentrating on accidents at work and transportation accidents. To encourage developments in delict law, two lines of thought emerged. The first aimed to broaden the notion of fault by accentuating the objective element – the breach of a duty or legal obligation – and by putting aside the subjective element that subordinates the existence of fault to the imputability of the injurious act to its author (i.e. to his ability to understand his fault). This objective notion of fault, which allows one to restrain the latter notion more easily, was defended by Planiol (at the beginning of the twentieth century), followed by H. Capitant and then by H. and L. Mazeaud.

The second line of thought sought to evade the requirement of fault itself. Taking as its basis the limitations of fault-based liability in dealing with the new compensatory needs arising from industrial accidents, academics propounded two solutions to escape the problem.

For certain authors (e.g. Sauzet, Sainctelette and Sarrut), recourse to contractual liability was appealing. The advantage was that article 1147, the primary relevant article of the Civil Code, presented the advantage of not requiring the victim to prove fault, but only the non-performance of a contractual obligation (of result). By grafting on to the contract of employment or contract of transport an *obligation de sécurité* owed by the employer or the transporter, the victim need only prove the non-performance of this obligation without having to meet the difficulties of proving the fault of his employer or the transporter.

For other authors, there was the possibility of escaping the fault-based straitjacket by developing the delictual idea of liability based on risk. Propounded by Saleilles and Josserand, the risk theory is a response to the idea that he who has control of or takes the profit of an activity ought to assume the concomitant risks. Primarily devised to meet the needs of compensating for accidents at work, this theory found itself called upon to cover all the accidents caused by the act of a thing, drawing on a broad interpretation of article 1384, paragraph 1 of the Civil Code.[1] Indeed, it

[1] In essence that, even if in the mind of the 1804 legislator, liability for the act of things was envisaged under the umbrella of fault, the formulation of article 1384, paragraph 1 makes no mention of fault, since it states that one is responsible for things in one's custody.

was possible to rely on the absence of the word 'fault' in the latter text to underline that it was not required and that, consequently, the person who causes loss through the act of a thing under his control could be held liable without the victim having to prove fault.

The case law, confronted with increasingly numerous accident victims, sought to take a decisive line amidst the doctrinal debate. It put forward case-by-case solutions, which eventually resulted in a rather disparate system. Accidents at work, which attracted much attention from jurists at the end of the nineteenth century, developed separately, since they were the subject of legislative intervention in 1898. But doctrinal arguments seeking to better the fate of victims in this area were able to contribute to debates on other types of accident – notably rail accidents, which, fortunately, became rarer with the growing safety in public transport, but also, and especially, in road traffic accidents, which, by contrast, multiplied from the beginning of the twentieth century. Moreover, until the legislator intervened in 1985 to regulate the compensation of road-traffic accident victims, sole responsibility was left to case law to rule upon the type of liability in these areas.

It is principally the case law of civil, as opposed to administrative, courts which for a long time determined principles to solve the problems. As to rail transportation, even if it was taken charge of very early on by companies linked to the state (today, united under the SNCF (Société nationale des chemins de fer)), it has always given rise to civil litigation. As to road traffic accidents, the litigation was initially divided between the administrative courts for accidents caused by state vehicles (the Blanco decision)[2] and the civil courts for other accidents, before being unified by the legislator in 1957 under the sole competence of the civil judge. This bifurcation of the litigation would not, however, have a great influence on the basis of the law since the administrative courts adopted solutions very close to those of the civil courts in this area.

In these two areas (rail accidents on the one hand and road traffic accidents on the other), case law demonstrates a development of French law on different foundations: the former accidents relied on contractual liability; the latter used delictual liability for the act of things before being the subject of special legislation in 1985. On the theoretical level, then, there are developments that appear divergent and contrasting for these two types of accident (see Section 2, below). However, despite these divergences, and even if they seem to have been accentuated by the legislator by the 1985

[2] TC, 8 February 1873, *Blanco*, S. 1873.3.153, conclusions David.

law on the compensation of road-traffic accident victims, the results of these developments are, on the practical level, very close (see Section 3, below, p. 69).

2 The divergences in the development of the French delict law in respect of rail accidents and road traffic accidents

These two types of accident are characteristic of the different paths taken by case law to remove civil liability from the original straitjacket of fault in order to respond to the problems not envisaged by the 1804 legislator. To illustrate, it is convenient to treat rail accidents first (in Section 2.a) then road traffic accidents (in Section 2.b).

2.a The development of liability in the field of rail transport accidents

The development of liability in the field of rail transport accidents is marked by the assertion of an essentially contractual liability (Section 2.a.i) which has little by little given up ground to delictual liability (Section 2.a.ii).

2.a.i The assertion of the contractual responsibility of the rail transporter

At the end of the nineteenth century, when rail accidents multiplied, it became imperative to rule on whether the liability of the rail company was contractual or quasi-delictual. The Cour de cassation then accepted that the obligation to compensate was of a delictual or quasi-delictual nature, which had as a consequence given the victim the burden of proving the transporter's fault or that of persons for whom the former had civil responsibility.[3] The solution rested upon the refusal to assimilate the transportation of persons with that of goods, which itself was regulated by special texts according to which the carrier, like any other depositary (bailee) of a specific thing, had to return the latter in good condition to the person who gave it to him, or justify the extinction of his obligation on the grounds of payment, *cas fortuit* or *force majeure*. The proof of fault of the transporter was not required, then, for damage caused to goods transported. But in the absence of special texts for the transportation of persons, it was held in the case law that this field could not be regulated by

[3] Cass. civ., 10 November 1884, S. 1885.1.129; DP 1885.1.279.

rules other than those of delictual responsibility.[4] The Cour de cassation thus left victims to the difficulties of proving the fault of the transportation and to the almost certain risk of not being compensated.

However, society came to regard such solutions as more and more intolerable. The lower courts offered strong resistance to them and attempted to attenuate the rigour of this body of case law by restricting its scope. Certain decisions thus held that the derailing of a train implied *a priori* the fault of the railway company. Others, always with the goal of evading fault-based liability, applied article 1384, paragraph 1 of the Civil Code in order to hold railway companies liable strictly as keepers (*gardiens*) of their carriages and their materials. As to legal writers, they were nearly unanimous in their acute criticisms.[5] To support the compensation of victims of these accidents, one doctrinal group proposed having recourse to the risk theory that had developed in the relations between factory workers and their employers to exclude fault. Others, criticising the use of delictual liability because such a solution did not respect either the nature of the relations between the passenger and the carrier that resulted in a contract, or the fact that the accident occurred in the course of the performance of this contract, pleaded for an overturning of the established case law, which would establish the contractual nature of the liability of the transporter and discover in the contract of the transportation of persons an *obligation de sécurité*.

The influence of Sarrut in the Cour de cassation would provoke this reversal of the case law in a decision of 21 November 1911 given on the subject of maritime transportation. In a case involving the steerage passenger of a General Transatlantic Company steamboat, whose foot was injured by the fall of a badly stowed barrel, the Cour de cassation explained that 'the performance of a contract of transportation involves, for the transporter, the obligation to take the passenger safe and sound to his destination'.[6] In 1913, the solution was reaffirmed more specifically in the context of rail transportation, in a decision involving a passenger of the Midi Railway Company.[7] The conclusions of the Advocate General Sarrut inviting the Court to hold to the direction taken in 1911 are particularly

[4] For an exposition of this case law, see Ch. Lyon-Caen, note under Cass. civ., 21 November 1911, S. 1912.1.73.

[5] See the conclusions of the Advocate General Sarrut on Cass. civ., 27 January 1913, S. 1913.1.177.

[6] Cass. civ., 21 November 1911, DP 1913.1.249, note Sarrut ; S. 1912.1.73, note Lyon-Caen.

[7] Cass. civ., 27 January 1913, S. 1913.1.177, conclusions Sarrut.

enlightening with regard to the reasoning of the judges. For him, indeed, it was indispensable

> to put an end to the just criticisms of la doctrine, to halt the divergences, discussions and subtleties. In an area as important as that of transportation, the law cannot remain uncertain, its practice wavering and confused. The law, as an applied science, requires clear and general rules, concordant theories. In deciding that from the point of view of the proof of fault of the carrier, the rules are the same, whether it be a matter of transport of persons or things, the Cour de cassation will formulate a simple, harmonious system, to which, without doubt, academics and practitioners will give their full support.

In support of contractual responsibility, he emphasised that

> the passenger has handed over his person and his goods; he has entrusted his person to the carrier for the journey; he has no control over the staff, no say on the organization of the equipment, over the train's movement, its direction, its speed. And … one cannot seriously contest that the accidents arise, 99 percent of the time, as a result of the fault of carriers or from circumstances outside the control of the passengers.

Sarrut concluded thus in these terms:

> [W]ithout the contract of transport, which connect the carrier and the passenger, which brought the passenger to the carrier, the passenger would not have suffered any damage … The contract of transport necessarily implies for the carrier the obligation to deliver the passenger to his destination in the state in which he was received – namely safe and sound. When that obligation alone is not performed, the carrier is liable. It is up to him to prove otherwise. This is the pure and simple application of the common law of contractual obligation (Civil Code 1147, 1315).[8]

From then on, the victims of railway accidents were liberated from the demands imposed by a fault-based regime of liability. The desired result was attained: fault-based liability was excluded. As soon as the carrier contracts to take the passenger to his destination safe and sound, the sole fact that an accident occurs proves that this obligation has not been performed and engenders the liability of the carrier, unless the latter demonstrates *force majeure*, *cas fortuit* or the fault of the passenger. In this regard, one must note that, by this solution, French law aligned itself with foreign law since, from the end of the nineteenth century, several legislative interventions in Germany, Belgium, Luxembourg and Holland had

[8] Cass. civ., 27 January 1913, S. 1913.1.177, conclusions Sarrut, p. 180.

created a strict liability for railway companies for the damage caused by their activities.[9]

From this time on, the field of contractual liability would expand with regard to rail travel. On the one hand, the case law retained an extensive conception of the contractual role, notably through a very broad definition of the idea of transportation. Thus, the *obligation de sécurité* benefited the passenger during the journey, but also covered his accidents at the station, from the moment he enters, supplied with his ticket, into the boundaries of the station until the time where he gets out, even when the passenger finds himself simply in an annex of the station.[10] On the other hand, bystanders injured by ricochet would also be able to bring actions since case law would recognise an *obligation de sécurité* for them by means of a tacit stipulation for another.[11] The contract of transportation was said to contain a tacit stipulation of the person transported for the benefit of persons towards whom he owed a duty of support by virtue of a legal relationship.[12] Persons intimately related to a passenger killed in an accident therefore also escaped from the rigours of fault-based liability. Recognised as beneficiaries of this stipulation for another contracted by the principal party, they were able to invoke the breach by transporter of the *obligation de sécurité* and thus to trigger the latter's liability without having to prove fault on his part.

In terms of this development, it was contractual liability that principally regulated the field of railway accidents. Having been called upon and brought into use to exclude delictual responsibility, which was deemed less favourable to victims, it offered the latter and their close relatives the possibility of triggering the liability of the transporter for the breach of an obligation of safety, grafted into the contract of transportation. The accident itself sufficed to establish its breach. From then on, the transporter was liable strictly, without fault, and could not escape from the obligation to compensate without establishing *force majeure*, *cas fortuit* or the fault of passenger. However, in parallel with this expansion of contractual liability, other developments modified the playing field somewhat, and

[9] See the various foreign legislative acts presented by Sarrut in his note on the decisions of 1911 and 1913, S. 1913.1.249, esp. p. 252.

[10] G. Viney and P. Jourdain, *Les conditions de la responsabilité* (2nd edn, Paris: Librairie générale de droit et de jurisprudence (LGDJ) 1998), n 551.

[11] In French law, the stipulation for another is the mechanism by which, in a contract, one of the parties (the stipulator) obtains from the other (the promissor) the promise that he will give or do something for the benefit of a third party (the beneficiary) who thus becomes a creditor without having been party to the contract (article 1121 of the Civil Code).

[12] Cass. civ., 6 December 1932, DP 1933.1.137, note Josserand.

once again made the growth of delictual liability, to the detriment of the contractual, a necessity.

2.a.ii The growth of the delictual liability of the rail transporter

Two movements explain the beginning of a movement away from contractual liability around the 1950s. The first relates to the development of the *obligation de sécurité*. When it appeared in the decisions of 1911 and 1913, the *obligation de sécurité* in the contract of rail transportation attracted the effects of what doctrinal writing would later call an 'obligation of result'. The transporter was thus required to perform a precise and fixed result, the absence of which would engage his strict liability. But when the distinction between obligations of means (*obligation de moyens*) and obligations of result (*obligation de résultat*) was proposed by Demogue in 1928, the existence of a possible *obligation de sécurité* as an obligation of means gradually won the day. Then there was no precise, fixed result that was demanded of the contractor, but rather that he act as a bonus *paterfamilias* (reasonable man) and perform his obligation with the diligence normally sufficient to satisfy the debtor.[13] Thus, with an obligation of means, the contractual liability of the debtor could only be invoked where one could allege against him some negligence or imprudence – which saw the return of fault. The Cour de cassation would affirm this distinction in the rail transportation context. Where it was a matter of 'movement', properly termed, the *obligation de sécurité* would remain an obligation of result, the contractual liability of the transporter would remain strict in the case of an accident. But the Cour de cassation, under the influence of doctrinal criticism of the obligation of result, decided to limit its field of application, thus the *obligation de sécurité* of result only bound the transporter from 'the moment where the passenger begins to enter the carriage until the moment he manages to exit it'.[14] One year later, the Court explicitly ruled that, with regard to station accidents, the transporter was only held to an *obligation de sécurité* of means.[15] The victims of those accidents again found themselves confronted with the difficulties of proving a personal fault of the transporter in order to be compensated. From then on, the restrictive domain of the *obligation de sécurité*

[13] Viney and Jourdain, *Les conditions de la responsabilité*, n° 521.

[14] Cass. civ. (1), 1 July 1969, D. 1969, 641, note G.MC; JCP 1969.II.16091, concl. Lindon: 'the contract of transport only exists from the moment where the traveller enters the carriage until the time he gets off it'.

[15] Cass. civ. (1), 21 July 1970, D. 1970, 767, note Abadie.

withdrew the advantages that contractual liability had been able to offer victims of station accidents.

The second movement that explains the beginning of the move away from contractual liability in respect of rail transportation has as its cause the development of delictual liability and more precisely to its detachment from fault. For, to the extent that the risk theory grew to be one of the foundations of civil liability, fault was no longer as indispensable to give rise to delictual liability. Above all, the rapid development of the liability for things under article 1384 started off a delictual responsibility far more favourable to victims. The first affirmation of a principle of liability for things, detached from fault, appeared in the Teffaine decision given on the case of a work accident caused by the explosion of the boiler of a tugboat.[16] From then on, it was accepted that article 1384, paragraph 1 of the Civil Code contains in itself an autonomous principle of liability for the acts of things whereby the regime derogates from that of article 1382, since it authorises the condemnation of the keeper of things without the thing's fault being established, on the proof solely of its possessing a 'hidden defect'.[17]

Following this, the Cour de cassation affirmed in 1919 that the presumption of liability founded upon article 1384, paragraph 1 could not be rebutted by the proof of absence of fault, and that it could only be removed by the presence of *force majeure*.[18] Furthermore, it gave to this principle of strict liability a large domain of application very favourable to victims who did not have to find proof of any fault what so ever.[19]

These two developments of French law of the contractual liability of the transporter on the one hand, and of the delictual responsibility on the other, worked in parallel. While contractual liability developed to allow victims to escape the harshness of a delictual liability regime anchored to the idea of fault, the growth of *obligation de sécurité* of means reintroduced that idea, only for delictual liability to remove the activity from fault. Save where the *obligation de sécurité* of result applied, delictual liability became more attractive to victims than contractual liability. To take this activity outside fault-based liability, it became necessary to give impetus to the expansion of delictual liability. This is the route that the case law would take from the 1950s onwards. Thus, injured bystanders

[16] Cass. civ., 18 June 1896, S. 1897.1.17, note A. Esmein; DP 1897.1.433, concl. Sarrut, note Saleilles.

[17] Viney and Jourdain, *Les conditions de la responsabilité*, n° 628.

[18] Cass. civ., 21 January. 1919, DP 1922.1.25, note G. Ripert.

[19] Viney and Jourdain, *Les conditions de la responsabilité*, n°s 630ff.

could consider the possibility of giving up the route of the tacit stipulation for another, if they preferred to base the transporter's liability in delict.[20] In practice, the stipulation in favour of another has practically fallen into desuetude in the contract for the transportation of persons, since injured bystanders prefer to waive it in favour of article 1384, paragraph 1 of the Civil Code.[21] In the continuation of this development, the Cour de cassation appeared to rule, in a decision of 28 October 2003, on the abandonment of the tacit stipulation for another in favour of victims injured by ricochet.[22] In addition, with regard to persons accompanying passengers and those travelling without a valid ticket, whenever a thing of which the transporter has custody caused them damage, the liability of the transporter can be delictual, and it was possible for them to take advantage of the delictual responsibility based on article 1384, paragraph 1 of the Civil Code.[23] In that respect, these people find themselves better treated than passengers who are victims of station accidents, since the latter could not rely on a contract and, there being an *obligation de sécurité* of means, had to prove the fault of the transporter. Thus, to remedy this incoherence and injustice, the Cour de cassation achieved a turnaround of the case law and endorsed the delictual nature of the liability of the transporter towards those passengers who were victims of accidents at the station.[24]

Today, then, in the field of rail transportation, the liability of the transporter may be analysed in the following way. As far as passengers with a valid authority to travel are concerned, and for the period of transportation only, the liability of the transporter is of a contractual nature. As a result of *obligation de sécurité* of result, he will be strictly liable in the case of an accident without the victim having to adduce proof of fault. However, all other possible accidents (station accidents of passengers and non-passengers, accidents with passengers without a ticket, victims injured by a ricochet) are based upon the delictual liability of the transporter.

[20] Cass. com., 19 June 1951, *Lamoricière*, D. 1951, 717, note G. Ripert.

[21] P. Jourdain, 'Vers l'abandon de la stipulation pour autrui tacite au bénéfice des proches de la victime directe', RTD. civ., 2004, 96.

[22] Cass. civ. (1), 28 October 2003, JCP 2004.I.163, n° 13f., obs. G. Viney; Jourdain, above note 21.

[23] R. Nerac-Croisier, 'Soliloque sur la responsabilité du transporteur de personnes', D. 1995, chr. 35.

[24] Cass. civ. (1), 7 March 1989, *Valverde*, D. 1991, 1, note Ph. Malaurie; RTD civ., 1989, 548, obs. P. Jourdain.

2.b The development of delict in relation to road traffic accidents

With respect to road traffic accidents, the development of delict law is marked by three main stages. The first is the expansion of delictual liability for the act of things under article 1384, paragraph 1 of the Civil Code (Section 2.b.i). The second is the emergence of a crisis (Section 2.b.ii), which led to the third – the intervention of the legislator in 1985 (Section 2.b.iii).

2.b.i The expansion of delictual liability for the act of things

Before being a matter of car accidents, traffic accidents involved horse-driven carriages. The question of liability was thus first of all brought within the field of liability for the act of animals in article 1385 of the Civil Code, since, according to this text, 'the owner of an animal, or the person using it, during the period of usage, is liable for the damage the animal has caused, whether the animal was under his custody, or whether it had strayed or escaped'. By a decision of 27 October 1885, the Cour de cassation declared that this rule was independent of the fault principle, affirming that it imported strict liability, the presumption of liability resting on the keeper of the animal, not removed by proof of absence of fault, but only by *cas fortuit* or the fault of the injured party.[25]

With the appearance of the motor car, the risks surrounding road traffic were increased. Early on, the use of motor cars was relatively isolated, as it was the preserve of a privileged few for whom it was more a sport or pleasure. The proposals for reform of delict law sought to base liability for car accidents on a property risk.[26] Progressively between the years 1900 and 1914, the motor car began to cause fear, its power and speed seeming to pose a real and violent danger, not only as a result of the sudden, instantaneous nature of a car accident but also because of its more and more imposing presence on public roads. To try and appease the hostility and growing fear towards the risks of the motor car, there were proposals to reform the principles of liability, which were as yet fault-based. They were concerned notably to take account of the difficulties of proof with which victims found themselves confronted. Certain authors were supportive of creating a presumption of fault in the driver. More ambitiously, A. Colin proposed establishing a special cause of action that would free

[25] DP 1886.1.207; S. 1886.1.33.

[26] A. Wahl, 'La responsabilité civile relative aux accidents d'automobiles', RTD civ., 1908, 24.

victims of the proof of a motor car driver's fault, whilst an insurance fund would step in where the driver was unknown or insolvent.[27]

After the First World War and in the decades that followed, the question of road traffic accidents changed in character. The motor car was no longer only a luxury – from then on it was considered useful, and soon indispensable. The production and distribution of motor cars would see an extremely rapid growth, which would resultantly integrate them into *la vie collective*. Traffic accidents consequently became rather normal due to the growing importance of victims in terms of their number. The imperative of compensating victims became yet more urgent and demanded reform of delict law in order to make it more favourable to victims. An important part of academic commentary encouraged case law to develop in the direction of applying strict liability based on article 1384, paragraph 1 to traffic accidents, and thus to transpose the case law on accidents at work (the *Teffaine* decision) to the field of traffic accidents.[28] Those who opposed this argument argued that such a regime of liability specially protecting the victim was only justifiable in the case where the thing escaped from the control of the individual. This reason was that when it is the action of the individual who controls the thing, it would be necessary to consider whether there was an act of the individual for which there is no place for a special regime. Refusing to limit the domain of application of article 1384, paragraph 1 only to things that are not driven by an individual, the Cour de cassation ruled in the *Jand'heur* decision of 1930 that the keeper of a car was strictly liable, that liability could not be lifted except by proof of an external, unforeseeable and unstoppable cause.[29] The field of traffic accidents was thus definitively removed from fault liability.

In parallel with this development of the law, Picard proposed in a series of articles the adoption of a special loi on motor car accidents, the aim being to make the compensation for traffic accidents independent from traditional fault-based regimes of liability.[30] Placing value on the societal nature of the risks associated with the motor car, the idea was to satisfy the social demand for compensation without disrupting the

[27] Analysis of all the reform proposals of tort law for traffic accidents can be found in F. Ewald, *L'accident nous attend au coin de la rue, les accidents de la circulation histoire d'un problème, Etude de sociologie juridique* (Paris: La documentation française, 1982).

[28] G. Ripert, L. Josserand, H. Capitant and P. Esmein.

[29] Cass. ch. réunies, 13 February 1930, DP 1930.1.57, note G. Ripert, rapport Le Marc'hadour; S. 1930.1.121, note P. Esmein.

[30] M. Picard, RGAT 1930, 259 and RGAT, 1931, 5f, 489ff.

entire legal edifice of delict law. More than a move from fault-based liability, this was to effect a move from the idea of liability itself, to spread the cost of damages linked to a social activity or to seek out 'better means by which one could help the economy, collectively taken, bear the weight of its own progress'.[31] Inspired by these ideas, a legislative proposal was conceived: victims would obtain a general right to indemnity unless they were inexcusably at fault, but the amount of compensation was limited and calculated on the basis of the victim's salary. This was the object of so much division and resistance from the class of professionals that it was not successful. Thus, for several decades, the case law solution went without reconsideration.

In a socio-legal study on the question of traffic accidents, F. Ewald underlined the fact that, at the time of these legislative proposals, the real question was not so much one of liability as that of the insurance of accident victims.[32] The majority of drivers were incapable of bearing the cost of a potential liability: incomes were insufficient and they might not pay the premiums for insurance. The problem was thus to make them solvent and, being a matter of setting up insurance for accident victims, the question could be made independent of the imputation of a liability.[33] It was possible to envisage the cause of action of the victim no longer arising only from fault, the error of a responsible driver, but from the accident itself, such that 'the solution to the problem of motor car accidents would no longer be in a law of liability, but in a law of insurance, not necessarily based on a particular liability, i.e. in the organisation of a form of social motor car insurance'.[34] In the organisation of this insurance, supporters of a compulsory liability insurance and supporters of a social insurance fund were for a long time opposed, impeding plans, which privileged one or the other, from coming into effect. This doctrinal movement, however, provoked a government intervention that sought to stabilise the insurance market. With the numerous bankruptcies of insurance companies covering the risk of motor car accidents, it was beneficial to stabilise the insurance market by establishing a regulator of insurance companies in

[31] Ewald, *L'accident nous attend au coin de la rue*, 39.

[32] Ibid., 42ff.

[33] Ibid., 43, citing the explanatory memorandum of the Doumergue bill.

[34] Ibid., 43, referring to the works of R. Savatier, *Du Droit civil au Droit public* (Paris: LGDJ, 1950); id., *Les métamorphoses économiques et sociales du Droit civil aujourd'hui* (3rd edn, Paris: Dalloz, 1964); also G. Ripert, *Le régime démocratique et le Droit civil moderne* (2nd edn, Paris: LGDJ, 1948).

order to protect the insured and to allow motor car users to insure themselves in better conditions.[35]

Then, in the aftermath of the Second World War, the increase in numbers of accidents and their seriousness emphasised once more the urgency of a solution to the problem of the insurance of traffic accident victims. And this time, compulsory liability insurance and a social insurance fund were thought to be cumulative solutions. The obligation to insure called for the creation of a fund to step in where the insurance was defective or where the insured driver runs off. Conversely, the creation of a *Fonds de garantie* presupposed the institution of obligatory insurance since the primary source of its nourishment was made up of the payments of insurers and the insured.[36] The government opted in 1952, however, only for the institution of a *Fonds de garantie*, whose goal was to take charge of the compensation of personal injuries that were not covered by any insurance, and where the person responsible was insolvent.[37] But the inconveniences of this system were quickly revealed. On the one hand, the number of persons not insured went beyond the 5 per cent estimated, seriously threatening the financial stability of the *Fonds*. On the other hand, the existence of the *Fonds* did not stir more motor car users to become insured: 'all things considered, the *Fonds* charged conscientious motor car users a premium for the non-insurance of others'.[38] Thus, to improve this, the legislator created in 1958 an obligation of insurance in respect of one's motor car 'as much as to maintain the financial stability of the *Fonds* as a matter of justice … in order to sanction motor car users who had not fulfilled their moral and social duty to insure and to guarantee an equitable distribution of the costs amongst motor car users'.[39]

Combining the obligatory liability insurance and the *Fonds de garantie*, the solution put in place to improve the situation of traffic accident victims appeared fairly comprehensive. Based on a system of strict liability, and thus detached from fault, it guaranteed, through the compulsory liability insurance, the solvency of the potential defendant. Moreover, in the case of unidentified or uninsured motor car users, the *Fonds* took the compensation of victims in hand. However, the development of this solution would hit a crisis.

[35] Décret-loi of 8 August 1935, ratified by the loi of 30 June 1936. For a discussion of its provisions, see Ewald, *L'accident nous attend au coin de la rue*, 51.

[36] Ibid., 53ff.

[37] Viney and Jourdain, *Les conditions de la responsabilité*, n° 963.

[38] Ewald, *L'accident nous attend au coin de la rue*, 56.

[39] Ibid., 57.

2.b.ii The emergence of a crisis

The seeds of the crisis appeared in the insufficiencies of the system put in place. They were numerous.[40] First of all, the compulsory insurance suffered from deficiencies and lacunae because the loi had kept the possibility of exclusion of quite a number of risks, in particular to the detriment of family members of the vehicle's owner. Then, even with the benefit of strict liability, victims always saw their compensation subject to the mechanism of a civil liability and its defences. Since it was a matter of delict law, where the car was stolen and the owner no longer considered as its custodian,[41] the insurer of the vehicle was relieved of the need to answer for the damage caused. It was the same where the vehicle had a passive role in the accident. But it was principally on the ground of defences that the system appeared deficient. Case law interpreted, more and more extensively, the exonerating '*cause étrangère*', thus permitting insurers to escape compensation in numerous cases (ice or a patch of oil on the road, game animals crossing the road or a storm).[42] Above all, the taking into account of the victim's fault in order to share out the liability occupied a greater and greater place. Certain insurers thus began the practice of systematically refusing to compensate entirely by invoking some carelessness, negligence or even a simple clumsiness of the victim, and the same if the latter was an elderly person, an invalid or a child. Aggravating again the situation of victims, the Cour de cassation held, from the years 1963 and 1964, that a simple 'faultless act' of the wictim (notably of a very young child not yet capable of real understanding) could, if it had contributed to the damage, justify reducing some of the compensation.[43] Worryingly for the guarantee of compensation for traffic accident victims, the whole system was thus evolving in a way unfavourable for victims, and became an increasingly important – in quantitative terms – cause of litigation.

As a result of these disadvantages, and because the risk surrounding the motor car was urged more and more as a social risk, presented sometimes as 'too great a risk' because the amount exceeded what individuals could bear, and as a 'risk to the population' in the same way as smoking or

[40] For a detailed description of the deficiencies and lacunae, see Viney and Jourdain, *Les conditions de la responsabilité*, n° 964.

[41] Cass. ch. réunies, 2 December 1941, *Franck*, DC 1942, 25, note G. Ripert ; S. 1941.1.217, note H. Mazeaud.

[42] Viney and Jourdain, *Les conditions de la responsabilité*, n° 964.

[43] Ibid.

alcoholism,[44] the Minister of Justice, Foyer, set up a commission in 1964 to consider an eventual legislative reform on the compensation for traffic accident victims. Before the commission, André Tunc presented an *avant-projet*, which proposed to remove traffic accidents completely from delict law and to place them within a regime of direct insurance whose operation would have been left to private insurance. His project spared victims all the difficulties linked to the application of delict law (proof of an act of a thing, determination of the guardian or, more broadly, the search for someone responsible) and, above all, he did not allow anything as a possible exonerating cause except the intentional fault of the victim. However, the compensation had some limitations, one of which was not awarding damages for non-physical loss. Finally, he advocated a simplification of procedure and encouraged settlement.

This proposal attracted attention and provoked numerous reactions and criticisms. Both lawyers and insurers, alarmed by the disruptive implications and the repercussions that the proposal could have on their professions, fiercely opposed and wrote against it. The majority of jurists were also angered by the threat to the principles of civil liability. Public opinion itself, badly informed by the media, which only gave a skewed picture of the proposal, opposed it. But the Tunc proposals set in motion a genuine process of reflection that was not about to be interrupted. In 1965, just as the work of Tunc on road safety was published, the book of the American Professors Keeton and O'Connell proposed abandoning delict law in the field of road accidents, its replacement being a form of direct insurance.[45] Strengthened by the study of reform realised in foreign countries in this field (New Zealand, Sweden, Israel and the United States), reflection upon the situation of traffic accident victims was prevalent as much as the imperative of improving their lot, and a solution had to be found.

Until the 1980s, the idea of a reform continued to progress in various forms. A conference of insurers in 1977 criticised the deficiencies of the existing system and made reform proposals similar to those American law[46] had made. A bill was proposed by Senator Chazelle in 1977 taking up Tunc's proposal. A conference in 1981 was organised by Tunc, at which he presented a barely modified version of his initial proposal. The legislature was anxious to avoid any reform that risked provoking opposition from insurers and lawyers. The only notable amendment of the law that

[44] On the frequency of this element, see Ewald, *L'accident nous attend au coin de la rue*, esp. 92ff.

[45] Viney and Jourdain, *Les conditions de la responsabilité*, n° 965.

[46] Ibid., n° 966.

came to the aid of victims was the adoption of the loi of 7 January 1981, which prohibited the exclusion, in the compulsory insurance of motor vehicles, of damages caused to the close relatives of the insured defendant when they travelled in the same vehicle.[47] With the change of the Minister of Justice in May 1981, the idea of a reform of the law relating to compensation of traffic accident victims was revived, but the commission set up for this purpose did not manage to develop a draft bill. As to the Cour de cassation, it remained impervious to the criticisms that had been made against its line of case law.

However, it was that Court which took the initiative in provoking a crisis, which led to the legislator's intervention. By a decision of 21 July 1982, known by the name *Desmares*, the Court decided that the fault of the victim would no longer have an exonerating effect on the liability of the keeper of an inanimate thing based upon article 1384, paragraph 1 of the Civil Code, unless it presented, for the said keeper, the characteristics of *force majeure*.[48] Inviting the Cour de cassation to adopt this solution, the Advocate General Charbonnier expressed himself in these terms:

> Since the defendant is no longer practically harmed by the consequences of his act, and since the insurer is not harmed either (since the latter varies the premiums in accordance with the number of materialised risks), from now on attention is focused on the victim. And in a world dominated notably by the – sometimes contradictory – values of individual happiness and social solidarity, our contemporaries have the tendency both to concern themselves over the fate of victims and to hope that they obtain more complete compensation, even if they have, by their own fault, contributed to their injury.

Also, if among the disadvantages of the solution proposed was the growth of costs on insurance companies and consequently a general increase in contributions, he concluded that if the solidarity effort began to appear excessive, 'it would be for the legislator to intervene ... [since in any case] it is not possible for us, within the state, having noticed the unjust consequences of a jurisprudential rule to let it stay as it is'.

Revolutionary in only exonerating the keeper where the fault of the victim amounted to *force majeure*, the widely publicised decision of the Cour de cassation was unanimously interpreted as a veritable provocation

[47] Viney and Jourdain, *Les conditions de la responsabilité*, n° 966.

[48] Cass. civ. (2), 21 July 1982, D. 1982, 449, concl. Charbonnier, note C. Larroumet; JCP 1982.II.19861, note F. Chabas.

aimed at the legislator – indeed, as 'genuine notice to take part at last in the regulation of traffic accidents'.[49]

Thus a crisis emerged. The lawyers and a section of the doctrinal writers rose up against this new line of case law, with many judges in the lower courts refusing to apply it. For several years, the lower jurisdictions were divided, and the situation became so confused that the legislator had to intervene. It was in this way that the loi of 5 July 1985 was born.[50]

2.b.iii The loi of 5 July 1985

The loi of 5 July 1985 dealing with the improvement of the situation of traffic accident victims and with the streamlining of procedures of compensation is the result of a number of compromises. If the intervention of the legislator was inevitable, the battle led against certain proposals by the lawyers and insurers caused it to recoil on certain points. Thus the measures intended to regulate the evaluation of damages and interests were abandoned. Similarly, the legislator finally decided to stave off from discarding the rules of delict law in favour of direct, pure and simple insurance, the system conserving the structure of an insurance based on liability.

As a result of this option in favour of liability insurance, the new provisions did not radically transform the system of compensation for traffic accident victims. They did, however, effect a development in two principal directions. The first was to make the guarantee of compensation firmer and more automatic in removing the majority of obstacles pertaining to the conditions of liability on which victims got caught up. The second direction was to place under stricter conditions the insurance of the debt of compensation, notably in extending the domain of compulsory insurance and in reducing the number of exceptions that the insurer could rely upon against victims. It was necessary that the latter were able to take advantage of insurance as much as possible. In addition, an obligation was imposed upon the insurer to make an offer of compensation to victims within a certain period after the accident. With the insurer being substituted in practice for the defendant, insurance is considered to have taken over the domain of liability.[51]

The rules laid down by the loi of 1985 were to be applicable 'even where they are transported pursuant to a contract, to victims of a traffic accident

[49] J.-L. Aubert, 'L'arrêt *Desmares*: une provocation … à quelles réformes ?', D. 1983, chr. 1.

[50] Two years after the promulgation of the loi, the Cour de cassation renounced its decision in *Desmares*, Cass. civ. (2), 6 April 1987 (6 decisions), JCP 1987.II.20828, note F. Chabas.

[51] Viney and Jourdain, *Les conditions de la responsabilité*, n° 972.

in which a motor vehicle is involved'. This included trucks and articulated lorries but excluded railways and tramways moving on their own tracks (article 1). In attaching liability to the occurrence of a purely objective fact (knowing if a vehicle was involved in the accident) the legislator allowed victims to avoid the difficulties linked with putting in place the establishment of liability prior to the intervention of the insurer. Numerous defences, which the keeper could invoke when his liability was alleged under article 1384, paragraph 1 of the Civil Code, were also removed. Thus, the driver or keeper could henceforth no longer rely on *force majeure* or the act of a third party (article 2). As to the fault of the victim, the defendant could invoke it to obtain total or partial releases, but only under very precise and very strict conditions. The scope of this fault was considerably reduced since victims, save for drivers, cannot have their own fault relied upon unless the double condition be met that it was inexcusable and that it was the exclusive cause of the accident. In addition, the loi marks out a certain number of victims (persons aged less than sixteen and older than seventy; or whatever their age, persons the extent of whose disability is greater than 80 per cent at the time of the accident) to which it attributes a special protection by ensuring that they will be compensated in all cases.

Despite these important changes, the importance of the loi seems limited. On the one hand, it puts to one side compensation for drivers who are the victims, presuming all fault on their part – the lack of any degree of seriousness can be relied upon against them to reduce or extinguish their right to damages (article 4). On the other hand, the measure remained based, at least in theory, on the idea of liability, and thus placed an obstacle before compensation of victims of accidents where there was no responsible other involved, which is the case where the vehicle of the proprietor is the only one involved and the proprietor is the sole victim, at least where the latter has no special insurance. In addition, the loi seems out of date today in various respects, and a reform is becoming necessary.

The respective developments in rail accidents and in traffic accidents thus have their differences. Despite a common endpoint, the improvement of the compensation of victims by a move from the harshness of a fault-based liability, the two areas have followed very different paths. For railway accidents, even if its domain was reduced in the course of time, the escape route was contractual liability, which presented over delictual liability the advantage of being based on the failure to perform a contractual obligation and not on fault. By affixing to the contract of transport an *obligation de sécurité* conceived as an obligation of result, case law allowed victims to avoid the pitfalls of proof of fault, and the liability of the transporter became a strict one from which one could be released only by proof of *force majeure*, *cas fortuit* or the fault of the victim. For road traffic accidents, it was recourse to delictual liability for the act of a thing based on article 1384, paragraph 1, which allowed victims to escape the fault. Interpreted as the statement of a general principle of strict liability from which the keeper of the thing could only release himself by proving *force majeure*, the text has for a long time regulated this area before giving way to the loi of 5 July 1985, which did not entirely detach itself from the idea of fault.

However, and although developing on two different grounds, the principles suggested to solve the problem of compensation of rail and road accident victims present points of convergence.

3 The convergence of the results of the developments of the liability in respect of rail accidents and road traffic accidents

As much as on the contractual as on the delictual plane, the principles of the solution finally adopted for rail accidents and for traffic accidents set up a liability both strict (Section 3.a) and limited in scope (Section 3.b).

3.a Strict liability

The liability seemed strict in as much as the proof of fault became unnecessary for the designation of the responsible person (Section 3.a.i) and because once the allegation had been made against him, the latter could only with difficulty release himself from liability (Section 3.a.ii).

3.a.i The removal of the need to prove the fault of the defendant

With regard to the liability of the railway transporter, the necessity of proving the latter's fault has been entirely removed thanks to the discovery of an *obligation de sécurité* of result in the contract of carriage. This contract obliges the transporter to carry the passenger safe and sound to his destination, and when this result is not attained, he is automatically liable, without the victim having to prove that the cause of his damage was the fault of the transporter. As to station accidents that lie outside contractual liability, they are most often dealt with by resort to the delictual liability for the act of things that, from this point of view, produce comparable results since the act of the thing gives rise to the liability of the keeper without the victim having to prove the latter's fault.

In the area of traffic accidents, it is now the simple involvement of the vehicle in the accident that suffices to engage the liability of the keeper or the driver for the damages resulting from the accident. With the act itself generating liability, the notion of involvement is detached entirely from the idea of fault; it supposes only some kind of participation of the vehicle in the accident.

3.a.ii A difficult route to release from liability

In the matter of release from liability, the principles regulating the compensation of rail accident victims and of traffic accidents are theoretically different. For railway accidents, the transporter can exonerate himself by proving *force majeure* and can obtain a share of the liability if he proves concurrent fault on the victim's part. However, for road traffic accidents, the legislator expressly eradicated release by *force majeure* in relation to victims who are not drivers. In addition, whilst some of this group (persons between the age of sixteen and seventy and those who are less than 80 per cent disabled) can find their own fault laid before them; that is only the case if it is both inexcusable and an exclusive cause of the accident. And the claim that the victim was at fault is less frequently made since judicial interpretation of its criteria effectively rules it out. It is only when the victim is a driver that the possibility of limitation or release from liability by virtue of the victim's fault regains its ground.

In practice, however, these real differences as to the possibilities of release from liability between the two types of accidents seem much more reduced than the statement of the principles allows one to believe. If the railway transporter benefits from the more important defences, case law requires the proof of such a high degree with regard to the SNCF that the liability of the latter is in reality much stricter than it appears. As to *force majeure*, it is hardly ever allowed as a release from liability for the SNCF, whose liability has been retained in case of terrorist attack and strike. As to the victim's fault, it is hardly ever successful when the victim is utilising a real freedom of movement, which confines it to accidents that happen whilst boarding or disembarking the train and to station accidents. In practice, therefore, the domain and operation of the defences is as much reduced for rail accidents as for traffic.

3.b A largely chanelled liability

Whether the rules be formulated by case law or by the legislator, liability in respect of rail transportation accidents and traffic accidents became largely channelled (3.b.i). This channelling is not, however, totally rigid, allowing victims the possibility of sometimes bringing claims against other potential defendants (3.b.ii).

3.b.i The reasons for the channelling of liability

The development of the principles of liability in respect of rail accidents and traffic accidents shows that the rules have quickly led to the channelling of liability onto a small number of persons. In the first case, this has as its object the rail transporter, which, in fact, is always the one entity since, in France, the SNCF has a monopoly as a rail transportation provider. With respect to tramways or some forms of urban train travel, it will be the company in charge. In the second case, before the legislator intervened in 1985, liability was to some extent focused on the keeper of the vehicle (i.e. on the person who, at the moment the damage was caused, independently exercised his 'power of use, direction and control' over the thing). In addition, with case law applying a presumption that the owner was the keeper of the vehicle, victims always benefited from the possibility of suing this defendant, even when he was not exercising such power or when there was a question over whether the person effectively possessed such a power. When, in 1985, the legislator settled the rules relating to compensation of victims of traffic accidents, it implicitly designated the keeper and the driver of the vehicle as defendants. This implicit channelling derives from article 2, which declares that victims cannot have *force majeure* or an act of a third party relied upon against them 'by the driver or the keeper'.[52] The loi of 1985 cannot therefore serve as a basis for putting in play the liability of other persons, and the Cour de cassation has thus refused to apply it to pedestrians, cyclists, drivers of vehicles other than motor-powered land-based vehicles within the scope of the loi, as well as to manufacturers, sellers and repair garages. To claim against these persons, only an action founded on the *droit commun* is possible.

In the two cases, the channelling of the liability on one of several determined persons serves to designate the persons who are best placed and able to master the potentially damage-creating activity, and consequently the better able to obtain insurance to cover the risks to which their activity gives rise. This is true for the rail transporter, which has complete authority over its staff and complete control over its operation. The SNCF must thus take the necessary measures, either by means of insurance or

[52] Viney and Jourdain, *Les conditions de la responsabilité*, n° 1004.

by internalising the risks within the business, to guarantee the debts of compensation that could be charged to it as a result of a liability action.

This is also true for the keeper-owner of the vehicle designated first of all by case law as the most likely person responsible for the damages caused by vehicles. Identified as such, the owner of the vehicle was strongly encouraged to insure himself and the market for motor car insurance to develop in that direction. By means of this sort of channelling of liability, the insurance of vehicle owners started to become widespread, thus offering victims a better guarantee of the solvency of the potential defendant. It is also as a result of insurance that the legislator of 1985 designated the responsible persons for traffic accidents as the driver and keeper of the vehicle involved. On the one hand, they are the people who are most often the cause of the risks of road traffic, which singles them out as answerable for the damages amounting to the materialisation of these risks.[53] On the other hand, and in consequence, they are naturally suitable to support the insurance network, the one and the other being from then on obligatorily insured; even in the case of theft or theft of the vehicle, the debt of compensation is insured: 'behind the driver and the guardian is the insurer who is becoming the person obligated to pay the compensation'.[54] The channelling of liability thus guarantees a close liaison between the right to compensation and motor car insurance (i.e., the guarantee of compensation).

In practice, the direct effect of this channelling and its primary purpose, which is to be found in the link that it allows to be established between liability and insurance, manifests itself in the existence of a procedure whereby an obligatory offer is imposed on the insurer of the defendant who must normally try to achieve a settlement. The insurer of the vehicle implicated in the accident therefore must, within a period of eight months from the accident, make an offer of compensation to direct victims who have suffered physical injury. This offer must include all the compensable elements of the injury, and the legislator has put in place a regime of sanctions for when the offer is late or is manifestly insufficient.[55]

In the field of rail and road traffic accidents, even if the channelling of liability, in practice and affirmed in the texts, appears to be the most

[53] Viney and Jourdain, *Les conditions de la responsabilité*, n° 1004.

[54] G. Viney, *Introduction à la responsabilité* (2nd edn, Paris: LGDJ, 1995), n° 25.

[55] On the compensation procedure, see articles L. 211–18 ff of the Code des assurances.

secure means of guaranteeing victims an action against a defendant who is solvent, because he is insured the channelling is not entirely rigid.

3.b.ii The other possible defendants

The victims of rail and road accidents most often have an interest in bringing an action against the persons that case law or the legislator has designated as the principal class of defendant. Other actions in delict, able to be brought by the victims themselves or by means of subrogation, remain possible. For rail accidents, however, one must observe that a liability other than that of the SNCF will rarely be engaged. Yet, for traffic accidents, actions in delict other than those founded on the 1985 loi are very much foreseeable. On the one hand, the common law of delict can serve as a basis for actions against all persons other than the driver or guardian. The loi not having placed 'any principle of liability-channelling on the head of those whom it designates as obligated to pay compensation', the Cour de cassation had the opportunity to retain the liability of pedestrians, cyclists or passengers of a land-based motor vehicle, notably on the basis of articles 1382ff of the Civil Code. In addition, it is clearly possible for the victim to take action both on the basis of the 1985 loi against the driver or the guardian and on the basis of the common law against another third party. Finally, actions in delict against the manufacturers of the vehicle against whom some safety default can be alleged, and against the garage and the mechanic, are very much possible under the common law.

It seems thus that the divergent developments in delict law in respect of rail and road traffic accidents have not led to very different results on the practical level. Notably, however, the differences in treatment of compensation according to whether the victim is one of a rail accident or a traffic accident can no longer seem justified. Thus, one could advocate a modernisation of the 1985 loi especially in order to unify the treatment of all victims, whether drivers or not, and to make the insurance of the driver compulsory. This reform would also be an opportunity to extend the benefit of this loi to the entirety of victims of land-based travel accidents without distinguishing according to whether they were by road or by rail. All the proposals emanating from the group of academics chaired by Professor Pierre Catala on the reform of the Civil Code were along those lines. More precisely, they amount to the following: on the one hand, the driver would be assimilated to other victims; on the other hand, rail accidents and tram accidents would be assimilated to other accidents in which a land-based motor vehicle is involved. Finally, the provision specially concerning infants, elderly persons and disabled persons would be deleted, a victim's fault not being able to be relied upon unless inexcusable and the exclusive cause of the accident.[56]

From this examination of the development of the law relating to rail and road traffic accidents in France, several factors of different types can be identified in relation to the development. In this regard, it is without doubt the area of traffic accidents that appears the most fruitful. Thus it is possible to observe some factors of a factual nature, such as the multiplication of motor car accidents and the increasing seriousness of their consequences. There are also sociological factors within the development. For example, some sociological studies have focused on when traffic accidents occur, and when society came to regard better compensation for victims as an imperative. Factors of a juridical nature inevitably come into play as the system of liability that no longer manages to provide compensation which is considered satisfactory is brought into question. Its problems are criticised, such as the difficulties of proof with which victims who have to prove the fault of the driver are confronted, or the excessive number of defences that stand in the way of compensation. And when victims suffer from the insolvency of the person deemed responsible under the relevant civil liability rule, the juridical factors in the development become aligned with economic factors. The latter manifest themselves in terms of the economic costs of traffic accidents, not only the individual costs for every person involved in a given accident, but also the social, collective cost for all the traffic accidents each year. Among these factors, it is also, above all, insurance that has a decisive place, not only as an actor in the developing system but also as an object of scrutiny, during the regulation of the insurance market or when it comes to protecting the insured. As for identifying precisely the role of each, the task is very much a delicate one, since these different factors in the development overlap, one becoming mixed up in the other.

[56] For all these proposals, esp. articles 1385ff of the *avant-projet*, see J. Cartwright, S. Vogenauer and S. Whittaker, *Reforming the French Law of Obligations* (Oxford: Hart Publishing, 2009).

4

The development of traffic liability in Germany

SEBASTIAN LOHSSE

1 Introduction

Right at the very beginning of the nineteenth century, German doctrinal writers started to concentrate on establishing a coherent system of liability based on the well-known principles of Roman Law, which had been passed down to them over the centuries. Derived from the Roman rules, this system quite naturally focused on fault liability.[1] Other types of liability were taken into account only as far as the Roman jurists' exceptions to their system of fault liability were concerned. Thus cases where there was liability for failure to exercise *custodia*[2] (which can approximately be defined as a strict liability for all loss not caused by *vis maior*, i.e. 'acts of God and the King's enemies')[3] were indeed taken into consideration, just like the law dealt with particular cases such as damage caused by animals (*actio de pauperie*), rainwater drained from a neighbouring property (*actio aquae pluviae arcendae*), things thrown down or liquids

[1] See, for example, Egid von Löhr, *Theorie der Culpa* (vols. I and II, Gießen: Heyer, 1806–1808); Johann Christian Hasse, *Die Culpa des Römischen Rechts* (2nd edn, Kiel: Marcus, 1838); Rudolf von Jhering, 'Das Schuldmoment im römischen Privatrecht', in Rudolph von Jhering (ed.), *Vermischte Schriften juristischen Inhalts* (Leipzig: Breitkopf and Härtel, 1879), p. 163.

[2] The most important case may have been the case of *locatio conductio*, where the 'conductor' was liable for *custodia* with regard to the objects he received from his customer in order to perform his work; furthermore, one has to bear in mind the liability of *nautae*, *caupones* and *stabularii* based on *receptum*, which originally appears to have been a strict liability. However, Labeo accepted that the debtor could exonerate himself if he could show that the incurred loss was the result of *vis maior*; thus, the classical jurists quite correctly thought of the liability based on *receptum* as being a type of liability for *custodia*; see Max Kaser and Rolf Knütel, *Römisches Privatrecht* (18th edn, Munich: Beck, 2005), § 46 no. 6 (p. 237), § 36 nos. 15–17 (p. 180).

[3] Fritz Schulz, *Classical Roman Law* (Oxford University Press, 1951), p. 515; Kaser and Knütel, Römisches Privatrecht, § 46 no. 6 (p. 237), § 36 nos. 15–17 (p. 180). This view has, however, not remained unchallenged; for details, see Reinhard Zimmermann, *The Law of Obligations* (Oxford University Press, 1990), pp. 193ff.

poured onto the street from a dwelling (*actio de deiectis vel effusis*) and so on. However, none of these cases prompted the nineteenth-century German legal writers to think of creating a comprehensive rule regarding strict liability. The prevailing doctrine adhered to the fault principle, which began to be regarded as an unquestionable, axiomatic truth. Cases of strict liability were either brought in line with this principle[4] or, at best, treated as extraordinary exceptions. One of the best-known examples of this development is the lack of attention Savigny gave to cases of strict liability in his 'Law of Obligations', referring to them as *obligationes ex variis causarum figuris* on a mere one and a half out of 331 pages.[5] The reasons are manifold, with the most important one probably being that the fault principle corresponded to the concepts of liberalism; it was widely regarded as the only means of providing adequate protection without unduly restricting economic activities.[6]

In the end, even though, meanwhile, several provisions introducing strict liability in the area of railway accidents had been enacted, the fathers of the German Civil Code (*Bürgerliches Gesetzbuch* – BGB) still stuck to the principle of fault liability for this very same reason: any liability going beyond negligence as defined in § 276 BGB, they argued, would result in an inappropriate constraint of freedom and would mean a burden on individual freedom, with incalculable responsibilities.[7] Thus, the only case of strict liability accepted in the BGB was the liability for damage caused by animals (§ 833 BGB). Against this background, the emergence of special rules concerning liability for railway and road traffic accidents during the nineteenth century and at the beginning of the twentieth century is all the more remarkable. Yet, at the same time, it is not surprising

[4] Esp. by means of a presumption of *culpa* (see von Löhr, *Culpa*, vol. II, pp. 163ff.); for a more detailed account, see Regina Ogorek, *Untersuchungen zur Gefährdungshaftung im 19. Jahrhundert* (Cologne: Böhlau, 1975), pp. 22ff., 28; Rudolf Müller-Erzbach, 'Gefährdungshaftung und Gefahrtragung' (1910) 106 *Archiv für die civilistische Praxis* (AcP) 309 at 327f.

[5] See Friedrich Carl von Savigny, *Das Obligationenrecht als Theil des heutigen Römischen Rechts* (Berlin: Veit, 1853), vol. II, pp. 330ff. Yet, as Zimmermann (*Obligations*, p. 1131, note 265) has pointed out, it would be unfair to argue that Savigny was insensitive towards the challenges of the industrial age; Savigny himself was one of the fathers of the first legal provision dealing with strict liability for damage resulting from railway accidents (see below, Section 2.b).

[6] For details, see Josef Esser, *Grundlagen und Entwicklung der Gefährdungshaftung* (2nd edn, Munich: Beck, 1969), pp. 50ff.; Hans-Peter Benöhr, 'Die Entscheidung des BGB für das Verschuldensprinzip' (1978) 46 *Tijdschrift voor Rechtsgeschiedenis* 1 at 8ff.

[7] See *Protokolle der Kommission für die zweite Lesung des Entwurfs eines Bürgerlichen Gesetzbuchs* (Berlin: Guttentag, 1898), vol. II, pp. 569, 585.

that 'the new forms of strict liability tended to be regarded, just as the old ones, as anomalous instances of a *ius singulare*; they were locked into special statutes and thus remained isolated from the mainstream of private law legal theory'.[8]

2 Railway accident liability

2.a The legal situation according to German common law

Due to the fragmentation of legal systems throughout Germany at the beginning of the nineteenth century, the situation concerning liability in railway accidents was quite complicated to start with. Wherever there were no special rules (for which, see below), the legal situation depended on the interpretation of the so-called Gemeines Recht (German common law, derived from ancient Roman law) in that particular territory. Generally speaking, the fault principle was applicable, with railway companies thus being liable for damages caused by the operation of railways only where the company in question had acted wilfully or negligently; the corresponding onus of proof rested on the victim. However, the practical application of this rule varied from state to state. This was mainly due to the fact that there was no uniform answer to the question of whether a person was responsible only for his own fault or could also be held liable, either in contract or in delict, where a third party had been employed in the performance of a contractual obligation and where the damage caused was the result of this party's fault. Furthermore, one had to distinguish between whether the damage had been inflicted on persons or goods transported on the train in performance of a corresponding contract (2.a.i) or to a third party (2.a.ii).

2.a.i Contractual liability

Where German common law was applicable, contracts for carrying persons or goods by rail were usually treated as contracts for work (*locatio conductio operis*).[9] According to the traditional doctrine, the railway company, being the conductor in these contracts, was responsible for its

[8] Zimmermann, *Obligations*, p. 1132.

[9] See Johann Adam Seuffert, *Praktisches Pandektenrecht* (4th edn, Würzburg: Stahel, 1867), vol. II, § 333, p. 236, note 2; Bernhard Windscheid, *Lehrbuch des Pandektenrechts* (2nd edn, Düsseldorf: Buddeus, 1868), vol. II, § 401, p. 459 and note 11.

own fault only.[10] Thus, where the damages resulted from the company's employees' fault, there was a contractual remedy only if the company had acted negligently in choosing[11] or supervising its employees (*culpa in eligendo vel custodiendo vel inspiciendo*).[12] Otherwise, the only obligation arising from the accident was a tortious obligation of the employee, who naturally did not have the necessary means to provide effective compensation for the loss incurred. Although this was the prevailing opinion, there were different approaches, on the basis of which an extension of the liability of railway companies was conceivable and was indeed approved by several courts.

Some scholars – without referring to railway-based liability in particular – took the view that one should not distinguish between the debtor's fault and the fault of those whom he employed in performing his contractual obligations.[13] In several cases, this general concept of vicarious liability was adopted by courts that had to decide on damage resulting from railway accidents.[14]

[10] See Hasse, *Culpa*, Ch. 12, pp. 404ff.; Windscheid, *Pandektenrecht*, II, § 401, p. 456, note 5.

[11] That is, if the company had not selected a so-called *homo idoneus*; see Paul D. 13.6.11.

[12] Accordingly, in 1855, the Oberappellationsgericht Celle – making reference to Paul D. 3.5.20(21).3 – did not hold responsible the Royal Hanover Railway Authority for an accident where two trains had crashed due to the fault of one of the Authority's communications officers; see *Aloise Spatzer-Gentiluomo* v. *Royal Hanover Railway Authority*, Seufferts Archiv, vol. 13, 188, no. 140. Similarly, several judgments outside the field of railway-based liability: the Oberappellationsgericht Dresden did not hold responsible a carrier of goods where his employee had acted negligently (Seufferts Archiv, vol. 7, 266, no. 224); likewise, the Oberappellationsgericht Lübeck, *D. Vollgold* v. *Emanuel Müller*, Seufferts Archiv, vol. 5, 422, no. 306.

[13] See Seuffert, *Praktisches Pandektenrecht*, § 333, p. 237, note 7 (referring to Ulpian D. 19.2.13 pr. and 5; Gaius D.19.2.25.7); Georg Friedrich Puchta, *Vorlesungen über das heutige römische Recht* (4th edn, Leipzig: Fischer, 1855), vol. II, § 302, p. 160; Rudolf Johann Burchardi, *Über die Verantwortlichkeit des Schuldners für seine Gehülfen* (Kiel: Schröder, 1861), pp. 133f. For an overview of the whole development, see Martin Schermaier, §§ 276–278 BGB, paras. 71ff., in Mathias Schmoeckel, Joachim Rückert and Reinhard Zimmermann (eds.), *Historisch-kritischer Kommentar zum BGB* (§§ 241–432 BGB) (Tübingen: Mohr, 2007).

[14] Based on Gaius D. 19.2.25.7 (a text that has been of the utmost significance for the discussion concerning vicarious liability in the nineteenth century); see Zimmermann, *Obligations*, pp. 399f. and the recent study of Hartmut Wicke, *Respondeat Superior* (Berlin: Duncker and Humblot, 2000), pp. 69ff. In 1858, the local court of Frankfurt am Main held a railway company liable for damage caused by its employees' fault; see Wilhelm Koch, *Deutschlands Eisenbahnen* (Marburg: Elwert, 1858–1860), annex XVIIIc, p. 212; Gustav Lehmann, *Körperverletzungen und Tödtungen auf deutschen Eisenbahnen und die Unzulänglichkeit des Rechtsschutzes* (Erlangen: Enke, 1869), pp. 22f.; likewise, the Oberappellationsgericht (Court of Appeal) Lübeck, in Sammlung der Entscheidungen des Ober-Appellationsgerichts zu Lübeck in Frankfurter Rechtssachen,

Other courts argued that the liability of *nautae*, *caupones* and *stabularii* based on *receptum* should not only be applied to contracts for carrying goods, but should also be extended to any contract for carrying persons, be it by cart or by rail.[15] This new type of liability based on *receptum*, however, did not exactly resemble the Roman jurists' understanding of *receptum*. According to Roman law, the company originally would only have been able to exonerate itself by showing that the loss was due to *vis maior*. The courts' approach, however, merely extended the debtor's liability by also asking for the fault of his employees. Accordingly, in effect, these courts introduced vicarious liability as well.[16]

2.a.ii Delictual liability

In principle, the claimants' situation was similar with regard to tortious remedies (i.e. the *actio legis Aquiliae*, where German common law was applicable), which, naturally, were the only remedies available to claimants who were not party to a contract with the railway company.

According to the traditional doctrine, plaintiffs in an action in tort could successfully claim damages only if they could prove[17] that the railway

vol. 6, pp. 116f. and 159f. As Lehmann, (*Körperverletzungen*, p. 15) has pointed out, the courts in Braunschweig would also have been ready to apply this concept. They generally held companies liable for the negligent behaviour of their employees as far as contractual liability was concerned; yet this question was not brought before them with respect to railway accidents.

15 This line of argumentation seems to have been particularly popular in those areas where the Badisches Landrecht (i.e. the French Civil Code) rather than German common law was applicable. According to arts. 1782 and 1784 Badisches Landrecht (provisions resembling *receptum*-based liability), a carrier was liable for any damage done to goods in his care, unless he could show that this damage had been inflicted accidentally or due to *vis maior*. The Oberhofgericht zu Mannheim, Seufferts Archiv, vol. 8, 78f., no. 52, for example, extended the scope of application of the aforesaid provisions so as to also cover any damage inflicted upon passengers, rather than just goods on the train. The courts of Wuerttemberg, where German common law was applicable, were also ready to apply the notion of liability based on *receptum*; according to their prevailing case law, a carrier was always liable for his employees' fault; see Obertribunal Stuttgart, Seufferts Archiv, vol. 2, 121, no. 93 – yet referring to D. 19.2.25.7 (see note 14, above); vol. 6, 346, no. 243 and Lehmann, *Körperverletzungen*, pp. 21f.

16 The Oberhofgericht zu Mannheim (above, note 15) even seems to suggest that – corresponding to what was common doctrine as far as contractual or tortious liability was concerned (see the following note) – the onus of proof of this fault rested on the victim (which would have been contrary to arts. 1782 and 1784 Badisches Landrecht).

17 According to common opinion, the onus of proof of fault in the *actio legis Aquiliae* rested with the victim; see Seuffert, *Praktisches Pandektenrecht* vol. I, § 99, pp. 122ff.; Carl Friedrich Ferdinand Sintenis, *Das practische gemeine Civilrecht* (3rd edn, Leipzig: Fischer, 1868), vol. II, § 101, p. 346, note 67.

company had failed to exercise the required standard of care in either operating the railway or in choosing or supervising its employees. However, several courts tended to relax these requirements in different ways.

Again, just as in cases concerning contractual liability, following Gaius D. 19.2.25.7,[18] a general concept of vicarious liability was occasionally adopted.[19] Rather more popular, though, was an approach reaching even further; courts started to operate with a reversal of the onus of proof as regards the requirement of fault. The railway companies were thus held liable under the *actio legis Aquiliae* unless they could show that every reasonable care had been taken.[20] These courts thereby introduced strict liability, except that the company in question could not only exonerate itself by showing that the damage inflicted was due to *vis maior*, but also by proving that it was due to lesser accidents (*vis minor*). The Munich Court of Appeal went still further in 1861 – even covering *vis minor*, though formally adhering to the fault principle. According to its judgment (which has become renowned for this very statement), 'the operation of a railway always amounts to *culpa*'.[21] The court's approach was based on the notion that *culpa* only required that the person acting could foresee that his actions could possibly result in damage.

In sum, several courts tended to rule in favour of the passenger or third party injured in a railway accident. But the extent to which there was a contractual or tortious obligation of railway companies to compensate their passengers or third parties for damage resulting from such accidents ultimately depended on the competent jurisdiction, and was thus more or less left to chance.[22]

2.b *The Prussian Railway Act of 3 November 1838*

Bearing in mind the German legal science's inclination to uphold the fault principle, it is not surprising that the first and most important

[18] See note 14, above.

[19] See Oberappellationsgericht München, Seufferts Archiv, vol. 10, 220, no. 164.

[20] See Oberappellationsgericht Braunschweig, *Wrede* v. *Ducal Railway and Postal Authority Braunschweig*, Seufferts Archiv, vol. 10, p. 221, no. 165; similarly, the Oberappellationsgericht Lübeck, Sammlung der Entscheidungen des Ober-Appellationsgerichts zu Lübeck in Frankfurter Rechtssachen, vol. 6, pp. 116f. and 159f. The latter court even extended this reversal of the onus of proof to contractual remedies.

[21] Seufferts Archiv, vol. 14, pp. 354ff., no. 208; similarly, the Oberhofgericht Mannheim, *Ettlingenweier* v. *Ducal Postal Exchequer*, Seufferts Archiv, vol. 13, pp. 328ff., no. 235.

[22] For further details concerning the situation throughout the different German territories, see Lehmann, *Körperverletzungen*, pp. 8ff. and Ogorek, *Gefährdungshaftung*, pp. 61ff.

step towards strict liability for damage caused in railway accidents was taken by the legislator. Merely four days after the opening of the first Prussian railway line on 29 October 1838 (stretching from Berlin to Potsdam, having a length of roughly 34 km, with the whole German railway network at that time amounting to about 140 km)[23] and a mere three years after the first German railway line had gone into service (stretching from Nuremberg to Fürth), the Prussian Railway Act (PRA)[24] came into force.[25]

In 1835, the Prussian King had ordered his ministers to submit a railway bill. Two years later, the Prussian Ministry of State put forward a first draft, according to which railway companies should be liable for all damage caused by their employees, provided that the victim could not successfully gain compensation from the employee himself. The Ministry's line of argumentation concentrated on the consideration that, without such a provision, railway companies could be held liable only if the victim could prove that the company had acted negligently in choosing its employees. This, in practice, would be impossible, however, and thus render useless any contractual or tortious remedies the victim might have. Furthermore, the Ministry specified the state's obligation to care for its inhabitants as a reason for a departure from the existing negligence rule. The Ministry's proposal was then brought before the Council of State, one of whose members was Friedrich Carl von Savigny. It is due to his dedication that the proposed subsidiary entitlement to damages from the railway company was eventually replaced by a strict liability of railway companies. Savigny pointed out that the Prussian Minister of Justice's original proposal of strict liability was highly preferable to the then present draft. In essence, he put forward two reasons: first of all, he argued, it would be impractical for a victim to have to sue the company's employee first. Due to the asymmetric

[23] See Rainer Fremdling, *Eisenbahnen und Deutsches Wirtschaftswachstum 1840–1879* (Dortmund: Gesellschaft für Westfälische Wirtschaftsgeschichte, 1975), p. 48.

[24] Gesetz über die Eisenbahnunternehmungen of 3 November 1838, Gesetzsammlung für die Königlich Preußischen Staaten 1838, pp. 505ff.

[25] For details on the process of its drafting, see Theodor Baums, 'Die Einführung der Gefährdungshaftung durch F. C. von Savigny' (1987) 104 *Zeitschrift der Savigny-Stiftung für Rechtsgeschichte (zss), Germ. Abt.* 277ff.; Martina Eckardt, *Technischer Wandel und Rechtsevolution* (Tübingen: Mohr Siebeck, 2001), pp. 220ff.; ibid., 'The Evolution of German Tort Law in the 19th Century', in Oliver Volckart (ed.), *Institutional Analysis of History, Homo Oeconomicus* (Munich: Accedo, 2004), pp. 83ff.; see further, Berthold Stumpf, 'Die Entstehung des preußischen Eisenbahngesetzes vom 3. November 1838', in *Die Reichsbahn, Amtliches Nachrichtenblatt der Deutschen Reichsbahn und der Reichsautobahnen*, vols. 44/45, pp. 7ff.

distribution of information, it would be virtually impossible for the victim to identify the person who could have been responsible for the damage. Thus, one should rather hold the company itself responsible, with the possibility of recourse against its employee. Secondly, and equally important, the company should also be liable for damage resulting from *vis minor*; otherwise, there would be no effective safeguards for passengers or third parties in cases where the reason for the accident was a purely technical one, such as unforeseeable defects in material or the like.[26]

In its plenary meeting, the Council of State adopted these arguments, additionally referring to several provisions of the Prussian codification, the *Allgemeines Landrecht für die Preußischen Staaten* (Prussian Civil Code 1794 – ALR), which – based on the concept of *receptum* liability – provided for strict liability of common carriers of goods.[27] Although these provisions were applicable only where the damage had been inflicted on a contracting party in fulfilment of the carrier's contractual obligations, it was argued that the Prussian Railway Act should be extended to damage done to third parties as well. If there was strict liability with regard to passengers who themselves had chosen to make use of the company's services, third parties who had not been in contact with the railway company before the accident would be all the more in need of effective protection. As far as the introduction of strict liability rather than a simple reversal of the onus of proof of fault is concerned, the Council put forward the additional argument that, due to the unmanageable dimensions of the railway network, damages resulting from the operation of a railway could hardly be prevented by public law provisions. Eventually, most of the Council's members were convinced. The strict liability rule (§ 25 PRA) was passed, with a majority of 29 votes to 4:

> The company is liable to pay compensation for all damages incurred by persons and goods during transportation by rail, regardless of whether or not the persons or goods were on the train. The company may exonerate itself only where it can prove that the damages were either inflicted due to the harmed person's own fault or caused by unavoidable external chance. The dangerous nature of railways itself does not constitute chance in this sense.[28]

[26] For the exact wording of Savigny's considerations, see Baums, 'Gefährdungshaftung', pp. 278f.

[27] That is, Part II Title 8, §§ 1734, 1735, 2459 and 2462 ALR and Title 15, §§ 185 and 187 ALR.

[28] Protocol of the Council's plenary meeting; see Baums, 'Gefährdungshaftung', pp. 280ff.; Lehmann, *Körperverletzungen*, pp. 45ff., note *.

2.c *The lack of effectiveness of the Prussian Railway Act and the call for a new provision*

The Prussian strict liability rule was soon adopted in other German territories.[29] Yet although, on the face of it, this rule seemingly provided for the effective protection of passengers as well as of third parties, it did not, in effect, work out as originally intended.[30] In the years after the coming into force of § 25 PRA, it turned out that the Prussian Railway Act had taken account of all but two things. Firstly, since § 25 PRA was not compulsory, the contracting parties could agree to make use of the traditional negligence rule instead. This possibility was widely used by the railway companies, which, due to their market power, were able to provide for the application of the fault principle in their terms and conditions.[31] Secondly, there was ample scope for interpretation of § 25 PRA by the courts. Especially harsh consequences arose from the Prussian Supreme Court's case law. According to this case law, railway companies were only liable to compensate for damage that had been inflicted on the injured person's body; they were not, however, liable to compensate the injured

[29] § 25 PRA was adopted by the declaration of 19 May 1840 (§ 22) in Holstein; Mecklenburg adopted the same rule on 23 May 1855; the Duchies and Grand Duchies of Saxony and Anhalt also enacted § 25 PRA, namely with regard to the Thuringian and Anhaltian railways; see Lehmann, *Körperverletzungen*, pp. 17f. The Kingdom of Hanover also enacted a similar rule by royal decree in 1856 (§ 30 of the 'Königliche Verordnung, die Anlage von Eisenbahnen durch Privatunternehmer betreffend' of 29 March 1856, in Sammlung der Gesetze, Verordnungen und Ausschreiben für das Königreich Hannover, 1. Abteilung, pp. 101ff.).

[30] On this point, see also the very detailed overview given by John M. Kleeberg, 'From Strict Liability to Workers' Compensation: The Prussian Railroad Law, the German Liability Act, and the Introduction of Bismarck's Accident Insurance in Germany, 1838–1884' (2003) 36 *Journal of International Law and Politics* 53 at 72ff.

[31] Kleeberg ('From Strict Liability to Workers' Compensation', pp. 70ff.) has suggested that the imposition of strict liability did not, to any great extent, meet resistance by the railway companies, because their business turned out to be so profitable that they could live with the law. Yet if railway companies were able to exclude strict liability in their terms and conditions, there was no need for resistance. The dispute as to whether or not such terms and conditions were valid (see Julius Hermann Beschorner, 'Von der Ersatzpflicht der Eisenbahnverwaltungen' (1858) 41 AcP 398ff. on the one hand, and Levin Goldschmidt, 'Ueber die vertragsmäßige Beschränkung der Ersatzpflicht der Eisenbahnverwaltungen' (1858) 41 AcP 406ff. on the other hand) did not, in practice, render these terms and conditions ineffective. Thus, eventually the Prussian legislator took action. The legislator's response, however, dates from as late as 1869: on 3 May 1869, a Prussian statute came into force prohibiting such terms and conditions (Preußische Gesetzessammlung (1869), p. 665, no. 38); this provision served as a model for § 5 RHPflG (see below, p. 86). Only as far as damage to goods on the train was concerned had the problem been solved earlier (by art. 423 ADHGB; see below, p. 84).

person for loss of profit, in particular for present or future loss of earnings resulting from the accident.[32]

Accordingly, even though the Prussian legislator had taken an important step in improving the protection of victims of railway accidents, by the middle of the 1850s, the legal situation throughout Germany with regard to liability in railway accidents was widely thought to be unsatisfactory. Very little of the problem was solved, when in 1861 the General German Commercial Code (*Allgemeines Deutsches Handelsgesetzbuch* – ADHGB) came into force in the different German territories. Henceforth, art. 423 ADHGB expressly prohibited the contractual exclusion of liability with respect to damage incurred to goods during transportation by rail. The entry into force of this provision has to be seen against the background of the formation of political interest groups in the years before. Whereas the chambers of commerce, which had grown in number since the middle of the century, had not been able to prevent the German Railway Association (which had been founded in 1847) from laying down in its conditions of the transportation of goods (1850) that § 25 PRA should not be applied, they had now been able to pursue their interests with the help of the political process and used the passing of the Commercial Code to achieve a tightening of the liability by statute rather than by contractual agreements.[33]

Yet, not only did the chambers of commerce push through their interests as far as the transportation of goods by rail was concerned. In fact, from the end of the 1850s onwards, legal writers also began to focus on the unsatisfactory situation concerning personal injuries.[34] They repeatedly pointed out the fact that, except for Prussia and those territories where

[32] Preußisches Obertribunal, Judgments of 24 April 1854 and 14 December 1857, in Entscheidungen des Königlichen Obertribunals, vol. 28, pp. 270ff. and vol. 37, pp. 42ff; cf. Koch, *Deutschlands Eisenbahnen*, annex XXXIVb; Lehmann, *Körperverletzungen*, pp. 67ff. The Court did to some extent, however, tend to rule in favour of railway companies' employees by allowing them to claim compensation for lost wages; see Kleeberg, 'From Strict Liability to Workers' Compensation', 72 at 78ff. Yet, at the same time, the Court, by means of a restrictive interpretation of the words 'during transport by rail', did not protect railway workers where the trains had not been in motion. This problem was solved only when the Imperial Law of Liability came into force (see below, pp. 86–87).

[33] See Eckardt, *Technischer Wandel*, pp. 239ff.; ibid., 'Evolution', Ch. 3.2.2. Eckardt gives a full account of the relevant circumstances.

[34] Amongst others, see August Bessel and Eduard Kühlwetter, *Preußisches Eisenbahnrecht* (Cologne: Eisen, 1855–1857); Koch, *Deutschlands Eisenbahnen*; Julius Hermann Beschorner, *Deutsches Eisenbahnrecht* (Erlangen: Enke, 1861); ibid., 'Ersatzpflicht'; Goldschmidt, 'Ersatzpflicht'; Lehmann, *Körperverletzungen*.

§ 25 PRA and the equivalent statutes, at least in theory, provided for effective protection in railway accidents, and except for the Rhine territories, where the Civil Code was applicable,[35] the legal situation was more or less disputed, and individuals could not be sure whether they would gain compensation at all. The most fundamental and substantial contribution to the further development probably has to be seen in the academic work of Gustav Lehmann.[36] In 1869, Lehmann brought forward a well-argued proposal to enact a new provision for strict liability as far as damage to persons was concerned, regardless of whether or not they were passengers on the train. This proposal took into account all of the previously mentioned difficulties and inadequacies that had been encountered. Accordingly, Lehmann suggested that railway companies should not only be liable for their employees' fault, but, on the contrary, should be strictly liable and allowed to exonerate themselves only where they could prove that the damage incurred was due to *vis maior* or the victim's own fault. Furthermore, railway companies should be liable for full damages including loss of profit. Ultimately, this proposal led to the adoption of the Imperial Law on Liability (*Reichshaftpflichtgesetz* – RHPflG) in 1871.

2.d The Imperial Law on Liability of 1871 and its aftermath

Whereas the Prussian Railway Act of 1838 had essentially been based on a political initiative, the drafting of a new provision at the beginning of the 1870s was in essence promoted by the legal profession.[37] In 1868, the Parliament of the North German Confederation was confronted with a petition by the National Liberal Party;[38] the father of this petition for a complete reform of the law of liability in accidents was Karl Biedermann, Professor at the University of Leipzig.[39] In essence, the petition criticised the fragmentation of legal systems throughout Germany and pointed at

[35] Which meant that arts. 1382, 1384 and 1782 (French) Civil Code (or Badisches Landrecht) provided for strict liability as far as common carriers of goods were concerned, and at least provided for vicarious liability in other cases.

[36] *Körperverletzungen*; id., *Der Nothstand des Schädensprozesses* (Leipzig: Fischer, 1865).

[37] Particularly interested in the insufficiencies of the legal situation as far as claims for damages are concerned were the practitioners at their annual meetings; see Verhandlungen des 4. Deutschen Juristentages, vol. 2 (Berlin, 1864), p. 278; Schaffrath, in Verhandlungen des 6. Deutschen Juristentages, vol. 3 (Berlin, 1868), p. 252ff.; Karsten, in Verhandlungen des 9. Deutschen Juristentages, vol. 1 (Berlin, 1870), p. 399.

[38] *Stenographische Berichte über die Verhandlungen des Reichstages des Norddeutschen Bundes* (1868), vol. II (annexes), pp. 188ff., annex no. 56B.

[39] See Ogorek, *Gefährdungshaftung*, p. 100, note 11.

the people's resentment resulting from these intolerable differences. From this point on, discussions were intensified on the political level as well. In 1871, the first Parliament of the German Reich was presented with a draft, which was ultimately adopted by a great majority of votes and came into force on 7 June 1871.

Paragraph 1 RHPflG[40] provided for strict liability of railway companies in cases of death or personal injuries caused during the operation of railways; railway companies could exonerate themselves only if they could prove that the damage was due to *vis maior* or the injured person's own fault.[41] Furthermore, the Imperial Law on Liability also provided a remedy for the problem that the Prussian Supreme Court, in applying § 25 PRA, did not hold railway companies liable to compensate for loss of profit. According to § 3, railway companies had to provide compensation not only for treatment expenses but also for loss of earnings – or, in case of death, had to pay for the relatives' subsistence. Finally, § 5 RHPflG made clear that railway companies were no longer allowed to 'opt out' of their liability by imposing any such terms and conditions on their passengers or any such contractual agreement on their employees.

Compared to § 25 PRA, there are two aspects of the Imperial Law on Liability that deserve closer attention. Firstly, unlike § 25 PRA, § 1 RHPflG was applicable to damage incurred 'through the operation of railways' rather than 'during transport by rail'. Secondly, § 1 RHPflG did not provide for an entitlement to damages in cases of damage to property. Ultimately, both differences can be ascribed to the same reason. When the legal profession had taken the initiative and proposed the adoption of a uniform rule for the liability of railway companies, the news had been dominated not by accidents resulting in damage to passengers or third parties, but rather by accidents resulting in injuries or death to employees of the railway companies themselves.[42]

[40] 'Gesetz betreffend die Verbindlichkeit zum Schadensersatz für die bei dem Betriebe von Eisenbahnen, Bergwerken, Fabriken, Steinbrüchen und Gräbereien herbeigeführten Tötungen und Körperverletzungen', Reichsgesetzblatt 1871, p. 207.

[41] As to the interpretation of *vis maior* by the courts, see below, p. 94.

[42] This is quite obvious when one takes into account that, in 1868, merely 4 passengers were killed and only 17 were injured on Prussian railways, whereas the numbers of railway employees killed and injured amounted to 183 and 320 respectively. The disparities were not as dramatic in other years, yet according to the statistical studies of Eckardt (*Technischer Wandel*, p. 253 and table 5 (pp. 322f.)), injuries to employees of the railway companies from 1851 to 1879 on average still accounted for 76% of all injuries suffered from railway accidents. Further statistical data is available in *Statistische Nachrichten von den Preußischen Eisenbahnen*, vol. 1 (1855) and vol. 27 (1880).

Naturally, this was all the more true in cases of accidents in other sectors of industry, such as mining,[43] where typically only employees were involved. These cases were the subject matter of the aforesaid petition as well. With regard to such accidents, the legal situation was particularly unsatisfactory,[44] since even § 25 PRA did not provide for effective protection of the employees themselves. This was not only due to the fact that railway companies, in employment contracts, regularly excluded their liability arising from § 25 PRA; the prevailing case law of the Prussian Supreme Court also played an important role. This case law favoured a restrictive interpretation of § 25 PRA as far as the words 'during transport by rail' were concerned, thereby excluding any such activities as the loading or unloading of carriages or other preparations for transportation, where trains were not in motion.[45] By choosing the wording 'through the operation of railways', the legislator made clear that, in the future, such cases should result in the railway companies being liable to compensate for damages too.[46]

That employees' injuries were one of the most important concerns of the legislator in 1871 is all the more apparent from the fact that the Imperial Law on Liability specifically dealt with such injuries in § 2, as far as accidents in mining, quarries or factories were concerned. It is probably for this very same reason that the discussions with respect to railway-based liability also focused on personal injuries rather than on damage to property, and that § 1 RHPflG thus dealt with personal injuries only. It needs to be borne in mind, firstly, that damage to property had been dealt with by the General German Commercial Code as far as the transportation of goods was concerned; secondly, that injuries to persons had been the people's primary concern in the 1860s; and thirdly, that the Imperial Law on Liability was the result of a reaction to this concern by the legal profession and the legislator rather than the result of efforts of organised

43 On these accidents, see Kleeberg, 'From Strict Liability to Workers' Compensation', pp. 86ff.

44 As Eckardt (*Technischer Wandel*, p. 254) has discovered, in cases of death, merely 6% of the employees' relatives were successful in claiming damages from the railway company. Likewise, only 17% of the injured employees were awarded damages.

45 See, for instance, the Prussian Supreme Court's judgment of 24 April 1854, in Entscheidungen des Königlichen Obertribunals, vol. 28, pp. 270, 273 and numerous other judgments as quoted by Georg Eger, *Das Reichshaftpflichtgesetz* (2nd edn, Breslau: Kern, 1879), p. 5.

46 This intention is quite clear from the statement of Dr Schwarze, Member of Parliament, in *Stenographische Berichte über die Verhandlungen des Deutschen Reichstags* (1871), vol. I, pp. 444f.

interest groups.[47] It is therefore reasonably understandable that the legislator did not focus on damage to property. Yet, at the same time, this clearly shows that the Imperial Law on Liability once again found a selective remedy only and did not provide for a comprehensive rule of railway accident liability.[48]

The courts, however, subsequently reacted to the inadequacies of the legal protection as far as damage to third parties' property was concerned. In 1886, the Reichsgericht held that, even in the absence of fault,[49] railway companies were to be held liable for damage inflicted on third parties' property where this property regularly came into close contact with the railway and was thus latently endangered by its operation. The corresponding line of argumentation concentrated on the fact that railway companies had been granted permission to operate railways by the state. If, by reason of this permission, the individual could not (on the basis of an *actio negatoria*) successfully claim that the railway company should cease to operate the railway, the individual should at least be entitled to claim damages, irrespective of the company's fault. Otherwise, the permission granted by the state would result in unjustified constraints on the claimant's property.[50]

After a comparatively short time, most of the Imperial Law on Liability was superseded by the Accident Insurance Act (*Unfallversicherungsgesetz*) of 1884.[51] The traditional path of coping with occupational injury was abandoned in favour of Bismarck's system of workmen's compensation

[47] Eckardt, *Technischer Wandel*, p. 268.

[48] This, however, quite conformed to the legislator's intentions. The primary concern was to provide for effective remedies in cases of injury or death, not to set on its way an overall reform of the law of tort with respect to 'accidents': see 'Motive zum Reichshaftpflichtgesetz', in *Stenographische Berichte über die Verhandlungen des Deutschen Reichstags* (1871), vol. III, pp. 69ff., no. 16.

[49] With respect to which the Reichsgericht made clear that the operation of railways in itself could not be treated as negligent behaviour; see the abovementioned judgments to the contrary (above, p. 80).

[50] See *Preußischer Eisenbahnfiskus* v. *Landschaftliche Brandkasse zu Hannover*, Entscheidungen des Reichsgerichts in Zivilsachen (RGZ), vol. 17, pp. 103ff.; see further RGZ 7, pp. 265ff.; 30, pp. 114ff.; 32, pp. 337ff.; 58, p. 130. A similar approach that did not, however, refer to the *actio negatoria* but simply to necessary limits in exercising one's own property had already been taken by the Prussian Supreme Court in 1852; see Theodor Striethorst (ed.), *Archiv für Rechtsfälle* (Berlin: Guttentag, 1852), vol. V, no. 52, pp. 282f. For further details, see Müller-Erzbach, 'Gefährdungshaftung', pp. 333ff.

[51] Unfallversicherungsgesetz of 6 July 1884, Reichsgesetzblatt 1884, p. 69. On its background and its emergence from the previous legislation in the field of railway accidents, see the detailed account of Kleeberg, 'From Strict Liability to Workers' Compensation', pp. 53ff., esp. pp. 98ff.

for occupational injury; instead of damages being paid according to delict law, a compulsory insurance for all employees (with the insurance contribution to be paid by the employer) was introduced, which provided for payment of treatment expenses as well as for the subsistence of injured workers and their relatives. A similar approach was also recommended with regard to the liability of railway companies for damage incurred by passengers. In 1884, Otto von Mühlenfels brought forward the proposal that every passenger on a railway should be obliged to enter into an accident insurance contract when buying a railway ticket.[52] However, this proposal did not find approval. The Imperial Law on Liability thus, in this respect, remained applicable.

Equally unsuccessful were proposals to incorporate § 1 RHPflG into the German Civil Code when it came to the drafting of the German Civil Code. These proposals were not thoroughly considered; instead, the vast majority accepted that it would simply require too much work to draft a sound piece of legislation in this respect.[53]

However, the Prussian Government was not prepared to accept that, due to the coming into force of the German Civil Code, the situation would have been worsened with respect to damage to property. Since § 1 RHPflG did not provide for any remedy with respect to damage to property and the General German Commercial Code was applicable with respect to the transportation of goods only, the Prussian Railway Act had not completely lost its scope of application. § 25 PRA had remained applicable with respect to such damage to property that was neither dealt with by the Imperial Law on Liability nor by the General German Commercial Code (i.e. damage to third parties' property as well as damage to such property that passengers kept with themselves on a train journey). The Prussian Government in this respect insisted on retaining the possibility of application of § 25 PRA. The fathers of the BGB thus made provision in Art. 105 EGBGB (*Einführungsgesetz zum BGB*) to make possible the application of laws of the German territories with respect to damage

[52] Otto von Mühlenfels, *Die Haftpflicht der Eisenbahnen und die Unfall-Versicherung* (Berlin: Reimer, 1884), pp. 72ff.

[53] See Bericht der XII. Kommission des Reichstages vom 12. Juni 1896, pp. 107f., reproduced in Benno Mugdan (ed.), *Die gesammten Materialien zum Bürgerlichen Gesetzbuch für das Deutsche Reich* (Berlin: Von Decker, 1899), vol. II, p. 1300. The true reason was probably somewhat different; one has to bear in mind that the legislator thought that the fault principle in the law of tort was an important achievement of the Roman as well as most modern legal systems and thus should not be questioned in principle by accepting any strict liability rule to be adopted in the Civil Code; see 'Bericht', p. 103 in Mugdan, *Die gesammten Materialien*, p. 1297.

to property resulting from railway accidents. Soon after the coming into force of the BGB, this possibility was made use of in several other of the German territories. In essence, their legislators provided for strict liability rules resembling § 25 PRA.[54]

2.e The development after the coming into force of the German Civil Code

The Imperial Law on Liability, as well as the fragmentation of remedies in the area of railway accidents, remained untouched until the 1940s. In 1940, however, a uniform regime of rules with respect to damage to third parties' as well as passengers' property[55] was adopted.[56] The main reason is quite obvious: the fragmentation of rules with respect to such damage was unanimously thought to be unsatisfactory;[57] even the courts had called for a reform.[58] Furthermore, even where there was strict liability with respect to damage to third parties' property, the corresponding rules, especially the Prussian Railway Act, did not necessarily apply to damage incurred by trams as well; this difference between trams and other types of railways had also been criticised.[59] Finally, in 1978, these new special rules were incorporated into the Liability Act of 1978.[60] Paragraph 1 of this Act now provides for strict liability of railway companies with respect to personal damage, as well as damage to property.

Since then, there have only been two further regimes of rules in the area of railway liability. Firstly, the Liability Act of 1978 does not deal with

[54] Mostly, these provisions were part of the territories' laws for execution of the EGBGB, for example Bavaria Art. 58; Hesse Art. 74; Braunschweig § 28; Saxony-Altenburg § 37; Saxony-Coburg and Gotha Art. 17 § 1; Saxony-Meiningen Art. 12 § 1; Saxony-Weimar/Eisenach § 90, Lübeck § 60. Württemberg adopted a special statute; see Arts. 1–3, 'Gesetz betreffend die Haftung für Sachschaden bei dem Eisenbahnbetrieb' of 4 June 1903, Regierungsblatt für das Königreich Württemberg 1903, p. 213.

[55] With respect to the latter, see Hans-Joachim Finger, 'Haftung der Eisenbahn und Straßenbahn für vom Reisenden mitgeführte Gegenstände' (1941) *Zeitschrift der Akademie für Deutsches Recht* (ZAkDR) 315f.

[56] 'Gesetz über die Haftpflicht der Eisenbahnen und Straßenbahnen für Sachschaden' of 29 April 1940, Reichsgesetzblatt 1940 I, p. 691.

[57] For the official reasons for its adoption, see (1940) *Deutsche Justiz* 544f.; for further details, see Elsa Koffka, 'Die Haftung der Eisenbahnen für Sachschäden' (1940) *Deutsche Justiz* 538ff.

[58] See RGZ 163, p. 65 at 67.

[59] See Josef Esser, 'Zur Neuregelung der Eisenbahnhaftpflicht für Sachschäden' (1939) *Deutsches Autorecht* (DAR), cols. 87ff.

[60] 'Haftpflichtgesetz' of 4 January 1978, Bundesgesetzblatt I 1978, p. 145.

damage to goods carried by rail. Such damage had, since 1938, been dealt with by the Railway Traffic Regulations (*Eisenbahnverkehrsordnung* – EVO) and the German Commercial Code (*Handelsgesetzbuch* – HGB), which provided for strict liability as well (§ 454 HGB and § 82 EVO). In 1998, most of these rules were abolished. Railway freight traffic now, in essence, is no longer subject to special rules, but rather is dealt with by the general principles of freight traffic law (§§ 407ff. HGB). In principle, these provide for strict liability. However, the railway company may exonerate itself not only in cases of *vis maior*, but also in cases where it can prove that the 'highest standard of care' (§ 426 HGB) has been observed.[61]

The second regime of rules to be mentioned is the ordinary law of delict as set out in §§ 823ff. BGB. These rules, being governed by the fault principle, come into play where there is no entitlement to damages under the strict liability scheme. Most importantly, this is the case where damages are limited to a certain amount (e.g. § 9 RHPflG, in case of death or injury, provides for a limit of €600,000 per person). The same situation arises in the area of road traffic accidents; the problems relevant to these accidents will be discussed in further detail, as will the whole development of strict liability in the twentieth century.

3 Road traffic accident liability

3.a Liability at the time of the German Civil Code coming into force (1900)

With Berta Benz making the first long journey with a motor vehicle in Germany on 5 August 1888 (from Mannheim to Pforzheim) and not more than 25 such vehicles having been built by Carl Benz before 1894, liability in road traffic accidents caused by motor vehicles had naturally not been a matter of concern during the process of the drafting of the German Civil Code. Thus, after the coming into force of the German Civil Code in 1900, liability in road traffic accidents was at first dealt with by the ordinary law of tort as set out in §§ 823ff. BGB. If a person had sustained physical injuries or damage to property, he could successfully claim damages only if he could prove that the driver had acted wilfully or negligently (§ 823, s. 1 BGB). Even where such behaviour could successfully be proven, it was only the driver who was liable. Due to the

[61] This rule has been adopted in view of Art. 17, s. 2(4) of the International Convention on the Carriage of Goods by Road.

legislator's reluctance to provide for true vicarious liability in the law of delict, it was nearly impossible, in practice, to make a claim on the owner of the car. For even if one could say that, in giving his car to a third-party driver, the owner had 'employed another person to do any work' and could therefore in principle be held liable (§ 831 BGB), he could, according to this provision, exonerate himself by proving that he had exercised the necessary care in the selection of the employee as well as in the supply of his equipment.

When road traffic quickly began to increase after 1900, this private-law liability regime was at first left unchanged. Notwithstanding several calls for special legislation in the field of private law,[62] the legislator focused on the adoption of public law provisions regulating road traffic. Since competence lay with the different territories, local rules were adopted at first; soon, there were miscellaneous road traffic regulations in the different German territories.[63] A uniform body of rules and regulations dealing with technical standards to be met by motor vehicles was first compiled by the Bundesrat in 1906 and subsequently adopted throughout the territories by statute or by-laws.[64] These rules and regulations, however, dealt with basic requirements only. A more diversified system of rules was established as late as 1910, when the Bundesrat framed general principles with respect to driving licences and requirements for ensuring the operational safety of motor vehicles.[65] Yet all these public law provisions did not change the legal situation for victims of road traffic accidents. These rules were regarded as rules designed to protect the individual in the sense of § 823, s. 2 BGB; their infringement thus, in theory, also gave rise to an entitlement to damages. According to § 823, s. 2, however, the injured person still had to prove that the infringement of any such rule by a driver had been due to the driver's fault.

[62] On which, see below, pp. 93ff.

[63] For example, the Bavarian 'Oberpolizeiliche Vorschriften über den Verkehr mit Motorfahrzeugen auf öffentlichen Wegen, Straßen und Plätzen' of 7 May 1902, Bayerisches Gesetz- und Verordnungsblatt 1902, p. 173; see also the 'Polizei-Verordnung für Berlin' of 15 April 1901, which not only dealt with speeding but also provided for a registration number to be attached to the car's rear side; in addition, drivers were obliged to carry a motor-vehicle registration certificate and a certificate confirming their ability to safely handle the car.

[64] 'Grundzüge betreffend den Verkehr mit Kraftfahrzeugen' of 3 May 1906.

[65] 'Verordnung des Bundesrathes über den Verkehr mit Kraftfahrzeugen' of 3 February 1910.

3.b *The Adoption of the Motor Vehicle Act (Kraftfahrzeuggesetz) of 3 May 1909*

With the increase of road traffic accidents in the first decade of the twentieth century,[66] the aforesaid situation was soon widely regarded as unsatisfactory. Once again, it was the legal profession that took the initiative. At their annual meeting in 1902, several practitioners called for the adoption of a strict liability rule in road traffic law resembling § 1 Reichshaftpflichtgesetz.[67] Nonetheless, it was not until 1906 that a first draft for a provision introducing strict liability in the field of road accidents was presented; as called for, this draft, in essence, provided for the same liability regime in road traffic accidents as had been introduced in railway accidents by § 1 RHPflG – with the only exception being that it was proposed that damage to property be covered as well. According to the 1906 proposal, the 'operator' ('*Betriebsunternehmer*') rather than the driver of a motor vehicle was to be held liable for any damage to persons or property incurred during the operation of a motor vehicle, unless the accident was due to *vis maior* or the injured party's own fault.[68] In its explanatory memorandum, the government referred to the difficulty that, even where the victim was able to provide evidence for the infringement of public law rules, he would, under § 823, s. 2 BGB, still have to prove fault on the part of the driver. Due to the agitated state of the parties involved,

[66] In 1907, there were 36,022 motor vehicles in the German Reich, with 4,864 road traffic accidents being recorded by the police. In these accidents, 145 people died and 2,419 were injured. By 1910, these figures had risen by roughly 50% and the road toll had doubled (49,941 motor vehicles, with 6,774 accidents; 278 people died and 3,651 were injured). These and further statistical data are available from the Statistisches Bundesamt: www.destatis.de (last accessed 20 May 2009).

[67] Cf. Karl Hilse, 'Gutachten über die Frage "Empfiehlt sich und in welchem Umfange die Ausdehnung der Haftpflicht auf Fahrzeuge, welche unabhängig von Schienensträngen auf öffentlichen Straßen durch elementare Kraft bewegt werden?" ', in *Verhandlungen des 26. Deutschen Juristentages* (Tübingen: Mohr, 1902), vol. I, pp. 27ff. and the discussions of the topic in vol. III (1903), pp. 163ff., 204ff., 596ff.; see also Friedrich Meili, 'Ein Reichsgesetz über die Haftung für Schädigungen durch Automobile' (1907) *Deutsche Juristen-Zeitung*, cols. 985ff. For an overall account of the development of Road Traffic Law in Germany until 1935, see Ludwig Trendel, 'Entwicklung des deutschen Kraftverkehrsrechts' (1935) ZAkDR 159ff; for all details concerning the adoption of the Motor Vehicle Act see Werner Schubert, 'Das Gesetz über den Verkehr mit Kraftfahrzeugen vom 3.5.1909' (2000) 117 *ZSS Germ. Abt.*, 238ff.

[68] Bundesratsdrucksache no. 7/1906. For the proposal, as well as the government's reasons, see also Fritz Müller, *Straßenverkehrsrecht* (12th edn, Berlin: Stilke, 1938), pp. 168f.; Werner Full, *Zivilrechtliche Haftung im Straßenverkehr* (Berlin and New York: Duncker and Humblot, 1980), pp. 92f.; Reinhard Greger, *Zivilrechtliche Haftung im Straßenverkehr* (2nd edn, Berlin and New York: Duncker and Humblot, 1990), pp. 4f.

the absence of witnesses and the complexity and speed of accidents, such proof of fault would often be virtually impossible. Moreover, the government also drew attention to the fact that the existing law did not provide for any remedies if the accident was due to unforeseeable defects in material, or even to the riskiness of road traffic itself rather than to the fault of any of the parties involved.

From the viewpoint of the car's owner, however, this proposal would have had rather harsh consequences. Common opinion acted on the assumption that the courts would apply their fairly narrow approach concerning *vis maior* – which they had developed in the application of § 1 RHPflG – in the field of road traffic liability as well, if the proposed provision was adopted.[69] According to this approach, a railway company was enabled to refer to *vis maior* only if the damage was due to an incident whose cause lay outside the operation of the railway and which could not have been avoided even by employing the highest standard of care, or which occurred so frequently that the railway company necessarily had to risk its consequences.[70] Adopting this approach in a road-traffic liability regime would have made it impossible, in practice, for a car's owner to prove that an accident had been due to *vis maior*, since most accidents were at least due to the riskiness of road traffic itself; as a consequence, car owners would almost always have been liable for damages.

Accordingly, this first draft quickly encountered the resistance of the car drivers' lobby. Under the supervision of the Imperial Automobile Association, a counter-draft was soon prepared, which not only objected to the liability being tied up to the 'operator' (which was thought to be rather too vague a wording), but also eased the liability. According to this draft, the custodian of a car (i.e. the person using the car for his own account), would have been liable only for his own and his driver's fault as well as for defects in material. Thus, roughly speaking, a kind of vicarious liability extending to the car itself rather than to employees only (i.e. the driver) was suggested. In order to secure effective protection for victims of car accidents notwithstanding this lessening of liability, the proposal provided for a reversal of the onus of proof.

The government at first adopted this counter-draft as its own,[71] pointing out that any liability that was stricter than the proposed one would mean imposing burdens on the users of motor vehicles that not only exceeded their financial capacity, but would also result in undesirable

[69] See Müller, *Straßenverkehrsrecht*, pp. 170, 198; Greger, *Haftung*, p. 6.

[70] For this approach, see RGZ 104, pp. 150ff.; 109, p. 172 at 173; 117, p. 12 at 13.

[71] Reichsanzeiger of 19 June 1908.

barriers to the development of the motor vehicle industry.[72] Subsequently, however, fears arose that the counter-draft's remedy would not be effective enough.[73] Thus, after lengthy discussions,[74] the custodian's liability was finally extended beyond fault and pure defects in material to all cases where the accident had not been due to an 'inevitable incident'. In order to ensure that the courts would not take this new criterion to mean any concept as narrow as *vis maior*, thereby rendering worthless all corresponding previous efforts of the car drivers' lobby, examples of such incidents were incorporated into the provision finally adopted on 3 May 1909. According to this provision (§ 7 Motor Vehicle Act),[75] the custodian to be held liable for damages could exonerate himself only if he could prove that the accident was due to an inevitable incident that was not based on defects in material or a malfunction of the vehicle's technical equipment. § 7 s. 2 additionally provided: 'An incident is deemed to have been inevitable especially if it is due to the injured party's action or the behaviour of an animal and if the custodian as well as the driver have exercised every care which in the circumstances of the case was necessary.'

In addition to this provision, the Motor Vehicle Act also provided for a tightened liability of the driver himself. The first draft from 1906 had not contained any such provision. However, the difficulties encountered by victims of road traffic accidents in proving fault were equally true as far as claims against the driver were concerned, which, until then, could only be based on § 823 BGB. Accordingly, in their counter-draft, the Imperial Automobile Association had called for a reversal of the onus of proof with respect to claims against the driver as well. In contrast to the custodian, however, according to this counter-draft, the driver should not be liable for defects in material, but rather for his own fault only. This proposal was adopted without alteration (§ 18 Motor Vehicle Act).

As pointed out, § 7 Motor Vehicle Act at the outset had been modelled on § 1 RHPflG. Even though § 7 Motor Vehicle Act thus referred to any accident incurred 'through the operation of motor vehicles', just as § 1 RHPflG referred to all accidents incurred 'through the operation of railways', and even though this wording in 1871 had been chosen in order to protect the railway companies' employees, the protection provided for by the Motor Vehicle Act in this respect was quite different. With § 8 s.1, the

[72] For these reasons, see Georg Eger, 'Der Entwurf eines Gesetzes über den Verkehr mit Kraftfahrzeugen' (1908) *Deutsche Juristen-Zeitung*, col. 995.

[73] See esp. the emphatic criticism by Eger, 'Entwurf', cols. 993ff.

[74] For details, see Müller, *Straßenverkehrsrecht*, pp. 169f., 197f.; Greger, *Haftung*, pp. 5f.

[75] 'Gesetz über den Verkehr mit Kraftfahrzeugen', Reichsgesetzblatt 1909, p. 437.

legislator made clear that the Act was not designed to protect any person engaged in the operation of the motor vehicle, nor even passengers of the motor vehicle, as far as these groups wanted to claim damages against the operator or the driver of the motor vehicle. Passengers as well as persons engaged in the vehicle's operation were thus able to claim damages under § 7 of the Act against a third-party operator or driver only (i.e. in such cases where their damage was due to an accident with a different motor vehicle).[76] The same was true for the owners of property being transported by motor vehicles. This rather narrow scope of application of the Motor Vehicle Act had already been proposed in the first draft in 1906 and was not questioned at a later stage; according to common opinion, this major deviation from the liability regime applicable to railway accidents was more or less self-evident. The reasons given for the first draft as well as for the government's final draft of 1908 concentrated on the line of argumentation that the proposed act aimed at the protection of the general public against dangers imposed on it by the operation of motor vehicles. As passengers, on the contrary, had voluntarily endangered themselves, they could not consequently be entitled to claim damages. Obviously, this would have been true for railway passengers as well. However, it was argued, railways had not only become an indispensable means of conveyance (thus, in effect, leaving no choice for passengers), but had also, from the outset, been dedicated to the transportation of passengers.[77] Notwithstanding all these arguments, the true reason for the act's limited scope of application with respect to passengers was probably somewhat different. In fact, it was widely thought that an extension of the liability to passengers etc. would unduly burden the owners of motor vehicles. Thus, in this respect, economic fears prevailed over the desire to provide for effective protection to road traffic victims. The idea of passengers voluntarily taking the risks was brought into play as a most welcome means of disguising this true reason and could, from a legal point of view, hardly be challenged.[78]

[76] This situation led to complications as regards the question of whether such a third-party operator was able to have recourse against the other operator under § 17 of the Act, even though the injured person was not entitled to a direct claim against the latter operator (§ 8 no. 1); for the different solutions, see Müller, *Straßenverkehrsrecht*, p. 333 (§ 17 C I a 5) on the one hand, and RGZ 146, pp. 97ff., 102f. on the other.

[77] For the official reasons for both drafts, see Müller, *Straßenverkehrsrecht*, pp. 238f. (§ 8 Vorbemerkung); Schubert, 'Kraftfahrzeuggesetz', 238ff.

[78] Cf. Müller, *Straßenverkehrsrecht*, p. 239 (§ 8 Vorbemerkung).

3.c *The further development of the Motor Vehicle Act*

In the years after the adoption of the Motor Vehicle Act, the statutes dealing with road traffic law in essence remained unchanged.[79] Instead of the legislator, the courts gained significant influence on the custodian's liability in road traffic accidents. In particular, they specified the notion of 'inevitable incidents'. According to their prevailing case law, an incident was inevitable only if the custodian as well as the driver had observed such a degree of care that the incident appeared to be due to completely unavoidable chance. The required standard of care thus by far exceeded the ordinary standard of care as applicable in the law of delict in general (i.e. as applicable in the area of fault liability (§ 823 BGB)). Most importantly, the driver of a motor vehicle always had to anticipate any imprudent action of pedestrians, even in the absence of the merest hint that such action was likely in the specific situation, as long as such action was foreseeable in general.[80] The liability in road traffic accidents thus, in practice, came close to the strict liability as provided for by § 1 RHPflG with respect to railway accidents,[81] except for the academically more than practically important difference that in railway accidents the railway company, in order to prove *vis maior*, could only bring forward as a defence external causes such as the force of nature, whereas for the custodian of a motor vehicle, internal causes, such as the riskiness of road traffic itself, constituted a defence if he and his driver had observed the special standard of care and if the accident was not due to defects in the vehicle's materials or its technical construction.

[79] That is, except for an amendment of the Motor Vehicle Act in 1923, which dealt with the question of the custodian's liability in the case of unauthorised use of his vehicle where the custodian's fault had rendered possible this use; see § 7, s. 3 Motor Vehicle Act as amended by the statute of 21 July 1923 ('Gesetz zur Abänderung des Gesetzes über den Verkehr mit Kraftfahrzeugen'), Reichsgesetzblatt I, p. 743; for details, see Full, *Haftung im Straßenverkehr*, pp. 201f. (§ 7 StVG, no. 242).

[80] See Reichsgericht (1926) *Juristische Wochenschrift*, p. 1191; Walther von Hellingrath and August Michel, *Kraftfahrrecht* (5th edn, Munich: Schweitzer, 1930), pp. 39ff., with further case-law at p. 45, note 3; Ludwig Trendel, 'Gefährdungshaftung – Zwangshaftpflichtversicherung – Reichskasse für Verkehrsunfälle' (1935) *Deutsches Autorecht*, cols. 145ff., 169; Full, *Haftung im Straßenverkehr*, pp. 210f. (§ 7 StVG, no. 260). See also note 90, below.

[81] As to this assessment, see the references in note 80, above, as well as Martin Isaac, rapporteur at the legal practitioners' annual meeting in 1928, in *Verhandlungen des 35. Deutschen Juristentages* (Tübingen: Mohr, 1928), vol. II, p. 224 and Uta Fromherz, 'Die zusammenfassende Neuregelung der Haftpflichtgrundsätze für Eisenbahnen, Kraft- und Luftfahrzeuge und der 35. Deutschen Juristentag' (1929) 130 AcP 73 at 88.

From the middle of the 1920s onwards, the legal profession once again increasingly focused on road traffic liability, mainly because the number of victims of road traffic accidents had risen to an unacceptable level.[82] Their discussion was given impetus when, in 1928, the question of whether the regimes of liability in the areas of railway, road and air traffic should be harmonised was put on the agenda of the annual meeting of legal practitioners. The expert opinions that were delivered to prepare the discussion pleaded in favour of such harmonisation. They did not, however, agree on the question of whether the liability standards of the Imperial Law on Liability or the Motor Vehicle Act should be applied in future. One of the experts pointed out that the courts, owing to their rather strict approach as to the notion of inevitable causes, had already drawn the custodian's liability in road traffic nearer to the railway-accident liability rules. He therefore called for the enactment of a rule whereby *vis maior*, rather than the inevitable causes, would be the only possible excuse with respect to road traffic accidents.[83] Another expert, on the contrary, argued that the application of the *vis maior* concept had led to some rather harsh results, in particular as far as trams were concerned, which were also believed to fall under the scope of application[84] of the Imperial Law on Liability; as trams, unlike railways, were operating amidst other road users, and any damage incurred by these users was thus normally, in one way or the other, due to the riskiness of the operation of trams, their operators had hardly ever been able to argue that they were not to be held liable because of *vis maior*.[85] Taking into account these consequences, it was argued, one

[82] As Isaac, *Verhandlungen des 35. Deutschen Juristentages*, vol. II, p. 209 pointed out, road casualties accounted for two-thirds of all fatal accidents (including mining, mountaineering, drowning accidents, etc.) at this time; in 1927 in Berlin, twenty-five persons on average were injured or killed in road traffic accidents every day.

[83] Robert Bartsch, 'Gutachten über die Frage: "Empfiehlt sich eine zusammenfassende Neuregelung der Haftpflichtgrundsätze für Eisenbahnen, Straßenbahnen, Kraftfahrzeuge und Luftfahrzeuge?" ', in *Verhandlungen des 35. Deutschen Juristentages*, vol. I/1, pp. 59ff., 74; cf. also Grünebaum, 'Empfiehlt sich …' (1928) 4 *Juristische Rundschau*, 153ff.

[84] See Eger, *Reichshaftpflichtgesetz*, p. 41 (§ 1 no. 3) for horse-drawn trams, and the 7th edn (Hanover: Helwing, 1912), p. 44 (§ 1 no. 3) for all other trams.

[85] See, for example, RGZ 50, pp. 92ff. Similarly, as far as railways were concerned, the *vis maior* concept in some cases led to liability, although, under the circumstances of the case, this was thought to be rather harsh a consequence. In RGZ 95, pp. 64ff., for example, the railway company was held liable where, as a result of dreaming of a railway accident, a passenger had smashed a window of the train and jumped out, even through the train was going at full speed. See also Isaac, *Verhandlungen des 35. Deutschen Juristentages*, vol. II, pp. 217ff.

should apply the regime of liability as set out in § 7 Motor Vehicle Act to railways as well.[86] Just like these experts, the jurists at their annual meeting did not come to an agreement either, and thus did not, in the end, suggest any alterations to the existing liability regimes.[87] The discussion concentrated on the issue of possible excuses for liability. According to the prevailing opinion, as far as railways were concerned, any lessening of liability with the result that internal causes also became possible excuses was not desirable. This formation of opinion was probably due to the line of argumentation of the rapporteur Isaac, who had drawn attention to the economic implications of the different liability regimes. As Isaac pointed out, the costs of liability of the German Reichsbahn accounted for as little as 0.13% of the Reichsbahn's operating expenses; thus, in practice, there was no necessity for a lessening of liability as far as railway accidents were concerned.[88] Owners of motor vehicles, on the contrary, depending on their yearly mileage, had to pay up to 7% of the total operating costs in order to obtain adequate insurance.[89] Bearing in mind that the interpretation of inevitable incidents by the courts was thought to be rather strict anyway,[90] it is quite clear that the proposal for stricter liability in road traffic accidents, so as to limit possible excuses to *vis maior* rather than accepting inevitable incidents, could not be successful either. On the other hand, a lessening of liability in road traffic was out of the question as well. However strict the courts' approach was thought to be, the necessity of effective protection for victims of road traffic accidents was beyond dispute.[91]

This situation changed when the discussion continued in the meeting's aftermath. In addition to the positions that had previously been adopted

[86] Friedrich Wussow, 'Gutachten über die Frage: "Empfiehlt sich eine zusammenfassende Neuregelung der Haftpflichtgrundsätze für Eisenbahnen, Straßenbahnen, Kraftfahrzeuge und Luftfahrzeuge?" ', in *Verhandlungen des 35. Deutschen Juristentages*, vol. I/1 pp. 81ff., 99f. and 103.

[87] See *Verhandlungen des 35. Deutschen Juristentages*, vol. II, p. 309.

[88] See Isaac, *Verhandlungen des 35. Deutschen Juristentages*, vol. II, p. 216; see also the consenting opinion of Flechtheim (p. 243) and the contrary opinion of Goltermann (p. 263).

[89] See Isaac, *Verhandlungen des 35. Deutschen Juristentages*, vol. II, pp. 227f.

[90] As Isaac put it (*Verhandlungen des 35. Deutschen Juristentages*, vol. II, pp. 227f.), according to the Reichsgericht, a motor vehicle driver, when sitting in the car, turned into a 'godlike creature', being able not only to handle the car safely but at the same time to foresee any action of any other driver on the road as well as pedestrians etc. Flechtheim (p. 247) suggested that this approach was quite contrary to the original intent of the legislator in 1909.

[91] Cf. Isaac, *Verhandlungen des 35. Deutschen Juristentages*, vol. II, p. 224.

and which continued to be discussed,[92] some jurists, obviously in particular those representing the automobile associations' interests, called for the repeal of § 7 Motor Vehicle Act. They argued that, due to the technical improvements motor vehicles had undergone in the meantime, and due to the fact that motor vehicles were now socially accepted, any liability other than fault liability was no longer justified.[93] Naturally, the whole discussion did not lead to the emergence of a uniform opinion that would have called for legislative action. Accordingly, the legislator did not see any necessity to react to the different proposals. The Motor Vehicle Act remained unchanged and, in 1952, was simply replaced by the Road Traffic Act (*Straßenverkehrsgesetz* – StVG).[94]

During the next decades, calls for a reform of the provisions dealing with liability in road traffic accidents were equally unsuccessful. The different proposals[95] in essence called for a tightening of liability, so as to abolish the excuse of inevitable causes and to provide for liability wherever the damage incurred was not due to *vis maior*. The primary intention of these proposals was to achieve uniformity throughout the different types of strict liability. The reason for the legislator's unwillingness to respond to these calls has probably to be seen in the courts' restrictive approach in interpreting the notion of inevitable causes. This interpretation, regularly leading to liability, guaranteed the effective protection of victims of road traffic accidents; a reform from the practical point of view was thus no matter of urgency. This was different with regard to one particular issue only. According to established case law, a driver had to take into account any imprudent action of other road users as well as pedestrians, and the custodian of a car could thus successfully invoke the excuse

[92] For a detailed account of the several approaches, see Hermann Gülde, 'Zur Erneuerung des Haftpflichtrechtes im Kraftfahrzeugverkehr' (1930) 132 AcP 70; see also Fromherz, 'Neuregelung der Haftpflichtgrundsätze', pp. 87ff.

[93] See, in particular, Trendel, 'Entwicklung', p. 163; id., 'Gefährdungshaftung', cols. 145ff., 169ff., 171.

[94] By means of the 'Gesetz zur Sicherung des Straßenverkehrs' of 19 December 1952, Bundesgesetzblatt I 1952, pp. 832ff., 937.

[95] See, for example, Karl Münzel, 'Zur Reform des Kraftfahrzeug-Haftpflichtrechts' (1963) *Neue Juristische Wochenschrift* (NJW) 1579; Hein Kötz, 'Haftung für besondere Gefahr' (1970) 170 AcP 1 at 41; Ernst v. Caemmerer, *Reform der Gefährdungshaftung* (Berlin: De Gruyter, 1971), pp. 21ff.; Erwin Deutsch, *Allgemeines Haftungsrecht* (Cologne: Heymann, 1976), vol. I, pp. 378f.; Hein Kötz, 'Empfiehlt sich eine Vereinheitlichung und Zusammenfassung der gesetzlichen Vorschriften über die Gefährdungshaftung im BGB und erscheint es erforderlich, das Recht der Gefährdungshaftung weiterzuentwickeln?', in Bundesminister der Justiz (ed.), *Gutachten und Vorschläge zur Überarbeitung des Schuldrechts* (Cologne: Bundesanzeiger Verlag, 1981), vol. II, pp. 1779ff.

of an inevitable incident only where his driver, taking into account such behaviour, had – as any perfect driver would have – acted in such a way as to avoid any accident resulting from such behaviour. But there was one particular situation where this approach did not provide for effective protection of the victim: in the case of a child running into the road unexpectedly, the custodian was able to identify an inevitable cause, and could thus not be held liable, if the child had not been visible to the driver, for example because the child had been standing between two parked cars.[96] A reform in this respect, calling for liability to be extended to all cases except for *vis maior*,[97] had been discussed since the end of the 1970s, especially after the German journal *Stern* had drawn attention to the frequency of road traffic accidents involving children.[98] As practitioners in the field of road-traffic accident law pointed out at their annual meeting in 1978, particular concerns arose from the fact that, according to statistics of the World Health Organisation, children below the age of 15 in Germany accounted for about 350 in every 100,000 road traffic victims, whereas these numbers were significantly smaller in other countries (Austria 270, Netherlands 190, the United Kingdom 110).[99] It was due to these cases of accidents involving children, rather than to the desire to provide for uniform rules in all fields of strict liability, that major amendments to the original statute came into force in 2002.[100] Since then, most importantly, the custodian's liability in road traffic accidents has extended to all cases except for *vis maior* (§ 7, s. 2 Road Traffic Act). Effective protection of children is thereby guaranteed; it corresponds to settled case law that

[96] See BGH (1985) NJW 1950; OLG Karlsruhe (1984) DAR 19ff.; OLG Köln (1980) *Versicherungsrecht* 338; OLG Hamm (1993) *Versicherungsrecht* 711.

[97] See Deutsche Akademie für Verkehrswissenschaft (ed.), *16. Deutscher Verkehrsgerichtstag 1978* (Hamburg: Deutsche Akademie für Verkehrswissenschaft, 1978), p. 14; id., *21. Deutscher Verkehrsgerichtstag 1983* (Hamburg: Deutsche Akademie für Verkehrswissenschaft, 1983), p. 10; id., *29. Deutscher Verkehsgerichtstag 1991* (Hamburg: Deutsche Akademie für Verkehrswissenschaft, 1991), p. 9.

[98] *Stern*, issue no. 27 of 23 June 1977.

[99] See Deutsche Akademie für Verkehrswissenschaft, in *16. Deutscher Verkehrsgerichtstag 1978*, p. 11 and Maria Limbourg, 'Die Leistungsfähigkeiten von Kindern als Fußgänger im Straßenverkehr', p. 267.

[100] By means of the 'Zweite Gesetz zur Änderung schadensersatzrechtlicher Vorschriften'; for details, see Gerhard Wagner, 'Das Zweite Schadensersatzrechtsänderungsgesetz' (2002) NJW 2049. Accordingly, the law has remained unchanged with respect to the question of the extent to which a custodian can recover damages he has paid to the victim from another custodian who is his joint tortfeasor; cf. § 17, s. 3 StVG. However, the legislator has, on the other hand, gone further than necessary in order to provide for effective protection to children; the amendment of § 7 StVG has not been limited to children, but rather affects all other road users.

children running into the road – even though this may have been unforeseeable under the circumstances of the case – do not constitute *vis maior*, because such behaviour is not exceptional and thus has to be accepted in terms of liability.[101]

Furthermore, it was not until 2002 that under the Road Traffic Act's liability scheme, custodians as well as drivers could be held liable to pay compensation for pain and suffering. Previously, victims of car accidents had only been able to claim compensation for such immaterial damages under the ordinary fault principle (§ 823 BGB) and therefore had to prove the custodian's or driver's fault. Accordingly, in actions for damages, courts regularly had to scrutinise the question of fault, even if the victim's claim was fairly clear with respect to material damages. In practice, therefore, the Road Traffic Act's liability scheme did not help to reduce the courts' workload. In essence, this was the reason for the second amendment of the Road Traffic Act.[102]

3.d *The application of the fault principle in road-traffic accident law and the influence of road traffic regulations*

Right from the very beginning, the Motor Vehicle Act did not provide for full protection of victims of road traffic accidents. Not only did victims have to rely on §§ 823, 847 BGB when they wanted to gain compensation for pain and suffering, but § 12 Motor Vehicle Act also provided for a maximum sum of damages to be claimed under this act. If a victim wanted to claim an amount exceeding this sum, he once again had to rely on fault-based liability as set out in § 823 BGB.

Fault liability has also always played an important role with respect to accidents of a legally more complex nature (i.e. accidents where the fault of another party is involved). If, in such a case, the custodian is not able to prove that from his point of view the accident constituted an inevitable incident, the extent of his obligation to pay damages depends on the extent to which he has contributed to the accident (§ 9 Road Traffic Act; § 254 BGB). In determining the custodian's quota of liability, the courts have to take into account not only the operational risk of his vehicle, but also the degree of fault involved on the part of the custodian or driver.

101 RGZ 54, pp. 404ff.; see also Adalbert Kunschert, 'Haftung des Kraftfahrzeughalters und Führers', in Reinhart Geigel (ed.), *Der Haftpflichtprozess* (24th edn by Günter Schlegelmilch (ed.), Munich: Beck, 2004), Ch. 25, no. 95, p. 882.

102 This is fairly obvious from the reasons the government has put forward; see Bundestags-Drucksachen 14/7752, p. 15.

Likewise, where the accident has taken place between different vehicles rather than between a vehicle and a pedestrian, cyclist etc., or where several custodians are liable to a third party as joint tortfeasors, the quotas of liability between the different custodians depend on the operational risk of their vehicles, as well as the degree of fault on the part of each custodian (§ 17 Road Traffic Act).

It is in these areas of fault liability, rather than within the mere scope of § 7 Road Traffic Act, that road safety regulations have come into play. Yet it would be inaccurate to say that such rules were of no importance in the field of § 7 Road Traffic Act. Any violation of such rule on the part of the custodian or driver rendered it impossible for the custodian to argue that the accident from his point of view had been an inevitable incident.[103] Likewise, these rules are of importance in so far as the driver's liability under § 18 Road Traffic Act is based on a rebuttable presumption of fault.

In practice, any violation of road traffic rules on the part of the driver results in an increase of his or the custodian's quota of liability, provided that this violation has had an impact on the accident.[104] Accordingly, the most important consequence of road traffic rules with respect to road-traffic accident liability has been that these rules have provided standards that are easy for the courts to apply when determining fault of the parties involved. Indirectly, these standards have thus had the effect of rendering more precise the notion of fault.

3.e *The influence of motor-vehicle liability insurance*

During the process of the drafting of the Motor Vehicle Act, there had already been a proposal to set up a fund for the compensation of victims of motor vehicle accidents.[105] According to this proposal, each custodian was to be obliged to make a contribution to the fund. The purpose of the proposed fund was to provide for compensation where the victim could not successfully recover damages from the custodian himself, be it due to his lack of funds or due to the fact that the custodian was unknown because the victim had not been able to identify the vehicle involved in the accident. This proposal, however, was not successful; the idea had at first been taken up by the Imperial Office of Judiciary, but had subsequently been

[103] See Reichsgericht, Höchstrichterliche Rechtsprechung 1930, no. 1504.

[104] See Entscheidungen des Bundesgerichtshofs in Zivilsachen (BGHZ), vol. 12, pp. 124 at 128; BGH (1957) NJW 99 and, most recently, BGH (2000) NJW 3069 at 3070.

[105] Petition no. 1289/3.

dropped.[106] Thus, when the Motor Vehicle Act came into force, victims of road traffic accidents could claim damages from insurance companies only where the custodian had voluntarily taken out a motor-vehicle liability insurance (which had been possible since around the turn of the century) and where the corresponding terms and conditions provided for the possibility of a direct claim of the victim against the insurance company.[107]

Subsequently, step by step, an obligation to enter into any such insurance contract was introduced on a territorial level; yet this obligation extended to cabs and vehicles used for the transportation of goods only.[108] It was not until 1936 that the situation changed; any driver who had not entered into an insurance contract and who was – due to his lack of funds – not able to fulfil his obligation to pay damages was thereafter threatened with the cancellation of his driving licence.[109] This was the government's first reaction to the legal profession's calls for the introduction of a compulsory insurance scheme. These calls had begun to emerge from the beginning of the 1930s, when more and more people had begun to purchase motor vehicles without having adequate funds to repair any damage resulting from the operation of their vehicle. Since then, it had been generally thought that the Motor Vehicle Act no longer provided for effective protection of victims of road traffic accidents since, even though in theory the victim was entitled to damages, such damages could not, in practice, be recovered.[110] Accordingly, by the end of the 1930s, the legislator took action and passed the Compulsory Insurance Act 1939 (Pflichtversicherungsgesetz).[111] With its coming into force on 1 July 1940, every custodian

[106] See Trendel, 'Gefährdungshaftung', col. 194.

[107] In the absence of such terms and conditions, direct claims did not arise from the insurance contract between the liability insurer and the custodian; see RGZ 124, p. 235 at 238; RGZ 141, p. 410 at 419 and Reinhart Geigel (ed.), *Der Haftpflichtprozeß* (3rd edn, Munich and Berlin: Beck, 1939), p. 305.

[108] See Gerhard Clase, 'Die Versicherungspflicht der Kraftdroschke', *Neumanns Zeitschrift für Versicherungswesen* 1928, pp. 1051 ff.; Herbert Kleinewefers, 'Zwangshaftpflichtversicherung für Kraftfahrzeughalter' (Dissertation, Bonn, 1938), pp. 16f.

[109] Erlaß des Reichs- und Preußischen Verkehrsministers, Reichsverkehrsblatt of 15 July 1936, no. 25; see Kleinewefers, 'Zwangshaftpflichtversicherung', p. 17.

[110] See, for example, Hans Kröner, 'Zur Frage der Einführung einer Zwangshaftpflichtversicherung für Kraftfahrzeughalter', (1938) ZAkDR 165f. For a compilation of the vast amount of literature with respect to this problem, see Kleinewefers, 'Zwangshaftpflichtversicherung', pp. 7ff.

[111] 'Gesetz über die Einführung der Pflichtversicherung für Kraftfahrzeughalter' of 7 November 1939, Reichsgesetzblatt 1939 I, p. 2223.

of a motor vehicle had to take out motor-vehicle liability insurance (§ 1). Yet the legislator had not, at that time, provided for a direct claim of the victim against the insurance company. Such claims were introduced as late as 1965 (§ 3 Compulsory Insurance Act), when a new version of the Compulsory Insurance Act was adopted[112] in order to implement the obligations arising from the 'European Convention on Compulsory Insurance against Civil Liability in Respect of Motor Vehicles' of 20 April 1959. As the convention also called for the establishment of a guarantee fund in order to compensate injured parties for damage where the obligation to be insured had not been complied with, such fund was provided for by § 12 Compulsory Insurance Act 1965.

Although it is quite clear from the development of motor vehicle insurance that, right from the beginning, it was designed to protect victims of road traffic accidents rather than to limit the financial risks of the custodian, the system established in 1939 was and still is based on the liability of the custodian and the driver, rather than being a no-fault accident insurance system provided for by a social security agency. As far as personal injuries are concerned, the victim at the outset has claims on the tortfeasor's motor-vehicle liability insurer as well as on the social security agencies that normally cover costs arising from personal injuries. However, as the benefits provided for by the social security agencies, being financed by the general public, are designed neither to double the claims of the victim nor to unburden the tortfeasor, the social security agencies have a vital interest in having recourse against the tortfeasor. § 116 Social Security Code X (*Sozialgesetzbuch X*)[113] in this respect provides for a subrogation of any claim the victim may have against the tortfeasor to the social security agency by means of a *cessio legis,* if and in so far as the social security agency provides for, or is obliged to provide for, the coverage of costs arising from the accident.[114] Bearing in mind § 3 Compulsory Insurance Act, this, in effect, means that the social security agency has a direct claim against the motor-vehicle insurance company. In order to

[112] 'Gesetz über die Pflichtversicherung für Kraftfahrzeughalter' of 5 April 1965, Bundesgesetzblatt 1965 I, p. 213.

[113] For damages arising from any accident before 1 July 1983, § 1542 Reichsversicherungsordnung (RVO) was applicable, which, however, in essence provided for the same legal consequence.

[114] Likewise, the tortfeasor does not have to pay lower damages because of any insurance the injured party has taken up privately. In cases of private insurance contracts, § 86 Insurance Contract Law (*Versicherungsvertragsgesetz*) thus provides for a similar subrogation of claims.

reduce costs and workload both for the social security agencies as well as for the liability insurance companies, they have entered into agreements according to which the liability insurer promises to pay for a certain quota of the expenses incurred by the social security agencies due to a road traffic accident, regardless of whether and to what extent the liability insurer would have actually been liable, provided only that certain maximum sums are not exceeded.[115] Such agreements of loss allocation had begun to emerge in the 1930s and had at first been held to be illegal, because it was thought that a social security agency would not be allowed to generally waive future claims.[116] Since the end of the Second World War however, such agreements have no longer been objected to and have regularly been entered into by all parties concerned.[117] The quota shares that the liability insurers have agreed to pay depend on whether the liability arising from the specific case is ordinary liability for fault, as set out in §§ 823ff. BGB, or strict liability, as provided for by the Road Traffic Act. In the case of ordinary fault-based liability, insurers typically agree to pay for a quota share of 50%; otherwise, a quota share of 60% corresponds to common practice.[118] This is different only as far as health insurance is concerned, where, commonly, quota shares of 45% and 55% have been agreed.[119]

Similarly, as far as the relation between different liability insurers is concerned, they have, by entering into so-called 'knock-for-knock agreements', waived their liability claims against each other. The intention is the same as in the case of the agreements between themselves and the social security agencies. The allocation of losses by means of quota shares is (according to the law of large numbers) in effect, thought to lead to the same balance between both parties as would be achieved if every single

[115] For details, see Werner Wussow, *Teilungsabkommen zwischen Sozialversicherern und Haftpflichtversicherern* (4th edn, Frankfurt: Robbers, 1975) and, more recently, Günther Schneider, 'Teilungsabkommen', in Werner Wussow (ed.), *Unfallhaftpflichtrecht* (15th edn, Cologne: Heymann, 2002), Ch. 76, pp. 1484ff.; Hermann Plagemann, 'Regress der Sozialleistungsträger', in Geigel, *Haftpflichtprozess*, Ch. 30 nos. 95ff., pp. 1441ff.

[116] See the Official Notification of the Imperial Insurance Office (Reichsversicherungsamt) of 6 January 1936 (1936) *Die Ortskrankenkasse* 295.

[117] See, for instance, BGH (1951) *Versicherungsrecht* 65 and Oskar Haidinger, 'Schadenteilungsabkommen mit Haftpflichtversicherern' (1951) *Versicherungsrecht* 57. By 1985, roughly 1,800 such agreements were in operation between the different social security agencies and liability insurers, by means of which claims amounting to DM 700 million (€350 million) were dealt with; see Alois Deichl, 'Die Schadenregulierung der KFZ-Haftpflichtversicherer' (1985) *Versicherungsrecht* 408 at 409.

[118] See Schneider, 'Teilungsabkommen', Ch. 76 no. 26, p. 1494.

[119] Plagemann, 'Regress der Sozialleistungsträger', Ch. 30 no. 95, p. 1441; see also Deichl, 'Die Schadenregulierung', 410.

case was settled appropriate to its specific circumstances. According to the relevant framework agreement of the association of liability insurers,[120] if two or more vehicles are involved in any incident, each of the insurers concerned has to adjust its quota share of the claim according to the number of motor vehicles involved.

The fact that, according to the aforesaid agreements, substantial amounts of damages were no longer dealt with by means of the law of tort, but rather by a simple allocation of losses between different insurers, played an important role in the calls for a reform of the system of liability as well as liability insurance in road traffic accidents, which began to emerge in Germany in the 1960s. If, due to the introduction of compulsory liability insurance, liability had shifted from the custodian and the driver to the insurer, and if, furthermore, as a consequence of the insurers' agreements with security agencies as well as with other insurers, loss distribution through tort law had been widely replaced by loss distribution based on economic considerations, it was argued that the 'merry-go-round of money' between insurers and social security agencies could be replaced by a loss insurance scheme covering all losses arising from road traffic accidents.[121] In Germany, the idea had first emerged as early as 1935, when Trendel had suggested the introduction of a system of loss insurance modelled on the system of workmen's compensation for occupational injury introduced at the end of the nineteenth century; according to this suggestion, any victim of a road traffic accident should have been able to recover full damages from the insurer, with the insurance contribution to be paid by all road users.[122] Similar proposals had been made in the so-called Columbia Plan in the United States even earlier (in 1932),[123] and it was due to the ongoing discussion, especially in the United States[124] as well as

[120] KH/KH-Rahmen-Teilungsabkommen, for which see Karl Heinz Hellwig, *Der Schaden*, (8th edn, Regensburg: Walhalla, 1993), part 22. The agreement in 1996 was applicable to 65% of all insurers, having a market share of 90%, see Lutz Heitmann, *Reform des Schadensrechts für Verkehrsunfälle* (Baden-Baden: Nomos, 1996), p. 40.

[121] For this line of argumentation, see Albert Ehrenzweig, *Full Aid Insurance for the Traffic Victim* (Berkeley and Los Angeles, CA: University of California Press, 1954), p. 25; Eike von Hippel, *Schadensausgleich bei Verkehrsunfällen* (Berlin and Tübingen: Mohr, 1968), p. 91.

[122] See Trendel, 'Gefährdungshaftung', cols. 135f.

[123] Columbia University Council for Research in the Social Sciences, Report by the Committee to Study Compensation for Automobile Accidents (1932).

[124] See, for example, Ehrenzweig, *Full Aid Insurance*. For further details, see Wolfgang Friedmann, *Law in a Changing Society* (London: Stevens, 1959), pp. 129ff.; von Hippel, *Schadensausgleich*, p. 54.

in France,[125] that the issue came back onto the agenda in Germany in the 1960s.[126] The proposal to abandon the principle of individual tort responsibility in road traffic accidents[127] in favour of the introduction of a social, no-fault accident insurance scheme did not, however, fall on fertile ground. The major concern right from the beginning, and still today, is that such a system would destroy any incentives to the careful handling of motor vehicles, as well as open up manifold opportunities for abuse.[128]

It is clear, in theory, that liability insurance does not modify the principles of liability; the insurer simply replaces the insured party in any tort claims that may arise. However, the fact that motor-vehicle liability insurance right from the very beginning has been thought of as a means of protection for victims of road traffic accidents, rather than as being designed to provide protection for the custodian, ties in with the fact that the awareness of the existence of such insurance has influenced liability in road traffic accidents. Yet, effects on the notion of fault itself have not been expressly made clear by the courts and, although, in principle, the introduction of a compulsory insurance system by the legislator may be taken as a reason for a restrictive interpretation of excuses for liability,[129] such reasoning has not taken place to any great extent as far as road traffic is concerned. This becomes fairly clear if one bears in mind that the courts' restrictive interpretation of the notion of inevitable incidents dates back to times not only when there was no compulsory insurance system, but when it was difficult, in many cases, to obtain damages at all, because such insurance contracts had not even been entered into voluntarily. However, as far as calls for a reform of motor vehicle liability are concerned, the

[125] André Tunc, *La sécurité routière. Esquisse d'une loi sur les accidents de la circulation* (Paris: Dalloz, 1966).

[126] With von Hippel (*Schadensausgleich*) being the most emphatic supporter of a reform; see also von Hippel, 'Schadensausgleich bei Verkehrsunfällen' (1967) NJW 1729; ibid., 'Allgemeiner Schutz vor Haftungsrisiken?' (1972) *Juristenzeitung* (JZ) 735 and Dirk Güllemann, *Ausgleich von Verkehrsunfallschäden im Lichte internationaler Reformprojekte* (Berlin: Duncker and Humblot, 1969). For a recent summary account, see Heitmann, *Reform*, pp. 144ff.

[127] The principle should, however, according to von Hippel's proposal, remain applicable with respect to the question of whether the insurer can have recourse against the tortfeasor, as well as with respect to the tortfeasor's insurance premiums and his possible no-claims bonus: see von Hippel, 'Schadensausgleich' (1967) NJW 1731.

[128] See Brigitte Borgmann, 'Soll unser System der Zuteilung von Unfallschäden reformiert werden?' (1973) *Zeitschrift für Rechtspolitik* 53; Heitmann, *Reform*, p. 155 and most recently Hein Kötz and Gerhard Wagner, *Deliktsrecht* (10th edn, Munich: Beck, 2006), pp. 219f.

[129] See Nils Jansen, *Die Struktur des Haftungsrechts* (Tübingen: Mohr Siebeck, 2003), pp. 116ff.

compulsory insurance system has had effects on the notion of fault. The existence of the insurance system has stimulated the readiness to call for possible excuses to be limited to *vis maior* instead of the inevitable incidents.[130] Apart from that, motor-vehicle liability insurance in general, and compulsory insurance in particular, have had an impact on the question of the extent of liability rather than on its requirements. Two issues in this respect deserve closer attention.

The most important influence of the compulsory insurance scheme on the practical application of road-traffic accident law can probably be found in the area of claims for compensation for pain and suffering. Originally, it had been common opinion that any insurance taken up by the tortfeasor was irrelevant in such claims. In assessing the tortfeasor's financial circumstances (which inter alia had to be taken into account in the assessment of such claims), according to this opinion, the fact that insurance had been taken up had to be disregarded.[131] Opinion gradually changed with the introduction of the compulsory insurance scheme. Supporters of the emerging new opinion pointed to the fact that the introduction of this scheme was based on the idea to provide for compensation, irrespective of whether or not the tortfeasor himself would have been able to pay damages; accordingly, the tortfeasor should no longer be allowed to defend himself with his lack of funds with respect to claims for compensation for pain and suffering.[132] This approach was subsequently adopted by the courts and is now common opinion, even in cases where insurance has been taken out voluntarily.[133]

The second and well-known practical influence of the compulsory insurance scheme arose in cases of damage to the occupants of a car. Before 2002, the fault principle of § 823 BGB was applicable in such cases; the Motor Vehicle Act as well as the Road Traffic Act did not provide for protection of the occupants.[134] In order to relieve the strains on the driver,

[130] This is abundantly clear, for example, from the statements of Münzel, 'Reform', 1581.

[131] RGZ 36, p. 104; Reichsgericht (1925) *Juristische Wochenschrift* (JW) 2599; (1933) JW 799; Paul Oertmann, *Das Recht der Schuldverhältnisse* (5th edn, Berlin: Heymann, 1929), p. 1493. For criticism, see, for example, Siegfried Schrammen, 'Ist wirklich bei der Bemessung des Schmerzensgeldes der dem Schuldner zustehende Schutz aus einer Haftpflichtversicherung auszuschalten?' (1935) DAR cols. 69ff.

[132] See Karl Sieg, 'Ist eine Haftpflichtversicherung bei Bemessung des Schmerzensgeldes zu berücksichtigen?' (1941) ZAkDR, 209f.

[133] BGHZ 18, p. 149 at 164; Hermann Lange and Gottfried Schiemann, *Schadensersatz* (3rd edn, Tübingen: Mohr Siebeck, 2003), § 7 (V) (3), p. 444.

[134] This was different, however, in the field of the transportation of passengers; see § 8 Motor Vehicle Act as amended in 1939 (Reichsgesetzblatt I, p. 2223); § 8a Road Traffic Act as amended by the statute of 16 July 1957 (Bundesgesetzblatt 1957 I, p. 710).

the courts took into consideration whether an implied exclusion of liability between the driver and the occupants could be assumed. The courts, however, were not prepared to make such an assumption where the damage incurred by the occupants was covered by the motor-vehicle liability insurance.

4 Conclusions

At the outset, railway as well as road-traffic accident liability was based on the fault principle. This situation, however, very quickly changed when the needs created by technical change became apparent. Notwithstanding the German doctrinal writers' inclination to the fault principle, the German legislator almost instantaneously provided for systems of liability that were thought to effectively protect victims of railway and road traffic accidents.

However, the development of both railway and road-traffic accident law in Germany also shows that the legislator has always confined itself to satisfying the most urgent needs rather than to providing for a coherent system of liability throughout the different areas of application. Accordingly, in reacting to calls for a reform, be it the issue of damage to property in railway accidents or the question of possible excuses for liability in road traffic accidents, the legislator has not been nearly as quick as it was in adopting rules at the outset. This is mainly due to the fact that the courts – with some exceptions at a very early stage – have tended to interpret the relevant provisions so as to provide for the most effective protection of victims. When the automobile associations, by means of their lobbying at the beginning of the twentieth century, prevented the Imperial Law on Liability's provisions from being adopted in the area of road traffic accidents (with the result of inevitable incidents rather than *vis maior* being accepted as a possible excuse for liability in road traffic accidents) they were thus only at first sight successful in promoting their interests. The restrictive approach taken by the courts in interpreting this excuse right from the beginning shows that the achievements of this lobbying were, in practice, rather insignificant. It is for this very reason that the dogmatic differences between the systems of liability in railway and road-traffic accident law, with the former system providing for true strict liability and the latter system being modelled on strict liability, yet incorporating – however strict the notion of inevitable incidents was interpreted – elements of fault, were able to persist for a whole century and were only abolished as late as 2002.

Calls for reform have proved to be successful only where the courts did not or could not provide for effective protection. This is true for the lack of effectiveness of the Prussian Railway Act, which led to the adoption of the Imperial Law on Liability in 1871, as well as for the introduction of the compulsory insurance scheme in 1939 and the latest reform of the Road Traffic Act in 2002. The courts had neither been able to deal with the unsatisfying situation arising from the fragmentation of legal systems throughout Germany in the nineteenth century, nor even been willing to widely interpret the Prussian Railway Act; they had not been able to deal with problems arising from insufficient funds being available to custodians of a motor vehicle in the 1930s and they had not, although such protection had long been called for, provided for the effective protection of children under the Road Traffic Act. All this shows that legislation dealing with the specific problems of a particular time has always been thought to be the proper means of responding to the needs of the Industrial Revolution. It is therefore not surprising that the legal situation in Germany, even nowadays, is rather complicated, and that road-traffic and railway accident liability are dealt with by similar yet, when it comes to details, all but identical rules.

5

The development of traffic liability in the Netherlands

CEES VAN DAM AND GERRIT VAN MAANEN*

This chapter analyses the development of liability for road traffic accidents and for railway accidents in the Netherlands over the past 150 years. It aims to set out, on the basis of legislation and case law, whether the basis for liability has changed from fault to risk and, if so, how. Subsequently, we will identify a number of 'external' factors that have probably or possibly influenced these developments (be it changes in the law or the lack of change), such as international developments and the role of key officials and key authors.

1 Railway accidents

1.a Statutory provisions on liability for railway accidents

Dutch law on liability for damage incurred by train passengers is currently governed by several provisions in Book 8 Dutch Civil Code (Burgerlijk Wetboek – BW), holding a rather strict liability rule for the railway company in respect of damage incurred by its passengers. Damage suffered by non-passengers is governed by article 6:162 BW, holding the general rule for fault liability, which applies to the liability of the railway company for damage caused to pedestrians, cyclists, motorised vehicles and their passengers.

This section of the chapter focuses on the liability of railway companies vis-à-vis their passengers. Liability vis-à-vis non-passengers will not be dealt with in this chapter.

Book 8 BW is part of the Dutch Civil Code that entered into force in 1992, introducing the new patrimonial law in Books 3, 5 and 6. Book 8 entered

* Section 1 (liability for railway accidents) has been written by Gerrit van Maanen; Section 2 (liability for road traffic accidents) has been written by Cees van Dam.

into force on 1 April 1991. The section on carriage by railway had (partly) already been brought into force in 1988.[1] The Dutch Civil Code is characterised by a layered structure: Book 3 contains the general part of patrimonial law; Book 6 contains general provisions on contract, tort and damages; and rules regarding specific contracts are laid down in Books 7 and 8.

This layered structure implies that the provisions of Book 7 have to be understood and interpreted in the context of the more general rules of Books 3, 5 and 6. Book 8, however, is more 'independent' of the other books of the BW. That is because a large part of Book 8 is, in fact, an incorporation of (international) transportation treaties to which the Netherlands is a party. In order to avoid, as far as was possible, a statutory interpretation that deviates from the original text, the Dutch legislator opted for a literal translation of the (English and French) text of the treaties.[2] The full text of the provisions is set out in the Appendix to this book (see p. 233).

1.a.i Liability of the railway company: strict liability?

Tort or contract? Fault or strict liability? The main provision in respect of the liability of the railway company for injuries suffered by its passengers is article 8:105 BW, which states that 'the carrier is liable for damage caused by the death of, or bodily injury to, the traveller as a consequence of an accident which has occurred in connection with and during the carriage'.[3] This liability can be rebutted by the defence that the accident has been caused 'by a fact which a prudent carrier has not been able to avoid'. Physical or mental disabilities of the driver, as well as technical defects, are the risk of the railway company.

Although this liability is attached to the contractual relationship that (normally) exists between the passenger and the railway carrier, it is not a standard contractual liability, nor a standard form of extra-contractual liability. Why is this so? The following considerations may clarify this:

- The liability provisions are mandatory law.
- Contractual stipulations concerning the limitation of liability are null and void (article 8:111).

[1] K. F. Haak, *De exceptie van de redelijkheid en billijkheid in het personenvervoer* (Deventer: Kluwer Law International, 2005), p. 7.

[2] N. M. van der Horst, 'Introduction', in P. P. C. Haanappel and E. Mackaay, *New Netherlands Civil Code. Book 8 Means of Traffic and Transport* (The Hague and London: Kluwer Law International, 1995), p. XVIII.

[3] This section will be restricted to death or personal injury claims and will therefore not cover related subjects such as damages for the loss of goods.

- Where the person or thing was on board otherwise than pursuant to a contract, a contract of carriage is deemed to be a contract referred to in article 8:364, section 1 (article 8:364, section 4).
- One of the main differences with the situation before 1988 – under the regime of the Railway Act 1875 – is that, in article 8:105 BW, the shift in the burden of proof not only covers those who are injured during the journey, but reference is now also made to the death of a traveller. So the carrier is (directly) liable vis-à-vis the secondary victims (wife, husband, children). There is no need to rely on specific provisions like article 1406 (old) BW or article 6:108 (new) BW.[4] These provisions – comparable to the English Fatal Accidents Act 1976 – provide for a claim in cases where someone is liable, vis-à-vis the deceased, for a specific next of kin group.[5]
- When extra-contractual actions against a servant of the party to a contract of operation are taken, the servant can invoke the defences of the contractual party, as if he were a party to the contract himself (article 8:365).
- The maximum amount of compensation in case of death or personal injury is €173,000.

Extra-contractual and strict liability Considering the above, we have a specific, rather strict liability, which also arises in situations where there is no contract at all, under terms that are not negotiable and with a substantial statutory limitation. The only contractual aspect is that this liability is attached – in normal situations – to the contract of carriage of the railway passenger, and that extra-contractual actions are limited in the same way as when they were contractual actions.

How strict is this specific form of liability? Taking into account that article 8:105 BW implies that the carrier is liable for damage caused by the death of, or bodily injury to, the traveller as a consequence of an accident, it looks like a form of strict liability. However, this liability can be rebutted. The available defence is that the accident has been caused 'by a fact which a prudent carrier has not been able to avoid'. So it is up to the carrier to show that he behaved like a prudent carrier; his wrongful behaviour is presumed. But his possibilities of rebutting his liability are limited by the

[4] It can be argued that the layered structure of the BW implies that article 6:108 BW applies. In practice, this means that only the specific class of persons mentioned in that article can claim damages, and then only for loss of maintenance.

[5] C. C. van Dam, *European Tort Law* (Oxford University Press, 2006), no. 1209.

fact that physical or mental disabilities of the driver, as well as technical defects, are no valid defences.

The carrier can invoke the defence of contributory negligence when the behaviour of the passenger was (in part) the cause of the damage (article 8:109 BW). This specific provision on contributory negligence deviates in some important aspects from the more general provision on that issue in Book 6 (article 6:101), which reads:

> When the damage is partly caused by an occurrence that can be imputed to the injured party, the obligation to pay compensation is reduced by apportioning the damage between the injured party and the liable party in proportion to the degree in which the occurrences that can be imputed to the parties have contributed to the damage, provided that account is taken of the disparity in the seriousness of the respective faults, or other circumstances of the case, to decide whether fairness demands that an alternative apportionment or full recovery takes place or that the obligation to pay lapses.

Article 6:101 BW holds a two-stage test: firstly, it has to be established what claimant and defendant each contributed to the damage. This includes all circumstances, not only the 'neutral' conduct and the degree of negligence, but also, for example in the case of road traffic accidents, the contribution to the damage of the so-called *betriebsgefahr.* This refers to the risk created by the weight and the speed of a motor vehicle, which can be a substantial causal factor as regards the damage. Secondly, fairness comes into play. The outcome of the first-stage test can be adapted if fairness so demands, because of the disparate seriousness of the mutual faults or other circumstances of the case. This can lead to a different apportionment of the damage: to a duty to compensate 100% or to the conclusion that the damage does not need to be compensated at all.

This last provision that equity or fairness can demand an alternative apportionment or full recovery is missing in article 8:109 BW. It is not clear whether this restriction can be invoked in case of railway accidents.

To summarise, we can fairly say that we are dealing here with a rather strict form of liability. In principle, the carrier bears the risk and his defences are limited.

1.b Legislative developments and case law in the nineteenth century

1.b.i 1859: statutory introduction of strict liability

In 1839, the first railway was opened between Amsterdam and Haarlem. This was not the start of a swift development; by 1859, only 337 km of (private) railway had been completed in the Netherlands, while in Belgium in the same year 1,713 km had been completed. From 1859 on, the state took responsibility for new railways. However, the exploitation was mostly a private initiative, although in 1860 a state-owned corporation was established for the exploitation of state-owned railways. There was heavy competition between more than ten railway companies. After 1938, the exploitation was centralised in one state-owned company: the Nederlandse Spoorwegen (NS).[6]

Meanwhile, the Railway Act of 1859 was enacted, creating in its very first provision a strict liability of the railway company: 'The undertakers of a railway service are liable for the damage inflicted on persons or goods in the exercise of the service, provided that this damage is not caused by their fault or the fault of their employees.' This provision was repeated in the Railway Act of 1875. An extra provision was added, however, stating that the entrepreneur of the railway was not allowed to limit his liability by contract, except where limitations were regulated in specific bylaws.[7]

Before the introduction of this strict liability rule in 1859, injured passengers had to prove negligence on the part of the railway company. Case law sometimes provided some help by accepting, in some situations, a shift in the burden of proof on the basis of *res ipsa loquitur*. This was, for example, allowed in a situation where a loose train wagon on a track caused an accident.[8] It is worth noting that the claims were made extra-contractually on the basis of the general liability provision of article 1401 (old) BW, a provision succeeded by article 6:162 (new) BW. Claims were never based on contract. Contract was seen as an obligation of transportation, but not as including 'safe' transport.[9] The discussion about the contractual or extra-contractual nature of this provision continued even after the Railway Act of 1875. One of the reasons for this was that this liability regime was considered to be of exceptional character.[10]

In spite of objections on the part of railway companies, Parliament agreed, in 1859, by a large majority (44 to 14) with the new statutory

[6] See, for an overview of the history of Dutch railways, A. J. Veenendaal, *De ijzeren weg in een land vol water. Beknopte geschiedenis van de spoorwegen in Nederland 1834–1958* (Amsterdam: De Bataafsche Leeuw, 1998).

[7] These restrictions mainly concern limitations to property damage, not death or personal injury.

[8] HR 11 June 1858, Nederlandse Regtspraak, deel 59, pp. 233–52.

[9] However odd this may seem to our modern eyes, contract was normally viewed in this way.

[10] J. Valkhoff, 'De invloed van de Spoorwegen op enkele gebieden van het Nederlands privaatrecht', *Rechtsgeleerd Magazijn Themis* (1939), 399–443.

regime of strict liability. It is interesting to see that the first drafts of this Railway Act did not provide for a strict liability regime (although, for property damage, this had already been the case for a long time, according to article 91 Commercial Code). Thanks to an amendment by MP Thorbecke (a former PM), the burden of proof for personal injury was shifted in article 1 Railway Act of 1859. The Minister (Boot) held the opinion that this amendment was contrary to established principles of good law. This reflected a long-standing debate about the aforementioned article 91 Commercial Code, which as early as 1838 had introduced a reversal of the burden of proof for the carrier of goods. Thorbecke's argumentation was that his amendment was in concordance with that provision of the Commercial Code.

The idea, however, of being responsible not only for one's own behaviour but also for that of one's employees, with the only exception being *overmacht* (an act of God or *force majeure*) was considered by many legal scholars in those days to be contrary to elementary notions of justice.[11] There were also more pragmatic objections to this strict liability, especially on the part of railway companies who were afraid of the economic consequences of this liability – consequences that might hamper the prosperous exploitation of their railways. This position was also advocated by some scholars.[12] Statistics show that there were about ten accidents per year involving personal injury, and a total of eight fatal accidents.[13]

1.b.ii The debate on liability in the nineteenth century

The discussion about (strict) liability for railway accidents formed part of a broader discourse on the nature and scope of extra-contractual liability in general. The BW of 1838 had introduced a rather general liability clause, with a wide scope of protection in articles 1401 and 1402, but had at the end of the nineteenth century moved towards a more restricted liability. Articles 1401 and 1402 were a translation of articles 1382 and 1383 of the French Civil Code, the first provision aiming at deliberate acts while the latter concerned negligent acts and omissions. This liability for negligence was questioned at the end of the nineteenth century, especially in cases of liability for unfair competition. The idea was that liability for unfair

[11] J. W. Karsten, 'De aansprakelijkheid van den voerman, krachtens art. 91 W. v. K.', *Rechtsgeleerd Magazijn Themis* (1873), 386–436.

[12] For example, R. van Rees, *Het spoorwegvervoer op de spoorwegen in verband met de wet van 9 april 1875* (Utrecht: van Hoften, 1875), p. 67.

[13] G. E. van Maanen, 'Stoomtreinen en aansprakelijkheid', Weekblad voor Prinaatrecht, Notariaat en Registratie (WPNR) 5742 (1985) 393.

competition would hamper the economy. Competition was good in itself, and judges should keep out of that playground. At the end of the day, this led to a more restrictive liability, in which article 1402 no longer played a substantive role.[14] It was not until 1919 that the Dutch Supreme Court, in the famous *Lindenbaum-Cohen* case, gave a new interpretation to article 1401 and, in doing so, broadened the scope of that provision to all kinds of wrongful behaviour, including unfair competition.[15] It is against this background that we have to consider the debate about the rule of strict liability in article 1 Railway Act of 1859, repeated in the Act of 1875.

In one of the first commentaries, this liability was seen as being based on a presumption of fault with a reversal of the burden of proof. The author, Dutry van Haeften, was in favour of a more generous interpretation of article 1 Railway Act 1859 in order to do justice to the fact that, in railway accident cases, it is hard for the victim to disclose what the actual cause of the accident was, due to the technical complexity.[16]

In 1874, the Dutch Association of Lawyers (NJV) put this issue of liability for railway accidents on the agenda of its annual meeting. The overall opinion was that the basis for this liability should be found in the contract of carriage. This contract, however, only entitled the passenger to a seat on the train, not 'to arrive at the place of destination unharmed'. The majority of the meeting was not in favour of a special liability for railway accidents in derogation from the general principles of tort law, as laid down in articles 1401 and 1402 BW of 1838.[17] This position was supported by Van Rees in his thesis published in 1875. He argued that the legal position for the railway company is an impossible one: 'their complaints that in most cases they are left to the mercy of their opponents are justified'.[18] Van Rees proposed to withdraw the strict liability provision and to leave this liability to the normal negligence regime in order not to hamper the 'natural' growth of this new mode of transportation. In a thesis defended one year later, we find the same opinion.[19] In 1889, another academic chose this liability rule as the subject of his research. Van Doorn held a view that was more favourable to the victim. In his eyes, the liability of article 1

[14] G. E. van Maanen, *De Zutphense juffrouw en de ontrouwe bediende van Lindenbaum* (Nijmegen: Ars Aequi, 1999).

[15] HR 31 January 1919, *Nederlandse Jurisprudentie* (NJ) (1919), 161.

[16] J. Dutry van Haeften, *De Spoorwetgeving in Nederland*, (Leiden: Noothoven van Goor 1863), p. 114; Van Maanen, 'Stoomtreinen en aansprakelijkheid', 413.

[17] Van Maanen, 'Stoomtreinen en aansprakelijkheid' 413, note 23.

[18] Ibid., 414.

[19] H. Pouw, *Eenige aantekeningen op de art. 1–9 der wet van 9 april 1875* (Amsterdam: van der Post 1876).

was of an extra-contractual nature, and it was also applicable in situations where railway workers incurred damage while working on the track. He proposed that this liability only be strict with the defence of an act of God (*force majeure*) and that of contributory negligence.[20]

In conclusion, we can say that only a small majority of the legal scholars was in favour of a stricter liability regime. It was still a point of debate whether this liability was of a contractual or a tortious nature. Some of the opponents in favour of a stricter form of liability had a clear eye for the financial consequences that strict liability might have for the prosperous development of railways.

1.b.iii Case law in the nineteenth century

Case law after the introduction of the 1859 Act reflects the idea that the main reason for the strict liability in article 1 is to urge the railway companies to exercise utmost care in order to provide the necessary safety of their passengers. This is why, in derogation from the ordinary negligence rules, the burden of proof is shifted from the victim to the tortfeasor.[21]

One of the main questions was which class of persons could benefit from this strict liability rule: only passengers, or every person who suffers damage from railway exploitation? Case law was unequivocally in favour of the restrictive interpretation: only passengers.[22] This was so despite contrary remarks by the Minister in Parliament. The reasoning for this restrictive interpretation is to be found in a judgment by the Dutch Supreme Court, stating that article 1 Railway Act of 1859 is a derogation from the normal rules regarding the burden of proof, and that this exception should therefore be interpreted in a restricted way. Only when it was crystal clear that the legislator intended an extension of liability was a broader scope of liability acceptable.[23]

The result of all this was that every passenger on a train could rely on this provision, whether he had a ticket or not, but that those outside the train could not. An unintended consequence of all this was that, in the case of death of a passenger, the descendants could not benefit from the reversal of the burden of proof provided by article 1 Railway Act of 1859. Case law at the beginning of the twentieth century shows that actions by the descendants were based on the general provisions of liability (articles 1401 and 1402 in conjunction with article 1407 (old) BW).

[20] W. Th. C. Van Doorn, *De Nederlandsche Spoorwegwet* (Arnhem: Cohen, 1889), p. 10.
[21] HR 28 March 1873, W. 3577; van Maanen, 'Stoomtreinen en aansprakelijkheid', 416.
[22] Van Maanen, 'Stoomtreinen en aansprakelijkheid', 416.
[23] HR 3 April 1890, W. 5856.

The available defence provided for in article 1 Railway Act of 1859 is that the damage is not caused by the fault of the railway company or by the fault of its employees. The fact that one of the iron rails of a railway track is broken is not considered to be a valid excuse that constitutes an absence of fault.[24] However, if a passenger sticks his head outside the window and injures himself, this will result in a valid defence.[25] The same holds true when a passenger puts his fingers between the closing doors when the train is about to leave.[26] When a passenger is hit by a ladder left unattended on the platform, the railway company is liable, even when it is unclear whether the ladder was left there by an employee.[27]

1.b.iv Conclusions regarding the strict liability regime in the nineteenth century

The strict liability regime introduced in the Railway Act of 1859 came into force due to the amendment of MP Thorbecke. This initiative was most likely stimulated by foreign legislation, which also protected the position of passengers in case of accidents. Thorbecke's explicit argumentation was that his amendment was in concordance with the principle of the reversal of the burden of proof for the carriage of goods in the Code of Commerce. We might assume that the (then recent) decision of the Hoge Raad of 11 June 1858 supported the idea that a stronger protection of the legal position of railway accident victims (passengers) was necessary.[28] The importance of this derogation from general tort law (articles 1401 and 1402 (old) BW) was seen as most remarkable, as is demonstrated by the large number of academic commentaries. We have seen, however, that the Hoge Raad took a restrictive position as regards to whom this protection applied: only the passengers and other persons on board.

1.b.v The strict liability regime in the twentieth century

International context of the strict liability regime in the twentieth century The regime governing railway accidents during most of the twentieth century is basically still that of the Railway Act of 1859, which contained the very first provision of the strict liability of railway companies: the operators of a railway service are liable for the damage inflicted on persons or goods in the exercise of their services, provided that this

[24] Hof Amsterdam 12 October 1883, W. 4992.
[25] Hof Amsterdam 23 February 1893, W. 6387.
[26] Kantongerecht Amsterdam 30 January 1906, MvH VIII, p. 31.
[27] Rechtbank, Amsterdam 25 May 1904, W. 8213.
[28] Van Maanen, 'Stoomtreinen en aansprakelijkheid', 417.

damage is not caused by their fault or the fault of their employees. This provision was repeated in the Railway Act of 1875. In this new act, a provision was added, stating that the railway operator was not allowed to limit its liability by contract, the exception being where limitations were regulated in specific by-laws.[29] This regime remained more or less the same in Book 8 BW, which is part of the Dutch Civil Code that entered into force in 1992, introducing the new patrimonial law in Books 3, 5 and 6. Book 8 entered into force on 1 April 1991. The section on carriage by railway had already been brought into force, in part, in 1988.[30]

This new regime, although in essence comparable to the old regime of the Railway Act,[31] is derived from several treaties on international railway transportation.[32] The International Convention on Transport by Rail (COTIF) came into force on 9 May 1980.[33] An annex to this treaty – the Additional Convention to the International Convention on the Carriage of Passengers and Luggage by Rail (1973) (CIV) – contains rules on liability in case of personal injury or death and loss of luggage. In article 26, section 1, the carrier is held liable for any damage suffered by the passenger during transportation. The defence in section 2 is that the accident has been caused by a fact that a prudent carrier has not been able to avoid, and to the extent that such carrier has not been able to prevent the consequences thereof, or contributory negligence on the part of the passenger. This is exactly what we find in article 8:105 BW.

In Dutch law, article 26, paragraph 2, sub-paragraph c, CIV holds that the carrier cannot raise the defence that, in case of a collision between two trains, the other train carrier is liable.[34] In the CIV, we also find a limitation of €70,000. In Dutch law, this has been raised to €173,000.

1.b.vi Various examples of case law in the twentieth century

One of the main questions in the nineteenth century case law on article 1 Railway Act 1875 was which class of persons can benefit from this strict liability: only passengers or each person who suffers damage from railway

[29] These restrictions concern mainly limitations to property damage, not death or personal injury.

[30] Haak, *De exceptie van de redelijkheid en billijkheid in het personenvervoer*, p. 7.

[31] Strangely enough, article 1 Railway Act 1875 was not repealed until 1 January 2005. Until then, article 1 was still in force under the condition that the regulation in Book 8 BW prevailed.

[32] A. W. Hagdorn, 'Aansprakelijkheden op het spoor', *Tijdschrift Vervoer & Recht* (2003), 151–57.

[33] Trb. 1980, p. 160; Dutch translation in Trb. 1981, p. 211.

[34] Hagdorn, 'Aansprakelijkheden op het spoor', 153.

exploitation? Legal scholars were in favour of the latter – broader – interpretation.[35] Case law, however, was unequivocally in favour of the restrictive interpretation: only passengers.[36] These precedents are still considered as being good law in twentieth-century case law. In a case decided by the Hoge Raad in 1903, it confirmed the ruling of the Court of Appeal, which denied the claim of a railway worker who had lost both legs whilst working on the track. As a result of the accident, the poor man was sacked. Article 1 Railway Act 1875 protects only those who are on the train and not those outside the train. This restrictive interpretation is in accordance with the exceptional character of the shift in the burden of proof set out in article 1. Another reason for denying the claim was that the accident was solely due to the negligence of the worker himself, and this excluded any fault on the part of the railway company.[37]

Closely connected to this question is the question of whether, in the case of the death of a passenger, the next of kin (husband, children) who suffer damage through loss of maintenance can base their claim on article 1 or whether they should be treated in the same way as victims outside the train. The latter seems to be the case.[38] A woman was fatally injured whilst trying to board a departing train. The husband claimed damages because he had to hire a maid to take care of their five children. The claim was denied, not only because article 1 was considered not applicable but also because of the specific provision in the case of death (article 1406 (old) BW) which held that the only damages available in case of wrongful death is the claim for loss of maintenance in favour of the married partner, the children or parents. In this case, the unfortunate wife was providing maintenance for neither the husband nor the children. Hence, the claim was denied.

Examples of first-instance court decisions show that the courts were not lenient towards victims who found themselves injured. A miller who broke his leg and lost his job because his horse was scared by the whistle of a train was not compensated because blowing the whistle was not forbidden.[39] The derailment of a tram was not seen as negligent vis-à-vis the victim because it was not proved that the tram was travelling above the speed limit.[40] More generous was the Court of Appeal for a two-year-old

[35] L. G. N. Bouricius, *De burgerlijk-rechtelijke gevolgen van de wet van 9 juli 1900* (Leiden: Van Doesburgh, 1902), p. 68.

[36] Van Maanen, 'Stoomtreinen en aansprakelijkheid', 416.

[37] HR 30 January 1903, Nederlandse Rechtspraak, deel 193, paragraph 20, pp. 180–85.

[38] HR 7 February 1906, W. 8324, p. 1.

[39] Rechtbank, Middelburg 10 June 1903, W. 7981, p. 2.

[40] Rechtbank, Haarlem 20 October 1903, W. 7983, p. 2.

child who lost his foot. The tram company was obliged to a lifelong payment of compensation for the disability in spite of its defence that even a child without a foot could find various jobs. The court stated that it was obvious that such a handicap would lead to serious damage.[41] When the damage was also due to the contributory negligence of someone crossing the railway track, the damage could be divided between the tortfeasor and the victim.[42]

Another tram accident led to an interesting Hoge Raad decision in 1914.[43] A passenger named Schoch was seated on the balcony of an Amsterdam tram. Due to sudden braking, he was thrown off the tram and lost his arm. The Court of Appeal allowed damages, a decision upheld by the Hoge Raad. Although a reference was made to article 1 Railway Act 1875, the claim seemed to be awarded on the basis of the general provisions of articles 1401 and 1407 (old) BW. The latter was the special provision for personal injury. The defence of the tram company was that nobody was obliged to take a seat on the balcony, which is less safe than seats inside. The Advocate General supported this idea by comparing this claim with the (ludicrous) claim of someone catching a cold whilst sitting on the balcony. The Hoge Raad was not convinced that the damage was only caused by Schoch's fault; on the contrary, it was the tram company's negligence that caused the damage.

In line with established case law was the Hoge Raad's decision in 1925 concerning a major accident near the city of Weesp.[44] The children of the parents who both died in the accident claimed damages on the basis of article 1406 (old) BW. This restrictive provision allowed claims for the loss of maintenance for the children, provided that they were in need of that maintenance. In this case, they inherited a large sum of money, the interest from which covered their costs of maintenance. Hence their claim was denied, as was their claim for the funeral costs.

Shortly after World War II, a tragic accident happened, partly due to the poor condition of the train and partly because of a temporary bridge that was taken too fast. The train shook heavily and a five-year-old boy was thrown out of the train because a door opened suddenly. The Court of Appeal denied the claim because the contract of carriage contained a time-limit clause of three years. The Hoge Raad, however, was of the opinion that the railway company was – irrespective of the contract of carriage – also liable on the basis of article 1 Railway Act 1875. The Court

[41] Hof Arnhem 15 April 1908, W. 8811, p. 1.

[42] HR 4 February 1916, NJ (1916), 450–3.

[43] HR 16 January 1914, NJ (1914), 407–10.

[44] HR 27 February 1925, NJ (1925), 566–71.

of Appeal was therefore wrong not to inquire whether the claim could be based on that ground.[45]

In the second half of the twentieth century (1971), we find a Hoge Raad decision in which the restrictive interpretation of the ninetheenth century that the contract of carriage does not imply the obligation to a 'safe' arrival is, finally, clearly abandoned.[46] In this case, a widow by the name of Johanne Ivens was severely injured on a Rotterdam tram. While paying for her ticket, the tram suddenly departed and she fell down. She based her claim on the contract of carriage with the tram company (and not on article 1 Railway Act 1875, because this did not directly apply in the case of tram transportation). She claimed that the tram company was obliged to provide her with a safe carriage. The court of first instance denied that, but allowed her to prove a claim based on fault. In appeal, however, her claim was allowed by arguing, like Ivens had done, that the contract of carriage implied a duty of safe transportation. The Court of Appeal also gave weight to the fact that, in article 1 Railway Act 1875, the burden of proof is shifted to the carrier. The Hoge Raad dismissed the appeal.

The issues at stake in the case law are not so much questions about the interpretation of article 1 Railway Act 1875, but are rather questions about related aspects, such as the claims of the descendants, and thus about the scope of articles 1406 and 1407 (old) BW and the relation to the contract of carriage. It is remarkable that, finally, the view was accepted that the contract of carriage does imply the duty of safe carriage.

1.b.vii Limiting the total amount of damages

It follows from article 8:105 BW that the carrier is liable for the damage caused by the death of, or bodily injury to, the traveller as a consequence of an accident that has occurred in connection with and during the carriage. However, the liability of the carrier referred to in this provision is limited to an amount to be determined by or pursuant to regulation. Since 1988, the maximum amount in case of death or personal injury has been €173,000.[47] This limitation was put to the test in a legal dispute in which a nineteen-year-old woman claimed damages because she had lost both legs in a horrible accident. While a train was departing, she tried to board the train but got stuck between the closing doors. An accumulation of errors and misjudgements contributed to the tragic result: the mobile phone of the person responsible for departure was out of order, the driver

[45] HR 7 November 1958, NJ (1960), 177.

[46] HR 26 February (1971), NJ 1971, 270 (Ivens/Gemeente Rotterdam).

[47] KB 15 March 1991, Stb. 1991, p. 114; KB 14 September 2001, p. 415.

of the train departed even though one of the doors was not yet closed (because of a special key held by the person responsible for departure) in spite of the signal to this effect, and there was no safety mechanism in the doors for this kind of situation.

The railway company (NS Reizigers) acknowledged liability for the accident but invoked the limitation of article 8:110 BW, set by by-law at €173,000. The actual damage inflicted upon the young woman was much greater and she therefore argued that the limitation did not apply. Her first argument was that, in this specific case, the person responsible for the departure behaved recklessly, in which case the railway company could not invoke this limitation (article 8:111 BW).[48] The second argument was that invoking this limitation was contrary to the principle of equity (article 6:2, section 2 BW) and was therefore not allowed in this specific case. A third argument was that the limitation rule violated article 1, First Protocol of the European Convention on Human Rights, which protects property, including matrimonial rights, such as the right to full compensation.

The Court of Appeal[49] accepted her arguments, although it held that the European Convention on Human Rights[50] was not directly infringed; this played an indirect role in the equity argument. The result was that the limitation was set aside and the young woman obtained full compensation.

The outcome of this case fits into the more general tendency to abolish or to reduce the effect of this limitation of compensation. For airline passengers, the absolute limitation was abolished by the EC Directive of 1997 (2027/97). The Treaty of Montreal came into force in the European Community in 2004 and replaced the Warsaw Treaty. Here we find an absolute liability for personal injury and death up to €117,000; over and

[48] This restriction is derived from various treaties such as article 25 of the Warsaw Treaty: 'an act or omission of the carrier done with intent to cause damage, or recklessly and with knowledge that damage would probably result'. See R. E. Japikse (ed.), *Mr. C. Asser's handleiding tot de beoefening van het Nederlands burgerlijk recht: dl. 1: algemene bepalingen en rederij: 7: verkeersmiddelen en vervoer* (Deventer: Kluwer Law International, 2004), no. 448.

[49] Hof Amsterdam 12 August 2004, Nederlandse Jurisprudentie Feitenrechtspraak (NJF) (2004), 543; comments by K. F. Haak in Nederlands Tijdschrift voor Burgerlijk Recht (NTBR) (2005), 34–9.

[50] See, in this respect, the decision of the Court of Human Rights 1 March 2005 (no. 69869/01), NJ 2006, 251 about a railway accident involving a fourteen-year-old boy alighting from the wrong side of the train. In accordance with the Öneryiliz decision, the Court states that article 2 of the European Convention on Human Rights implies that the state has to take precautionary measures to protect the lives of its citizens. However, this does not imply that the state also has to take action to prevent situations where citizens themselves are careless about their own safety.

above this amount, the air carrier can only raise the defence of an act of God. The same tendency can be found in international railway treaties such as the COTIF Treaty of 1999 in which the minimum amount was raised to €200,000. The European Commission has proposed accepting fault liability for personal injury on top of the €220,000 limit for which absolute liability exists.[51]

1.b.viii Fault liability for non-passengers

Although not the main focus of this chapter, a brief diversion on fault liability for non-passengers is illuminating. In cases in which the relevant provisions of Book 8 do not apply, the victim has to base his claim for damages on the general fault liability rule of article 6:162 BW. This concerns accidents involving trains or trams on the one hand, and motor vehicles, cyclists and pedestrians on the other. If, for example, a motor vehicle collides with a train on a railway track and the passengers and driver suffer damage, they can file a claim against the railway company on the basis of article 6:162 BW. This means, firstly, that they have to prove an unlawful act (*onrechtmatige daad*) of the company. This implies that a right (to bodily integrity) has been infringed, a statutory rule has been violated or that the driver has acted contrary to the care that is required in society. Secondly, the victims have to state and, in principle, also prove that the unlawful act can be attributed (*toerekening*) to the railway company. Only 'legal' blameworthiness is required in road-traffic accident cases based on article 6:162 BW.

The most important difference between article 6:162 BW and article 8:105 BW is the burden of proof that, in the former case, is, in principle, on the victim and, in the latter, on the defendant. In practice, this could be a very important difference, since the success of many – if not most – claims in road traffic accidents depends on the burden of proof. However, there is some evidence that courts take the position that the driver of a train or tram has to take the utmost care. In a case involving an Amsterdam tram hitting a pedestrian crossing the road without really paying attention, the Court of Appeal stated that the driver has a high duty of care and has to take into account that pedestrians will not always pay attention and will make errors in judgement.[52] Hence, in practice, this liability comes close to a form of strict liability.

[51] COM (2004) 143; see www.europa.eu.int/eur-lex/nl/index.html (last accessed 27 May 2009).

[52] HR 3 June 2005, NJ 2005, 286; H R 14 July 2000, NJ 2001, 417.

When the claim based on article 6:162 BW is successful, there is no limitation as to the amount of damages, as is the case in article 8:105 BW, in conjunction with article 8:110 BW (€173,000). Other restrictions, like those of article 6:108 BW that limite the class of persons that can claim for loss of maintenance and the amount of damages, still apply in both situations.

1.b.ix International developments from 1999 to 2006

In accordance with Directive 91/440/EEG, the EU member states are obliged to make a separation between the exploitation of railway transportation by carriers and the exploitation of the railway infrastructure.[53] In 1999, this development led to an adaptation of the COTIF Treaty with agreement on a new Protocol, which came into force on 1 July 2006. The liability regime remained the same.[54] The amounts of damages were left to the national law of the member states. In the case of personal injury or death, the maximum amount according to the Protocol is €210,000.

If the accident is caused wholly or partly by defects in the infrastructure, the company responsible for the exploitation of the infrastructure is considered to be an assistant to the carrier. This means that the carrier is the person responsible.

Meanwhile, the European Union has produced a new regulation on international train transportation.[55] The liability of a railway company for damages sustained in the event of the death of, or bodily injury to, a passenger is not subject to any financial limit. The railway company may not exclude or limit liability for death or personal injury below €220,000 for each passenger. Above that amount, the railway company is not liable for damages if it proves that it was not negligent. Passengers are entitled to advance payments, to cover immediate needs following an accident, within fifteen days from the identification of the person entitled to compensation. In the event of death, this payment may not be less than €21,000.

1.b.x Number of accidents and fatalities

In 2000, the number of fatal railway accidents in the European Union was 0.3 per billion passenger km. This was even lower than the ratio for airline

[53] Amended by Directive 2004/51/EU of 29 April 2004, PbEU 2004, L 220. See A. W. Hagdoorn and Th. J. J. Kramer, 'Het gewijzigde verdrag betreffende het internationale spoorwegvervoer (COTIF)', *Tijdschrift Vervoer & Recht* (2006), 71–83.

[54] With a minor exception: see Hagdoorn and Kramer, 'Het gewijzigde verdrag betrefferde het internationale spoorwegvervoer (COTIF)', 75.

[55] Regulation 1371/2007/EC on Passengers' Rights and Obligations, OJ 2007 L 315.

travel, which was 0.4 per billion passenger km. The figures for road accidents were much higher: up to more than ten times as many for car passengers (5.9 per billion passenger km) and up to a hundred times as many for pedestrians (45 per billion passenger km). The total number of fatal railway accidents in the Netherlands in the same period (2000 to 2003) was an average of one fatal incident per year and about 100 injured.[56]

Compared to the situation in the first half of the nineteenth century, the total number of fatal accidents remained more or less the same, although the total number of train passengers multiplied.

1.c Some concluding and analytical remarks

Considering the above, the most remarkable conclusion is that the liability of the railway carrier has, in essence, remained the same since it was introduced in the Netherlands in 1856. It recurred in the Railway Act of 1875, and at the end of the twentieth century it was enacted in Book 8 BW and modelled after the COTIF Treaty. One of the main differences from the situation before 1988 is that, in article 8:105 BW, the shift in the burden of proof is not only addressed to those who are 'injured' during the trip, but reference is now also made to the 'death' of a traveller: 'The carrier is liable for damage caused by the death of, or bodily injury to, the traveller as a consequence of an accident which has occurred in connection with and during the carriage.' So the carrier is – directly – liable vis-à-vis the secondary victims (wife, husband, registered partner, unmarried partner and children). There is no need to rely in this respect on specific provisions like article 1406 (old) BW or article 6:108 (new) BW. These provisions – comparable to the English Fatal Accidents Act 1976 – provide for a claim in cases where someone is liable, vis-à-vis the deceased, for a specific next-of-kin group.[57] This, however, does not mean that *all* secondary (*ricochet*) victims can claim damages. Because of the layered structure and the system of the Dutch Civil Code, the restrictions of article 6:108 BW still apply.

The explanation for the fact that the relation with article 6:108 BW is left unclear is probably that article 8:105 BW is modelled after the international treaty. This treaty is in force in a large number of countries all over the world. A lot of countries – like France – do not have a provision like article 6:108 BW or like the English Fatal Accidents Act 1976.

[56] K. Peijs, *Veiligheid op de rails. Tweede Kadernota voor de veiligheid van het railvervoer in Nederland* (The Hague: Ministerie van Verkeer en Waterstraat, 2004), p. 27.

[57] Van Dam, *European Tort Law*, no. 1209.

The Netherlands was, of course, not the only country where in the nineteenth century the judiciary was confronted with the dangers of the new technical development. We can fairly assume that the Dutch legislative response to this development was inspired by legislation in neighbouring countries like Germany. The importance of accepting – in the middle of the nineteenth century – a strict liability provision supersedes that of the stronger legal position of railway accident victims in those days; it was a major breakthrough on the subject of extra-contractual liability, where the dominant view still was that liability was only acceptable where the victim could prove fault on the part of the tortfeasor. This specific derogation from the 'holy' general principles of tort law served as a strong example for future discussions where a higher level of protection for the victim was advocated. It turned out to be a major breakthrough.

In Germany also, the only exception to fault liability was found in the Prussian Railways Act 1838. This is generally explained by the fact that its regime of strict liability hardly affected the – mainly land-owning – dominant class, because of the moderate territorial length of the railway tracks in those days.[58] The liability of railway companies was intended by its instigator and Berlin professor Von Savigny to protect only passengers and landowners (whose estates could catch fire from the sparks from locomotives' funnels). The Prussian Supreme Court, however, reinterpreted this provision to include the protection of workers. Other workers were still forced to base their claim on fault liability.[59] The Prussian Railways Act 1838 led to the (more general) *Haftpflichtgesetz* of 7 June 1871.

In the Netherlands, article 1 Railway Act 1875 served as a source of inspiration for the employer's liability for accidents at work (article 1638x (old) BW; article 7:658 (new) BW). The introduction in 1924 of strict liability for the keeper of motor vehicles (section 3.2.1) was also inspired by article 1 Railway Act.

However, the actual role of article 1 Railway Act should not be overestimated. In the nineteenth century and a large part of the twentieth century, the advantage of shifting the burden of proof was only available for injured passengers. In the case of death, the descendants were considered not to come under the protection of this article. Their claim was treated as a normal negligence claim; they had to prove negligence on the part of the carrier and were bound to the restrictions of article 1407 BW. Hence, in practice,

[58] See Chapter 4, above (p. 75).

[59] See E.F.D. Engelhard, 'Background Analysis: the Concurrence of Compensation Schemes', in T. Hartlief and S. Klosse (eds), *Shifts in Compensating Work-Related Injuries and Diseases* (Vienna: Springer ECTIL, 2007).

only when a breadwinner died could his wife and children expect to obtain damages. Funeral costs were excluded by article 1407 BW. Railway workers and other persons outside the train (or tram) were also excluded from the protection of article 1. More recent case law, specifically on tram accidents, indicates that the law is more favourable for non-passengers. The Amsterdam Court of Appeal – sanctioned by the Hoge Raad – stated that the driver has a 'high duty of care' and has to take into account that pedestrians will not always pay attention and will make errors in judgement.[60]

It can be argued that this very high standard of care will not automatically be applied in accidents involving trains. Trains run on a closed track, unlike trams, which can run through busy streets and whose driver has more options for making emergency stops. There is some case law that indicates that a railway company is not liable when a car crossing the track is hit by a train.[61]

The rationale for article 1 Railway Act is therefore not (or not only) the inherent danger (*betriebsgefahr*) of railway transportation. If this was the underlying idea, then people outside the train especially would deserve protection! According to article 185(1) Road Traffic Act, people outside a motor vehicle (pedestrians, cyclists) are the ones who receive protection. Here, the underlying idea is clearly the *betriebsgefahr*. The driver and the passengers, on the contrary, are not covered by this strict liability rule, because they themselves are considered to benefit from this dangerous machine.

It can be argued that the reason for introducing article 1 Railway Act in the middle of the nineteenth century had to do with the dominant view that the contract of carriage did not, as such, imply a duty to a 'safe' arrival at the destination; the obligation was merely that one was transported from A to B. This resulted in an unsatisfactory situation, in that injured passengers had to rely on the general fault provisions such as those in article 1401 (old) BW and were thus usually confronted with the problem of being unable to prove the actual cause of the accident and which servant was at fault. This specific problem was then solved by introducing article 1 Railway Act 1875. The underlying argumentation for deviating from the 'holy' principle of tort law, that the burden of proof is on the victim, is provided by Thorbecke in his reference to the contract of carriage of goods, which already implied a shift of the burden of proof.

[60] HR 3 June 2005, NJ (2005), 286; HR 14 July 2000, NJ (2001), 417.

[61] In HR 8 April 1988, NJ (1988), 659, it was decided that the Dutch Railway Company (NS) was liable, however, for 25 per cent because a truck had stopped on the track crossing and was hit by the train. This judgment was, however, not based on negligence on the part of the driver or the NS, but was based on article 33 Railway Act 1875, which holds that the

The conclusion is that the underlying rationale for article 1 Railway Act was closer to the principles of contract law than to the principles of tort law, notwithstanding the fact that this liability was designed to be more or less independent from the contract of carriage. Later on in the twentieth century, railway companies were state-owned in most European countries. It was the government that negotiated the treaties on railway liability. It was not in their financial interest to increase their liability in the case of railway casualties.

The situation changed somewhat with the implementation of the COTIF Treaty into Book 8 BW. Since 1988, the descendants of fatally injured train passengers can now profit from the strict liability rule provided for in article 8:105 BW. However, persons injured outside the train are still excluded from this protection. They need to rely on the general fault-based liability of article 6:162 BW. In exceptional cases, they may benefit from specific strict liability provisions, such as those in article 6:173 BW (liability for defective movable objects) if it can be shown that the train had a defect that caused the accident.

2 Road traffic accidents

2.a *Statutory provisions since 1994*

The Dutch law on liability for damage caused by motor vehicles is mainly governed by three provisions: article 185 Wegenverkeerswet 1994 (Road Traffic Act – WVW), creating a strict liability rule for the owner or keeper of a motor vehicle towards pedestrians and cyclists; article 6:162 BW, setting out the general rule for fault liability which applies to the liability of the driver towards other motor vehicles and their driver and passengers; and article 6:101 BW, setting out the general rule for contributory negligence, which applies in both categories. The three provisions are set out in full in the Appendix to this book.[62]

2.a.i Article 185 WVW: strict liability

Article 185 WVW provides as the main rule that the owner or keeper of a motor vehicle is liable for damage caused in a road traffic accident to pedestrians and cyclists, unless the accident amounted to *overmacht* for the driver, including situations where the accident was caused by someone for whom the owner or keeper was not liable.

NS is responsible for the fencing of the track. In this situation, the crossing was not sufficiently protected by barriers.

[62] Below p. 233.

The key word in article 185 is '*overmacht*'. *Overmacht* is typically translated into *force majeure*, but this might not be entirely accurate. Over the years, the Hoge Raad has limited the possibilities for successfully invoking *overmacht*, thus providing more protection to victims of road traffic accidents (i.e. cyclists and pedestrians) by gradually changing the definition of *overmacht*.

It is important to emphasise that the scope of application of article 185 WVW is limited. It only applies to damage suffered by a pedestrian, a cyclist, the owner of a leashed animal and a highway authority. The provision is not applicable to passengers or drivers. If a passenger or driver suffers damage in a road traffic accident, he has to file a claim on the basis of article 6:162 BW. This provision holds the general rule for negligence liability, although in road traffic accidents a very high level of care applies. The main difference is that in article 6:162 BW, the burden of proof of negligence is on the claimant, whereas in article 185 WVW it is up to the owner or keeper to prove *overmacht*.

A second defence in article 185 WVW for the owner or keeper is to invoke the pedestrian's or cyclist's *eigen schuld* (contributory negligence: see article 6:101 BW). Usually, this leads to a reduction of the amount of compensation to be paid.[63] Next to the development of the word *overmacht* in article 185 WVW, the development of the concept of contributory negligence has played a major role in the case law of the Hoge Raad. In the course of time, the Hoge Raad has substantially limited the scope for the contributory negligence defence in order to improve the position of pedestrians and cyclists, particularly those under the age of fourteen, who have been victims of an accident. This will be set out in more detail in the following sections.

2.b *Legislative developments before 1994*

2.b.i 1924: introduction of a rule of strict liability

The first rule of strict liability for damage caused by motor vehicles was enacted in article 25 Motor- en Rijwielwet (Motor Vehicles and Cyclists Act – MRW). Although this Act had already been in force for some time, article 25 was only inserted in 1924. This rule of strict liability was not initiated by the government but by some members of parliament (MPs) (Van Rapperd and Van Sasse van Ysselt).[64] The main rule was virtually the same

[63] See below.

[64] A. S. Hartkamp, *Mr. C. Asser's handleiding tot de beoefening van het Nederlands burgerlijk recht. Verbintenissenrecht. Deel III. De verbintenis uit de wet* (12th edn, Deventer: Tjeenk Willink, 2006), vol. III, no. 219; J. H. Ekering, *Motorrijtuig en aansprakelijkheid naar*

as the current article 185, § 1: the keeper of a motor vehicle was liable for damage caused to pedestrians and cyclists, unless it was plausible that the accident was due to *force majeure* (*overmacht*), including situations where it was caused by someone for whom the owner or keeper was not liable.

A rule of strict liability had been advocated by the legal literature since the beginning of the twentieth century, with the aim of providing victims with a stronger position for claiming compensation for damage suffered as the consequence of an accident involving a motor vehicle.[65] These ideas had been the basis of the MPs' initiative for new legislation.[66]

There was confusion and discussion about the basis of the new rule on this point. There was not even consensus between the MPs who contributed to the text of the Act. The two main advocated theories were the 'theory of increased danger' (*gevaarverhoging*) and the 'theory of a presumption of fault' (*vermoeden van fout of schuld*). In the latter view (supported by MP Van Rapperd), it would be possible for the defendant to escape liability by proving that he had done everything that was reasonably possible to prevent the accident. In the former view (supported by MP Van Sasse van Ysselt), the defendant would be liable on the basis that using his motor vehicle increased the danger, even if preventing the accident was beyond his control.[67] The Minister of Justice added to the confusion by initially taking the first view (theory of increased danger) and later emphasising that correct driving could also be a defence against liability.[68]

After the statutory strict liability rule came into force, it was renumbered twice, firstly as article 31 WVW and then, in 1994, as article 185 WVW.[69] On the second occasion, a number of editorial changes were made.

Nederlandsch burgerlijk recht (Amsterdam: Paris, 1941), pp. 27ff.; W. J. M. Weersma and N. J. Polak, *De wegenverkeerswet verklaard* (Groningen: Wolters, 1950), pp. 177ff.; E. F. D. Engelhard and G. E. van Maanen, *Aansprakelijkheid voor verkeersongevallen* (Nijmegen: Ars Aequi, 1998), pp. 14ff.

[65] C. W. Star Busmann, 'De aansprakelijkheid der automobiel in het verkeersrecht', *Rechtsgeleerd Magazijn* (1908), 395: 'dat het publiek … zekerder dan tot dusver ter zake van de veroorzaakte schade zijn verhaal zal kunnen vinden' ['that the public can find a claim more easily for injuries caused than was hither the case'].

[66] See, in particular, C. W. Star Busmann, 'Moderne verkeersmiddelen en schadevergoedingsrecht', *Vragen des Tijds* (1922), pp. 163–84; *Handelingen der Staten-Generaal* 1923/24, Tweede Kamer, no. 52, p. 1986. See also Engelhard and Van Maanen, *Aansprakelijkheid voor verkeersongevallen*, p. 15.

[67] See, for an overview of the opinions in the legal literature, Weersma and Polak, *De wegenverkeerswet verklaard*, pp. 199ff. See, for an overview of the way the provision has been interpreted by the Hoge Raad, below.

[68] *Handelingen der Staten-Generaal* 1923/24, Tweede Kamer, no. 1, pp. 20–1. See also Engelhard and Van Maanen, *Aansprakelijkheid voor verkeersongevallen*, p. 15.

[69] Act of 21 April 1994, Stb. 1994, p. 475, entering into force on 1 January 1995.

2.b.ii 1960 to 2000: failed proposals for a new liability regime

In the 1960s, a new liability regime for damage caused by motor vehicles was considered in the framework of the drafting of a new BW. This new regime was embodied in the proposed article 6.3.14 and differed substantially from the by then applicable article 31 WVW. The first sections of this proposed provision ran as follows:

> (1) Without prejudice to the provisions of the foregoing articles, the possessor of a motor vehicle which in traffic causes damage to persons or things outside that vehicle is liable if the accident is due to a defect in the vehicle or to a fault of a person to whom it was entrusted by the possessor …
>
> (2) Even if no defect or fault as referred to in the foregoing paragraph is established, the possessor is liable if the danger to persons or things constituted by a moving motor vehicle has materialised in his motor vehicle, except for damage occasioned to motor vehicles engaged in the traffic or to persons or things carried in them.[70]

This proposal introduced a strict liability for a defect in the motor vehicle (paragraph 1) and for the danger caused by the motor vehicle (paragraph 2). Paragraph 1 would protect drivers and passengers, whereas paragraph 2 would not. This proposal was withdrawn because it was considered preferable to have a new regime adopted in Book 8 (Traffic Measures and Transport), rather than in Book 6 (Obligations).

Around the time of the withdrawal, in 1973, the Minister of Justice established a study group to advise him on a new liability regime for road traffic accidents. The study group produced two reports: one in 1978 on personal injury, and one in 1980 on property damage. These reports helpfully clarified the situation and advocated a system of strict liability and a no-fault system (first-party traffic insurance), but did not make a choice between these possible solutions. The Commission made some general recommendations, such as abolishing the defence of contributory negligence and the general negligence claim in road traffic accidents.

Although Parliament and the legal authors were anxious to know what the Minister was going to do with the reports, it was only in 1987 that the Minister promised Parliament a memorandum to set out his views on the possibility of drafting a system that would provide compensation as fully as possible for the protection of road-traffic accident victims. This memorandum was presented to Parliament in 1990.[71] In this memorandum, the Minister set out his preference for a system of strict liability; a no-fault

[70] Translation in Ministry of Justice, *The Netherlands Civil Code: Book 6 The Law of Obligations. Draft Text and Commentary* (The Hague: Ministry of Justice, 1977), p. 48.

[71] Kamerstukken II, 1989–1990, section 21 528, no. 1.

system had several drawbacks: higher premiums, particularly for mopeds and motor cycles, and lower amounts of compensation available for the most seriously injured victims. A system of strict liability would be in accordance with systems in other countries and would avoid making the difference with victims of other accidents too big.

Again, it took a number of years before the idea was turned into a bill. The key provision in that bill was that the possessor or the keeper of a motor vehicle that is involved in a road traffic accident was liable for damage suffered by pedestrians, cyclists and passengers, unless the damage was caused by their intentional or knowingly reckless behaviour. The defence of *overmacht* would be abolished. This rule was very similar to the French (1985) and the Belgian (1994) liability regimes for road traffic accidents.

Although strongly supported by the legal literature, the proposal was not warmly welcomed in Parliament. In the eyes of some, abolishing the contributory negligence defence, or rather, reducing it to intentional or knowingly reckless behaviour, was a step too far. The successor Minister therefore decided to extend this defence to intentional and reckless behaviour. This step was a sign that ideas about 'victim friendliness' were changing. The political support for the proposal started to evaporate and eventually the bill was withdrawn.

2.b.iii 2005: minor changes to the strict liability regime

The latest legislative development was a minor reform of the law in 2005.[72] Firstly, the old rule limiting the recovery of property damage was abolished. Since 2005 there is no longer any limitation as to the recovery of property damage. The main beneficiaries of this legislation have been the highway authorities, which can now more easily recover damage to the highway caused by motor vehicles.

Secondly, article 6:173 (new) BW (strict liability for defective movable goods) was made applicable to defective motor vehicles. In the 1970s, it was decided to exclude motor vehicles from the application of article 6:173, awaiting a new liability regime for motor vehicles. This reform may therefore be a signal that such a new liability regime is, at best, at the very bottom of the political agenda. It is, however, more likely that it has, in fact, already fallen off.

This overview shows that the legislator has struggled to create a new liability regime since the 1960s. There were some preparatory activities in

[72] Wet van 16 juni 2005, houdende wijziging van de Wegenverkeerswet 1994 en het Burgerlijk Wetboek teneinde het verhaal van schade die wordt veroorzaakt als gevolg van een ongeval met of een gebrek aan een motorrijtuig te vergemakkelijken, Stb. 2005, 357.

the 1970s, but it was only in the late 1990s that, after much hesitation and cautiousness, a bill was presented to Parliament. In the end, the fate of the bill was that it never reached the status of Act and that the legislation will remain as it has been since 1924.

2.c Case law

2.c.i 1924 to 1980: from 'presumption of fault' to 'increased danger'

As has been pointed out above, the basis for the liability rule of article 25 MRW was not entirely clear: on the one hand, there was the 'theory of increased danger' (*gevaarverhoging*) and, on the other, the 'theory of a presumption of fault' (*vermoeden van fout of schuld*). In the latter view, the defendant can escape liability by proving that he did everything that was reasonably possible to prevent the accident. In the former view, the defendant would be liable on the basis that using his motor vehicle increased the danger, even if preventing the accident was beyond his control. This problem had to be solved by the courts, particularly by interpreting the concept of *force majeure* (*overmacht*). Very briefly summarised, the courts initially embraced the theory of a presumption of fault but ended up, in the 1990s, with the theory of increased danger.

The first landmark case on the interpretation of the word *overmacht* in article 25 MRW was handed down in 1937. In this case, the Hoge Raad clearly adopted the presumption of fault theory (see above, Section 2.b.i), holding that *overmacht* implied an event for which neither the owner or keeper, nor someone for whom he is liable, was to blame.[73]

In 1942, however, the Hoge Raad changed its position. Reasoning on the basis of the provision's scope rather than its literal wording, the court limited the meaning of *overmacht* by ruling that a defect in the steering column of a motor vehicle could not amount to this defence.[74] This decision was an application of the theory of increased risk (*theorie van de gevaarverhoging*), rather than the theory of the presumption of fault (*theorie van het vermoeden van schuld*). The Hoge Raad considered that the risk created to persons by motor vehicles on public

[73] HR 16 April 1937, NJ (1937), 490, note EMM: 'een gebeuren waarvan men noch de eigenaar of de houder zelf, noch iemand voor wie hij aansprakelijk is, een verwijt kan maken'.

[74] HR 16 April 1942, NJ (1942), 394 (Torenbout): 'dat een eigen gebrek van het motorrijtuig geen overmacht opleverend feit is'.

highways justified a liability that goes further than the general fault liability rule.[75]

It is not clear whether the interpretation in this decision, handed down during the German occupation of the Netherlands, had been influenced by German law. In a later decision in 1943, the Hoge Raad acknowledged the right to compensation for pain and suffering, referring not only to what had applied in the Netherlands before the enactment of the BW of 1838, but also to the law in the surrounding countries that acknowledged such a right.[76]

In the subsequent case law, the Hoge Raad narrowed the possibilities for defendants to invoke the defence of *force majeure.* Until the early 1970s, the defendant had to show that he was not at all to blame for his driving, as far as this was relevant for the cause of the accident. In this sense, the basis was partly the theory of the presumption of fault (albeit with a high standard of care) and partly the theory of increased risk (with regard to technical defects).[77]

Two 'waves' of the Hoge Raad's case law, one in the early 1980s and one in the early 1990s, have shifted the centre of gravity of the rule's basis to the theory of increased risk. This means that there does not seem to be an immediate connection between this emphasis on increased risk and the introduction of compulsory liability insurance for motor vehicles in the mid 1960s.

2.c.ii 1980s: limiting the defence of *overmacht*

Since the 1980s, the Hoge Raad has held that the defence of *overmacht* can only be invoked if the driver shows that: (i) he could not 'legally' be blamed for his conduct, a standard of reference that allows for a comparison with the perfect driver; and (ii) that the accident was solely due

[75] HR 16 April 1942, NJ (1942), 394 (Torenbout): 'art. 25 berust op de overweging, dat het gevaar dat het verkeer met motorrijtuigen op den openbaren weg voor anderen oplevert, een aansprakelijkheid rechtvaardigt verder gaande dan die van het gemeene recht'.

[76] HR 21 May 1943, NJ (1943), 455 (Van Kreuningen/Bessem): 'dat in overeenstemming met hetgeen van oudsher in ons land gegolden had en met hetgeen volgens wet of rechtspraak in de naburige landen geldt, het toekennen van vergoeding voor ideëele schade, geleden tengevolge van voormelde daden [moedwillige of onvoorzichtige kwetsing of verminking van enig deel van het lichaam en misdrijven tegen de persoon, SDL], als redelijk en billijk valt te beschouwen'.

[77] A rare example of successfully invoking the *overmacht* defence is HR 11 February 1977, NJ (1977), 511; see also A. T. Bolt and J. Spier, *De uitdijende reikwijdte van de aansprakelijkheid uit onrechtmatige daad* (Deventer: Kluwer Law International, 1996), p. 210, and Hartkamp, *Mr. C. Asser's handleiding*, vol. III, no. 223 *in fine.*

to another person's fault (including the victim's own fault), that was so improbable that the driver could not reasonably have taken them into account whilst driving.[78]

As regards (i), parallel to the case law of article 6:162 (see 2.c.iv), the Hoge Raad developed a distinction between conduct that is humanly blameworthy (*menselijkerwijs verwijtbaar*) and conduct that is legally blameworthy (*rechtens verwijtbaar*). In road traffic accidents, only legal blameworthiness is required. The standard of reference is that of the perfect driver.[79]

As regards (ii), it has to be shown that the accident was solely caused by someone else's fault; this includes the victim's fault (*uitsluitend te wijten aan de fout van een ander, inclusief het slachtoffer*). The other persons' faults must have been so unlikely that the driver could not reasonably have taken them into account (*de fouten waren voor de bestuurder zo onwaarschijnlijk dat hij bij het bepalen van zijn verkeersgedrag naar redelijkheid geen rekening behoefde te houden*). In the case law, this standard was set very high. The driver has to take into account that other people (in the framework of article 185 WVW, pedestrians and cyclists) make mistakes, even if these mistakes are very unlikely. According to the case law, a driver needs to anticipate that pedestrians and cyclists violate traffic regulations, for example driving through red traffic lights, changing directions without indicating, crossing the road without looking, riding a bicycle at night without lights, etc. More particularly, a moped driver has to anticipate that if he overtakes pedestrians on a moped and cycle track, they may suddenly move sideways.[80] And a car driver has to anticipate that a pedestrian may suddenly cross the road in front of his car.[81] There

[78] HR 22 May 1992, NJ (1992), 527 (ABP/Winterthur): 'indien aan de bestuurder rechtens geen enkel verwijt kan worden gemaakt, daar de aanrijding uitsluitend is te wijten aan fouten van een ander (inclusief de gelaedeerde) die voor de bestuurder zo onwaarschijnlijk waren dat deze bij het bepalen van zijn verkeersgedrag met deze mogelijkheid naar redelijkheid geen rekening behoefde te houden'. See, in this sense, HR 24 December 1982, NJ (1983), 443; *Verkeersrecht* (VR) (1983), 40 (Wijman/Corten); HR 23 May 1986, NJ (1987), 482, note CJHB (Frank van Holsteijn). See also HR 26 March 1971, NJ (1971), 262, note GJS (Jan de Waard); HR 16 February 1996, NJ (1996), 393 (Staat/Royal Nederland); HR 4 October 1996, NJ (1997), 147, note CJHB (Dijksma/Klaverblad); H. Bouman, 'Artikel 31 WVW: Van bewijslast naar bescherming', VR (1987), 85–9. See, for an overview *Mr. C. Asser's handleiding*, vol. III, no. 224 and M. van Dam, *Verkeersongevallen*, (Den Haag: Boom Juridische Uitgevers, 2001), pp. 82ff.

[79] HR 11 November 1983, NJ (1984), 331 (*meppelse reel*crossing deer). On this case, see below, p. 141.

[80] HR 22 May 1992, NJ (1992), 527 (ABP/Winterthur).

[81] HR 24 December 1982, NJ (1983), 443, VR (1983), 40 (Wijman/Corten).

are, however, also a few examples of cases in which a driver has successfully invoked *force majeure*, for example when a cyclist drove through a red traffic light and was hit by a bus driving at low speed and whose driver only saw the cyclist at the very last moment.[82]

2.c.iii 1990s: the 100% rule and the 50% rule

In the second wave, in the early 1990s (the 'roaring nineties'[83]), the Hoge Raad took an unprecedented role as substitute-legislator by developing the law as regards the liability for damage caused by motor vehicles to vulnerable road traffic users such as pedestrians and cyclists along strict lines. In a series of decisions, it virtually abolished the defences of *force majeure* and contributory negligence towards children and it guaranteed most adult pedestrians and cyclists at least 50% compensation.

Firstly, in 1990, the Hoge Raad limited the defence of contributory negligence towards pedestrians and cyclists under the age of fourteen to the youngster's intentional behaviour or intention approaching recklessness.[84]

Secondly, in 1991, the Hoge Raad extended this standard to the requirement of *force majeure*, limiting this defence to cases in which the child had acted intentionally or with intention approaching recklessness.[85] This made the defence virtually impossible: it hardly ever happens that a court decides that a child acted (almost) intentionally.

Finally, in 1995, the Hoge Raad decided that, even in the case of an unforeseeable fault of a third party, the defence of *overmacht* cannot be invoked towards a child under the age of fourteen, unless it had acted (almost) intentionally.[86] This interpretation of *force majeure* towards children is also known as the 100% rule.[87]

This interpretation by the Hoge Raad of the word *overmacht* in article 185WVW as regards youngsters implied an extension of the statutory provision beyond its text and scope. However, there were hardly any protests to be heard; on the contrary, many authors welcomed the moves. This development added to the popularity of the Hoge Raad (at least amongst legal

[82] HR 16 February 1996, NJ (1996), 393, VR (1996), 195 (Plomp/Ketelaar).

[83] Engelhard and Van Maanen, *Aansprakelijkheid voor verkeersongevallen*, p. 17.

[84] HR 1 June 1990, NJ (1991), 720, note CJHB (Ingrid Kolkman).

[85] HR 31 May 1991, NJ (1991), 721, note CJHB (Marbeth van Uitregt).

[86] HR 2 June 1995, NJ (1997), 700, note CJHB (Marloes de Vos); in the same sense, HR 17 November 2000, NJ (2001), 260, note CJHB (FBTO/Delta Lloyd).

[87] See van Dam, *Verkeersongevallen*, pp 90ff. with further references.

authors), to the detriment of that of the legislator. It was not long after this case law was created that the legislator started to prepare new legislation.

This case law only applies to victims under the age of fourteen. To persons of fourteen years and older, the 'external cause' rule applies: *overmacht* can only be invoked if the driver, from a legal point of view, cannot be blamed at all because the accident was solely due to other persons' faults (including the victim's fault), and these faults were so unlikely that the driver could not reasonably have taken them into account whilst driving.[88] However, the defence of contributory negligence has been strongly restricted. If the driver cannot show that there was force majeure, the adult pedestrian or cyclist is entitled to compensation of at least 50% of his damage (unless he acted intentionally or with intention approaching recklessness).[89] This interpretation of *force majeure* towards adults is also known as the 50 per cent rule.[90]

The age limit of fourteen years in the Hoge Raad's case law is related to article 6:164 BW. This provision holds that a child under fourteen years of age cannot be liable for damage caused by his own conduct (*[e]en gedraging van een kind dat de leeftijd van veertien jaren nog niet heeft bereikt, kan aan hem niet als een onrechtmatige daad worden toegerekend*). The parent or the custodian is liable for the child's objectively negligent conduct. Hence, a child cannot be liable for his own personal conduct; neither can it be contributorily negligent unless it acted intentionally or with intention approaching recklessness. These rules apply not only in road traffic accidents, but also more generally in accidents with young victims.[91]

In various decisions the Hoge Raad has laid down a number of considerations for developing the case law: hard and fast rules contribute to a less time-consuming settlement of claims; the scope of article 185 WVW is to protect (by definition, vulnerable) pedestrians and cyclists against the far-reaching consequences of an accident with a motor vehicle (this is particularly relevant for children who are impulsive, playful and imprudent); and, finally, motor vehicles are compulsorily insured against liability. This approach became particularly clear in the Hoge Raad's position in a number of cases, holding that the so-called 50% and 100% rules cannot

88 See HR 28 February 1992, NJ (1993), 566, note CJHB (IZA/Vrerink). In the same case, the Hoge Raad held that, as regards the contributory negligence of an adult victim, the so-called 50 per cent rule applies.

89 HR 24 December 1993, NJ (1995), 236, note CJHB (Anja Kellenaers).

90 See van Dam, *Verkeersongevallen*, pp 86ff. with further references.

91 See Hartkamp, *Mr. C. Asser's handleiding* (2004) vol. I, no. 451a.

be invoked by social or private insurance companies seeking recourse for damages paid to insured road-traffic accident victims.[92]

2.c.iv Article 6:162 BW: fault liability

In cases in which article 185 WVW does not apply, the victim has to base his claim for damages on the general fault liability rule of article 6:162 BW. This concerns accidents between motor vehicles, between cyclists and between cyclists and pedestrians.

If, for example, two motor vehicles collide and the passenger and driver suffer damage, they can file a claim against the owner or driver of the other vehicle on the basis of article 6:162 BW. This means, firstly, that they have to prove an unlawful act (*onrechtmatige daad*) of the owner or driver. This implies either that a right (to bodily integrity) has been infringed, a statutory rule has been violated (in particular a road traffic rule) or that the driver has acted contrary to the care that is required in society. Secondly, the victims have to state and, in principle, also prove that the unlawful act can be attributed (*toerekening*) to the owner or driver on the basis of fault, of a statutory provision or of the opinion of society.

Over the course of time, just as in the case law regarding article 185 WVW, the Hoge Raad developed the requirement of attribution (*toerekening*) (previously fault (*schuld*)) along the lines of the requirement of *force majeure* in article 185 WVW. It developed the requirement of fault into an objective test, which culminated in the landmark case of the crossing deer (*meppelse ree*). In this case, the Hoge Raad made a distinction between conduct that is humanly blameworthy (*menselijkerwijs verwijtbaar*) and conduct that is legally blameworthy (*rechtens verwijtbaar*). In road-traffic accident cases based on article 6:162, only legal blameworthiness is required.

The case concerned a driver who was suddenly confronted with a crossing animal and swerved into the oncoming traffic. This was humanly an understandable – and perhaps even inevitable – reaction. However, it was legally blameworthy because the driver could have chosen a better (safer, less dangerous) reaction by swerving onto the hard shoulder or even colliding with the animal.[93]

92 HR 1 June 1990, NJ (1991), 720, note CJHB (Ingrid Kolkman); HR 31 May 1991, NJ (1991), 721, note CJHB (Marbeth van Uitregt); HR 28 February 1992, NJ (1993), 566, note CJHB (IZA/Vrerink); HR 24 December 1993, NJ (1995), 236, note CJHB (Anja Kellenaers); HR 2 June 1995, NJ (1997), 700, note CJHB (Marloes de Vos); HR 5 December 1997, NJ (1998), 209 and 400–2, note JH. See, for an overview, van Dam, 93ff. with further references.

93 HR 11 November 1983, NJ (1984), 331 (*meppelse ree*/crossing deer).

It goes without saying that a high level of care is owed not only to other road users, but also towards passengers. Mr Wenmakers was driving on an unlit motorway when he suddenly saw a large object in front of his car. He swerved in order to avoid the object but this caused an accident, as a consequence of which his passenger suffered serious injuries. The Hoge Raad considered that Wenmakers had not adapted his speed to the range of visibility. For this reason he was liable for the damage caused to his passenger.[94]

So, even if someone cannot be blamed for his conduct from a human point of view, he can still be liable because his conduct was legally blameworthy. This is not a normal objective standard, but rather one of the 'perfect driver' who knows and foresees almost everything and is able to avoid almost all possible risks: it is the robot type of comparison. In fact, it is the car's 'conduct', rather than the driver's conduct, that is taken into consideration.

The most important difference between article 6:162 BW and article 185 WVW is the burden of proof, which, in the former case, is, in principle, on the victim and, in the latter, on the defendant. In practice, this is a very important difference, since the success of many, if not most, claims in road traffic accidents depends on the burden of proof.[95]

Unlike in article 185 WVW, liability on the basis of article 6:162 BW does not imply that it has to be guaranteed that a motor vehicle is without any defect. Until recently, strict liability for defective movable objects did not apply to motor vehicles (see article 6:173 BW). This meant that if someone suffered damage as the consequence of a defect of a motor vehicle, a claim had to be based on article 6:162 BW requires, in principle, that the owner or driver has breached his duty to sufficiently maintain the vehicle.

A case from the 1960s illustrates this. Due to defective shock absorbers, the bonnet of a car became loose and an accident was caused. The Hoge Raad agreed with the Court of Appeal (Gerechtshof) that one cannot expect a driver who is not an engineer to know that defective shock absorbers can cause a bonnet to become loose.[96]

[94] HR 26 March 1982, NJ (1982), 292, VR (1982), 51 (Wenmakers/Smeets). See C. C. van Dam, 'De Hoge Raad op zoek naar de perfekte automobilist. Drie recente arresten', VR (1985), 261–4.

[95] HR 15 January 1993, NJ (1993), 568, VR (1993), 76 (Puts/Ceha); HR 11 November 1983, NJ (1984), 331, VR (1984), 56 (*meppelse ree*/crossing deer). H. A. Bouman, 'Van bewijslast naar bescherming – Artikel 31 Wegenverkeerswet', VR (1987), 86. See also HR 23 October 1992, NJ (1992), 813, VR (1993), 93 (Centraal Ziekenfonds/Van der Velden).

[96] HR 7 April 1967, NJ (1967), 282, VR (1967), 109, note P. (Bonnet Daf): '... dat van een op het gebied van de autotechniek niet deskundige bestuurder niet zonder meer kan worden

Illustrative of the changing views in this respect is, however, the decision in the 1990s of a lower court that a spontaneous shortcut in a car, as a consequence of which the car started moving, can be generally considered to imply a lack of maintenance, for which the owner of a car is liable.[97]

Since 2005, these cases are governed by article 6:173 BW (strict liability for defective movable objects, including defective motor vehicles).

2.c.v Article 6:101 BW: contributory negligence

The general provision on contributory negligence is article 6:101 BW. It holds a two-stage test: firstly, it has to be established what the claimant and defendant each contributed to the damage. This includes all circumstances, not only the 'neutral' conduct and the degree of negligence, but also, for example, the contribution to the damage of the so-called *Betriebsgefahr.* This refers to the risk created by the weight and the speed of a motor vehicle, which can be a substantial causal factor as regards the damage.

Secondly, fairness comes into play. The outcome of the first stage test can be adapted if fairness requires this, because of the differences in seriousness of the mutual faults or other circumstances of the case. This can lead to a different division of the damage, to a duty to compensate 100 per cent or to the conclusion that the damage does not need to be compensated at all.

The Hoge Raad had already anticipated this rule before the entry into force of the new BW in 1992. It considered the new rule to reflect the law as it stood under the old law.[98]

It was particularly the second-stage test that the Hoge Raad applied to provide cyclists and pedestrians with a stronger position to recover their damages. In 1990, the Hoge Raad limited the defence of contributory negligence for drivers towards pedestrians and cyclists under the age of fourteen to the youngster's intentional behaviour or intention approaching recklessness.[99] This meant that, regardless of the mutual attribution of causal circumstances at the first stage, fairness required that the loss of the youngster should be fully compensated by the owner or keeper of the motor vehicle, or, rather, his liability insurer. This is what became known

gevorderd, dat hij enig verband tussen het niet behoorlijk werken van schokbrekers en het loswerken van deksel en motorkapsluiting voorziet'.

97 Rechtbank Breda 25 October 1994, NJ (1995), 506 (Hooge Huys/Hennen).

98 Hartkamp, *Mr. C. Asser's handleiding* (2004), vol. I, no. 450.

99 HR 1 June 1990, NJ (1991), 720, note CJHB (Ingrid Kolkman).

as the 100% rule. The rule applies not only in road traffic accident cases, but, in principle, in all cases in which a child under the age of fourteen suffers personal injury as the consequence of machines or activities with an increased risk.[100]

The Hoge Raad not only improved the position of the young victim within the framework of contributory negligence; as regards pedestrians and cyclists fourteen years of age and older, the Hoge Raad created the so-called 50% rule. In two decisions, the court held that the age limit is a sharp one and that contributory negligence of persons of fourteen years and older, in principle, cannot be higher than 50%.[101]

In other words, the owner or keeper of the motor vehicle has to pay at least 50% of the damage of a victim over fourteen years of age, unless the victim acted intentionally or knowingly recklessly. Whether the owner or keeper can be obliged to pay more depends on the mutual causal contributions to the damage (the first stage of article 6:101, section 1). This implies that if the victim has contributed to the damage by 50% or more, he will still have 50% of his damage compensated. If he has contributed to the damage by less than 50%, he will have 100% less his percentage contribution; for example, if the victim has contributed 20% of the damage, 80% of his damage will be compensated.

Hence, adult victims are less strongly protected than young victims: as regards the former category, the defence of *overmacht* is *force majeure* instead of (almost) intentional conduct, and the defence of contributory negligence leads to a minimum of 50% instead of a general rule of 100%. Although similar arguments for protection have been put forward for both groups (vulnerability of pedestrians and cyclists, compulsory liability insurance of the motor vehicle, easy establishment of liability), the argument for extra protection of youngsters is their extra vulnerability because of their lack of experience and their childish impetuosity.

2.c.vi Analysis of possible change initiators

In many respects, it will be hard to provide evidence for possible change initiators, not only because of a lack of empirical information (e.g. as regards personal views, particularly from the Government Commissioner and the members of the Civil Chamber of the Hoge

[100] Hartkamp, *Mr. C. Asser's handleiding* (2004), vol. I, no. 451a.

[101] HR 28 February 1992, NJ (1993), 566, note CJHB (IZA/Vrerink) and HR 24 December 1993, NJ (1995), 236, note CJHB (Anja Kellenaers).

Raad), but also because many of these change initiators cannot be isolated but are part of a more complicated process of intertwined change factors.

It is submitted here that at least four aspects may have been relevant:

(1) the tension or 'battle' between a passive legislator and an active Hoge Raad
(2) the personal influence and authority of Wouter Snijders who, during two decades, combined the position of Government Commissioner for the new BW and membership of the Hoge Raad, most of the time as Chairman of the Civil Chamber
(3) the influence of the legal literature, in which a system of no-fault compensation was almost unanimously advocated
(4) the influence of developments in neighbouring countries, particularly France and Belgium, members of the same legal family.

'Battle' between legislator and judiciary It can be concluded from the outline above that there might have been a relation between the inactivity of the legislator on the one hand, and the activity of the judiciary on the other. For a long time, the legislator remained undecided about the way ahead as regards liability for damage caused by road traffic accidents. In the 1960s, the provisions in the draft new BW were withdrawn, and in the 1980s two Commission reports were published, but these did not invoke any visible activity by the legislator. It was only in the early 1990s that the Minister of Justice set out his preference for a strict liability regime in a memorandum for Parliament. At last, in 1997, his successor sent a bill to Parliament which some time later was withdrawn. This meant that the legislator did not show any substantial progress in developing the law until the mid 1990s.

From the 1960s and 1970s onwards in particular, after a substantial growth in the number of motor vehicles and the number of accidents, the urge for a stricter liability regime became apparent. This was the case not only in the Netherlands, but also in many other European countries. In the Netherlands, eminent authors like Bloembergen and Van Wassenaer van Catwijck advocated a new regime that would provide better protection for victims. The idea of a no-fault liability was adopted from abroad (Saskatchewan (Canada), New Zealand and Scandinavia) and became an important issue for further discussion in the Dutch legal literature.

This lack of activity by the legislator, the development of road traffic accidents as a social problem and the 'pressure' from the doctrine to reform the system brought the Hoge Raad to a position in which it could legitimately stretch the limits of the existing liability system of article 185 WVW. The limits of its competence and the limits of the interpretation of the wording of article 185 formally prevented the Hoge Raad from going so far as to create a no-fault liability system. However, in fact it did so for children under fourteen years of age. Although the system for adult victims remained a strict liability system, even here article 185 WVW was stretched to its limits. One can even argue that, for this category of persons, the system is halfway to being a no-fault system, since, in most cases (*overmacht* being very difficult to establish), adult victims have at least half of their damage compensated.

Role of the Government's Commissioner/Chair of the Civil Chamber of the Hoge Raad Wouter Snijders is regarded as one of the most eminent, if not the most eminent, Dutch civil lawyer of his time. After having worked as a judge in the Court of First Instance in Rotterdam, he was appointed as an assistant to the so-called 'troika': three Government Commissioners (*Regeringscommissarissen*) who were working on the draft of the new BW, particularly Books 3, 5 and 6 on property law and the law of obligations. This 'troika' did not work very effectively, and in the 1970s Snijders was appointed as the only *Regeringscommissaris* for Books 3, 5 and 6 of the new BW. He stayed in office until the mid 1990s.

Also in the 1970s, Snijders was appointed judge in the chamber of the Hoge Raad. In the 1980s, he became chair of this civil chamber. Snijders's unsurpassed knowledge and overview of civil law matters probably made him the most influential and authoritative member of the civil law chamber. The combination of being Government Commissioner for the new BW and being chair of the Hoge Raad's civil chamber might have also made him the most powerful and influential lawyer in civil law matters for at least two decades.

It is not unlikely that Snijders was the main *autor intellectualis* of the case law the Hoge Raad developed as regards liability for damage caused in road traffic accidents. Whether this is indeed the case is hard to prove, because the Hoge Raad decides on a collective basis and gives just one decision. There are no individual opinions, as is the case in common law.

In a couple of landmark cases, the Hoge Raad mentioned a number of considerations for its case law: the personal interests of the victim (pedestrian and cyclist) to receive compensation rather easily; the social interest of proper victim protection; the vulnerability of pedestrian and cyclist in today's road traffic (especially the young pedestrian and cyclist); and the fact that the driver's, keeper's and owner's liability is compulsorily covered by liability insurance.

As Government Commissioner, Snijders was only responsible for the technical part of the work on the new BW. The Minister of Justice was, of course, responsible for the political aspects. Compensation for road traffic accidents was, no doubt, a politically sensitive issue in which the Commissioner could only make proposals as long as he was backed by the Minister. Hence the Memorandum on Traffic Liability, published in 1990, was written under the auspices of both the Commissioner and the Minister. It is not clear what Snijders personally considered the most desirable way to deal with liability for road traffic damage. However, it is obvious that the Hoge Raad, directed by Snijders, made the maximum possible use of the possibilities provided by the existing regime (article 185 WVW and article 6:101 BW). The reason for this will have certainly been a genuine desire to improve the position of road traffic victims as set out in the decisions. However, it might very well be that, at the back of their minds, the members of the Hoge Raad also wanted to put some pressure on the legislator to decide on a new statutory system or to compensate for the legislator's slowness.

Role of the legal authors During the 1960s, 1970s and 1980s, two authoritative lawyers led the discussion about the reform of the law on road traffic accidents: Auke Bloembergen, Professor of Civil Law at the Rijksuniversiteit Leiden and, from the late 1980s, member of the civil chamber of the Hoge Raad, and Otto van Wassenaer van Catwijck, Professor of Civil Law at the Vrije Universiteit in Amsterdam. In various publications, they continuously advocated a no-fault system for road-traffic accident victims.

Bloembergen's first proposal for a no-fault system (a system that would be additional to the existing social security payments) dates from 1965 (in an inaugural lecture).[102] Van Wassenaer van Catwijck presented a similar compensation system in 1977 (also in an inaugural lecture), and he elaborated his thoughts in a publication in 1989, as well as in his valedictory lecture in 1993.[103] Many other authors such as Salomons, Van

[102] A. R. Bloembergen, *Naar een nieuw ongevallenrecht* (Deventer: Kluwer Law International, 1965).

[103] A. J. O. Baron van Wassenaer van Catwijck, *Verkeersverzekering* (Alphen aan den Rijn: Tjeenk Willink, 1977); id., *Verkeersverzekering in Nederland: Is no-fault geschikt*

Dam, Hartlief and Tjittes joined the chorus, singing the praises of the no-fault system.[104] The dissenting opinions (such as from Kottenhagen and Kottenhagen-Edzes) came in the mid 1990s, at a time when a no-fault system was already disappearing from the political agenda.[105] Their plea concerned an improvement of the existing strict liability regime.

The case law of the Hoge Raad was generally warmly welcomed by the legal literature, which applauded the Hoge Raad's creativity. However, the authors did not regard this case law as the most ideal liability system, but considered it the best possible solution until such time as the legislator undertook to develop a new statutory liability, which should then preferably be a no-fault system.

The concerns about the Hoge Raad's case law were expressed by the drivers, and particularly by the liability insurers who saw their payments rise. However, there is no clear evidence available as regards the consequences of the Hoge Raad case law for the insurance business. The lobby position of insurers towards the Hoge Raad is non-existent, but they have, of course, lobbied the legislator. It is not unlikely that one of the delaying and complicating factors in the legislative process was overcoming the objections of the insurers. The insurers were not in favour of a first-party insurance system, and this may have been a reason for the delay in the legislative process. Although initially there might have been a preference for a first-party insurance system, the insurers would not have wanted to give the go-ahead for such a proposal.

Influence of international developments, particularly in France and Belgium In 1985, France enacted the *loi Badinter*, which embodied a new regime for compensation for damage caused by motor vehicles. Since the 1960s, the discussion for reform had been led by the godfather of French tort law, Professor André Tunc. In the *loi Badinter*, many of his ideas were recognisable, though at the same time different choices had been made by the legislator. The French legislation impressed the Dutch,

voor export naar Nederland? (Deventer: Kluwer Law International, 1989); ibid., *Naar een Europees verkeersschaderecht* (Deventer: Kluwer, 1993).

[104] R. A. Salomons, 'Verkeersverzekering', *VerzekeringsArchief* (1974), 197–202; C. C. van Dam, *Zorgvuldigheidsnorm en aansprakelijkheid* (Deventer: Kluwer Law International, 1989); T. Hartlief and R. P. J. L. Tjittes, *De invloed van verzekeringen op de civiele aansprakelijkheid* (Deventer: Kluwer Law International, 1990).

[105] R. J. P. Kottenhagen and P. A. Kottenhagen-Edzes, 'Eindelijk naar een nieuw verkeersongevallenrecht?', Nederlands Juristenblad (NJB) (1995), 1115–23; Van Dam, *Zorgvuldigheidsnorm en aansorakelijkheid*; Hartlief and Tjittes, *De invloed van verzekeringen op de civiele aansprakelijkheid.*

probably not only the legal writers (they still preferred a no-fault system, but the difference between that and the French 'nominal' liability system was relatively small), but also the judges in the Hoge Raad. Or was it pure coincidence that the Hoge Raad stepped up its efforts to limit the defences of article 185 WVW and article 6:101 BW as from the mid 1980s?

In 1995, Belgium enacted a system for compensation for damage caused by motor vehicles. This system deviated from liability and, in fact, adopted a new insurance system in which the liability insurer of the motor vehicle had a duty to compensate road-traffic accident victims, be it pedestrians, cyclists or passengers. The defences for the liability insurer were extremely limited. Belgium followed the French example in article 29 bis of the Act on Liability Insurance of Motor Vehicles (WAM)).

The Belgian legislator was inspired by the wish to improve the position of social security funds, rather than to protect victims of road accidents. A strict liability for owners and keepers of motor vehicles, combined with a right of recourse for healthcare and disability insurers, implies that a bigger part of social security expenses is shifted to liability insurers.[106] Unlike the French system, the obligation to compensate does not rest on the driver or keeper of the motor vehicle, but rests solely on the liability insurer of the motor vehicle that is involved in an accident.[107] Whereas the French approach implies an almost absolute liability system, Belgian law provides for an insurance system in which the liability insurer has an obligation to pay compensation for the damage suffered. This difference is, however, not a matter of principle. In hardly any other area of tort law are insurance and liability so closely connected as in the law regarding compensation for road accidents.

Although preparations for the Dutch bill on liability for road traffic accidents had already started in the early 1990s, the Belgian experience will certainly have fertilised the ground for the proposal of the Dutch legislator, containing a very strict liability system for damage caused by motor vehicles.

[106] H. Bocken and I. Geers, 'De vergoeding van letselschade en schade door overlijden bij verkeersongevallen', Tijdschrift voor privaatrecht (TPR) (1996), 1199–263; B. Tuerlinckx, 'Artikel 29bis W.A.M.-Wet: Toepassing in de praktijk na de wetswijziging van 13 april 1995', TPR (1996), 11–27.

[107] Another difference is that, in Belgium, pedestrians, cyclists and passengers have a right to compensation, unless the liability insurer can prove intentional conduct of the victim. The initial defence of inexcusable fault was abolished in 2000: see (the former version of) Belgian law in C. Von Bar, *The Common European Law of Torts* (Oxford: Oxford University Press, 2000), vol. II, no. 369.

3 General observations

Over the past 150 years, rules of strict liability have been enacted both for motor vehicles and trains. A stricter liability rule for trains was introduced in 1856 and for motor vehicles in 1924. In the course of time, these rules have been adapted slightly, but no major changes have been adopted, despite serious efforts in the area of liability for motor vehicles in the last part of the twentieth century.

A remarkable difference in application of both regimes is that the strict liability for motor vehicles only protects road users outside the vehicle: passengers have to rely on the general fault liability rule of article 6:162 BW. In railway accidents, the special liability regime protects passengers, whereas people outside the train have to rely on the general fault liability rule of article 6:162 BW. Hence, in road traffic accidents, the strict liability regime is based on the protection against the motor vehicle's *Betriebsgefahr*, whereas in railway accidents the focus has remained on the contractual relationship between the operator and the passenger.

In principle, both rules for road traffic accidents and for railway accidents, provide liability for damage caused, unless this liability is rebutted. For the keeper of a motor vehicle, the abundant case law has substantially reduced his possibilities of rebutting liability, and in some instances they are virtually abolished. The railway operator still has slightly better opportunities to rebut liability. Here, the case law (in a much smaller quantity) has been less active in applying the liability rules in a stricter way. This may be explained by the fact that, unlike in road traffic accidents, the rules for railway accidents are based on international treaties.

6

The development of traffic liability in Spain

ISABEL GONZÁLEZ PACANOWSKA

1 Introduction

1.a Fault liability as a basic principle of tort liability versus strict liability as the result of specific statutes

The keystone and starting point of the Spanish system of fault-based liability, article 1902 Código Civil 1889 (CC), reflects a general clause, according to which any kind of damage caused to another by a negligent or faulty act or omission is to be compensated.

Notwithstanding the indisputable influence of the French Civil Code, legal writing in the nineteenth century delivers a thorough definition of *quasi delito* as a 'wrongful action' that causes damage to another without intent, but as the result of carelessness (*descuido*), imprudence (*imprudencia*) or lack of adequate professional skills (*impericia*) for which 'any man' will be held responsible.[1] In addition, in the decisions of the civil division of the Tribunal Supremo (Supreme Court, hereinafter 'TS'), the general principle of fault as the necessary support for damages is anchored on *Leyes de Partida* (thirteenth century) (Partida 15, 7, 2–3).[2]

Strict liability, therefore, was treated as an exception – notwithstanding a few cases included in the Código Civil – and has developed outside the codified rules by way of specific statutes. Road traffic, nevertheless, waited until 1962 (coming into force in 1965), and trains have not been subject to any particular tort rules at all.

The fault requirement, however, has undergone, as in many other countries, steady erosion. The steps and turns of (civil) court law towards

[1] J. Escriche, *Diccionario razonado de legislación y jurisprudencia* (Madrid: Imprenta de Eduardo Cuesta, 1874), vol. II, *s.v.* '*cuasi-delito*' at p. 587, thus reflecting the three typical roman hypotheses of 'culpa'.

[2] STS 12 May 1891, *Colección Legislativa. Jurisprudencia Civil* no. 144: 'It is an unquestionable legal principle, admitted as such by Roman Law and by our national legislation (Partida 7, 15, 3) that (a person) who by his fault or negligence brings forth damage … is obliged to repair it or compensate for it.'

today's '*quasi*-strict' liability for dangerous activities and the technical devices used in the process are well known.[3] Scholars usually point out that the civil division of the TS moved from the traditional regime of fault rather late; the process towards a '"stricter' approach, despite a few forerunners, only began to take shape after the second half of the twentieth century. Most of the legal recourses applied therein, without forsaking fault, had quite an early start in damage caused by trains or, later on, in road accidents. Indeed, some of the most relevant decisions, considered to be the milestones of this evolution, deal with traffic. So, even before the law introducing strict liability for road injuries came into force, courts were not likely to leave the claimant without some sort of compensation – notwithstanding the ever-extending resort to 'contributory negligence' – unless proof of complete lack of negligence could be afforded by way of an act of God (*fuerza mayor*) or the sole fault of the victim (*culpa exclusiva de la víctima*). Damage caused by trains, on the other hand, was quite quickly treated as a risk internal to the functioning of the railway company. The fact that the defendant was either a private company – concessionaire of a public service – or, by the 1940s, a public body, seems to have favoured the judges' propensity not to leave death or personal injury unattended.

The so-called 'risk theory', along with *cuius commoda, eius incommoda*,[4] has been a favourite argument in case law, whilst the burden of proof of the appropriate standard of care falls upon the defendant, and compliance with (administrative or public) regulations will not exclude fault. Negligence (elevated to the heights of *culpa levissima*) is asserted when the accident can be described as the foreseeable result of the hazard inherent in motor-vehicle traffic or the 'exploitation' of the railways. A quite early reluctance to an analogous application of the 'strict liability' imposed upon the 'possessor' of an animal in article 1905 CC on the one hand, and the lack of a general provision in the Código Civil on which to build the owner's/keeper's liability for *fait des choses* on the other, has not restrained case law from attending to the demands of society and the pleas of scholarship *pro damnato*, at least when physical harm was at stake.

[3] See S. Cavanillas Múgica, *La transformación de la responsabilidad en la jurisprudencia* (Pamplona: Aranzadi, 1987), *passim*. See also L. Díez Picazo, *Derecho de daños* (Madrid: Civitas, 1999), pp. 118ff; M. Martín-Casals and J. Solé Feliu, 'Fault under Spanish Law', in P. Widmer (ed.), *Unification of Tort Law: Fault* (The Hague: Kluwer Law International, 2005), pp. 227ff.

[4] In particular if the victim is trying to reach the owner (of the motor vehicle) or the employer in a private or public company.

1.b Security standards and highway codes

The first 'general' laws on 'railway policing' (*Ley de policía de ferrocarriles*, 14 November 1855, amended by the *Ley de Policía de Ferrocarriles*, 23 November 1877) provided for vicarious liability of concessionaires and lessees in the case of damage caused by administrators, directors and other employees (article 14). This provision, together with others on security measures, such as barriers, fences, level-crossing guards or clearing-up duties in order to prevent fires, was to be frequently invoked in order to recover damages.

Regulations on the safety requirements of public road transportation that had been in force since 1858[5] were applied to motor vehicles by 1902 (*Reglamento* 12 April 1902). The *Reglamento* of 17 September 1900 introduced legal conditions for the maintenance of the roadworthiness of vehicles on public roads (such as a driving licence, regular maintenance, a maximum speed limit of 12 km/h in towns and the duty to slow down, or even stop, if there is reason to fear any kind of difficulty or accident: articles 5 and 11). Since 1918,[6] the Highway Code has stipulated that the driver must be, at all times, 'absolute master of the vehicle's motion' and must reduce speed and even stop whenever it seems necessary to preserve the safety of people or property.

This 'general' regulation of railways, safety rules and highway codes has, to some extent, played a relevant role in facilitating the compensation of primarily personal injuries. Firstly, it must be emphasised that it opened the door to the application of the Criminal Code provisions on liability and compensation within the criminal justice procedure, which brought procedural advantages and at the same time secured a decision on damages. An outstanding peculiarity of the Spanish codification of tort liability rules is that the first enactment of provisions on 'civil responsibility' did not wait for the Código Civil (1889), but was included in the (second) Criminal Code (1848),[7] and it was for the criminal court to

[5] RD 13 May 1858, *Reglamento para el servicio de los carruajes de conducción de viajeros*, in M. Alcubilla, *Diccionario razonado de la Administración española*, 3rd edn (Madrid: Administración Arco de Sta. María, 1892), vol. II, heading '*Carruajes públicos*'.

[6] *Reglamento para la circulación de vehículos con motor mecánico por las vías públicas de España*, article 17. *Reglamento*, 16 June 1926 (article 16), *Reglamento*, 17 July 1928 (article 15); *Código de la Circulación*, 25 September 1934 (article 17). The current *Ley*, 2 March 1990, on *Tráfico, Circulación de vehículos a motor y seguridad vial* still prescribes that drivers must be in a condition to control their vehicles at all times (article 11).

[7] Legal writers, and also the members of the Law Commission who prepared the Criminal Code, describe the section on 'civil' compensation as being the most advantageous for securing adequate recovery. As J. De Castro y Orozco and M. Ortiz de Zúñiga, *Código*

decide on damages accordingly (including instances of vicarious liability of employers) – unless the civil action had been reserved. If such was the case, the victim was then entitled to bring a claim for damages before the civil courts. This so-called 'civil liability' derived from crime has survived, basically for 'procedural economic' reasons, despite it being a source of confusion and being subject to severe criticism.[8]

Here it is important to stress that the broad description of imprudence (*delito imprudente*), which had been in the Criminal Code since 1848 and which encompassed 'simple imprudence in breach of regulations' as a criminal offence and 'simple imprudence' as *falta*,[9] allowed most traffic accidents with personal injuries to be labelled as some sort of criminal offence. Absence of 'acoustic signals', for instance, was 'reckless imprudence' according to the criminal division of the TS, and the

penal explicado (Granada: Manuel Sanz, 1848), vol. I, p. 233, explain, when the harm flowing from crime is of a moral nature or when it spreads to the victim's family, 'courts seldom give it heed and when they do are inclined to bestow but a meagre amount'. Article 123 Codígo Penal, 1848 (CP) even foresaw a 'future statute' by which the victim would have subsidiary recourse against the state, in case the defendant was insolvent. The law authors pointed out that such a 'beautiful theory' would encounter insuperable inconvenience (De Castro y Orozco and Ortiz de Zúñiga, *Código penal explicado*, p. 239); 'miracles are not to be expected', according to T. Mª. Vizmanos and C. Álvarez Martínez, *Comentarios al Código penal* (Madrid: J. González y A. Vicente, 1848), vol. I, p. 380. There were even less-refined precursors in the first Criminal Code in 1822; see articles 93 and 94 and refer to M. Roig Torres, *La Reparación del daño causado por el delito* (Valencia: Tirant lo Blanch, 2000), pp. 40–6.

8 See F. Pantaleón, 'Causalidad e imputacion objetiva', in *Comentario del Código civil* (Madrid: Ministerio de Justicia, 1991), vol. II, pp. 1973ff. Extensively, M. Izquierdo Tolsada, 'La responsabilidad civil en el proceso penal', in L. F. Reglero Campos (ed.), *Tratado de Responsabilidad Civil*, 3rd edn (Cizur Menor: Thomson Aranzadi, 2006), pp. 539ff.

9 'Regulations' is to be understood as any kind of provision dictated to prevent damage and common dangers, according to A. Groizard, *El Código penal de 1870 concordado y comentado* (Salamanca: Hijos de J. A. García, 1899), p. 398. The penalty for infringement is described as a 'legal warning for the ignorant and indolent' by De Castro y Orozco and Ortiz de Zúñiga, *Código penal explicado*, vol. I, p. 86. Not to abide by regulations is evident recklessness: Vizmanos and Alvarez Martínez, *Comentarios al Nuevo Código Penal*, vol. II, p. 528. Indeed, in the nineteenth century, decisions of the civil division on personal injuries caused by horse-drawn carriages were rare, whereas in the criminal division the breach of any kind of administrative norms of local authorities permitted not only the penalty, but also monetary compensation to the victim. See SSTS (criminal division) 16 November 1876, JC no. 3611; 19 March 1877, JC no. 3857; 20 January 1880, JC no. 5329; 19 December 1883, JC no. 7528; 27 March 1888, JC no. 253; 19 April 1892, JC no. 199; and 12 November 1904, JC no. 144. As for trains, article 21 of the *Ley de Policía de Ferrocarriles*, 23 November 1877 prescribed that the penalty of the Criminal Code for 'reckless imprudence' be applied to the person who, due to 'ignorance, imprudence, carelessness *or breach* of administrative laws or regulations, causes damage to trains or their surroundings that brings harm to people or property' (emphasis added).

tram company was liable for the damage caused to the carriage it ran into while the latter was overtaking an obstacle and got in the tram's way.[10] As Borrell Maciá wrote in 1942, referring to road traffic, many accidents for which the driver would perhaps not be held liable under the negligence rule of the Código Civil are pronounced a criminal offence in order to allow the victim to recover damages. If the law neglects its duty to protect citizens, 'the rules will be disregarded, but justice is saved'.[11] By the 1950s, this 'incrimination' of even *culpa levissima* in the field of traffic accidents and the 'compassionate' attitude of courts to victims seeking monetary compensation were thought best to be rechannelled instead into civil transactions by the introduction of compulsory insurance.[12]

As for the civil division of the TS, breach of such rules and regulations, considering their 'administrative' scope, was not construed as an instance of strict liability. Infringement, however, was used in courts' decisions up to the first third of the twentieth century to embody the requisite of *culpa*, but treated as a criterion for 'objective imputation' (*imputación objetiva*): it is not necessary to inquire how or why the breach arose. Therefore cases in which no compensation was granted at all, despite the existence of some sort of flaw, might be explained as falling out of the 'scope of protection' of the norm. Equally, it could have been that the breach itself had not played a part in the occurrence of the event or the harm, as happens when compliance with regulations could not have prevented the hazard,[13] or the

[10] STS 22 January 1896, JC no 67. For similar cases, see SSTS 3 April 1884, JC no. 7871; 14 February 1902, JC no. 78. Other decisions deal with defective chains or barriers contributing to harm at level crossings: SSTS 3 May 1875, JC no. 2761; 22 March 1899, JC no. 121. If regulations did not even require a guard, the officially appointed engineers in charge of technical aspects of the line could nevertheless be held responsible for 'recklessness': STS 22 January 1900, JC no. 39.

[11] A. Borrell Maciá, *Responsabilidades derivadas de culpa extracontractual civil* (Barcelona: Bosch Casa Editorial, 1942), p. 36. The work of E. Colom and F. Marimom, *Compendio Jurídico del accidente del automóvil* (Barcelona: Librería Bosch, 1933) refers to many of the cases decided by the criminal division of the TS; the authors point out (in vol. I, p. 102) that it is nearly impossible to run someone over without violation of an article on the very detailed and extensive regulations on road traffic. For an account of the decisions of the criminal division of the TS on road traffic and train accidents between 1930 and 1956, see J. Canals Martí, *Los accidentes de automóvil* (Barcelona: Bosch Casa Editorial, 1957). The so-called *numerus apertus* system of 'imprudencia punible' was suppressed by the Criminal Code of 1995.

[12] See A. Quintano Ripollés, *Derecho penal de la culpa (Imprudencia)* (Barcelona: Bosch Casa Editorial, 1958), pp. 365ff.

[13] As, for instance, in the STS 29 May 1915 *Colección Legislativa. Jurisprudencia Civil* no. 78: several bulls in panic running across the tracks on their way to a bullfight could hardly have been stopped, even if chains had been in place; or when the damage is due

accident or subsequent damage could be attributed to the victim's reckless carelessness.[14] If, indeed, the courts appreciate the absence of transgression and therefore of *culpa*, as is the case in most car accidents that reached the TS up to 1930, there is no liability.[15]

Notwithstanding some 'civil' decisions in which the breach of a legal duty was given as an alternative to fault as a source of liability, the weight attached to the former seems to have lessened as the domain of fault expanded.[16] In this process, two points must be highlighted.

The STS 20 December 1930[17] granted compensation to the widow and children of the victim, despite claims of very slow driving, on the basis that 'the concepts of fault and negligence of art. 1902 CC encompass such a wholesale or extensive range, that it is not possible to reduce or summarise their broad meaning into a closed set of rules ("*reglas precisas*")'; the standard of care is to be fixed, taking into account all the particular circumstances of 'persons, time and place', according to article 1104 CC, and the categories of negligence are not closed.

But even earlier, the STS 13 February 1928[18] delivered a judgment that was to turn into one of the most repeated case rules in the process of

to an external event, such as the unforeseeable collapse of a trench that someone else has built: STS 27 December 1923 *Colección Legislativa. Jurisprudencia Civil* no. 172.

[14] See SSTS 22 October 1864 *Colección Legislativa. Jurisprudencia Civil* no. 306; 12 June 1900 *Colección Legislativa. Jurisprudencia Civil* no. 14: the lack of chains was not proven to be the 'cause' of the accident; 27 December 1928 *Colección Legislativa. Jurisprudencia Civil* no. 167: despite the overcrowding on the train, the victim should not have travelled with his arm hanging out of the window, and the eventual amputation was due to his having sought advice from a *curandero* (quack doctor), instead of seeking proper medical treatment.

[15] The complete diligence of the driver and compliance with regulations were defence enough in the very few road traffic decisions that reached the civil division before 1930: SSTS 27 March 1909 *Colección Legislativa. Jurisprudencia Civil* no. 35; 27 October 1909 *Colección Legislativa. Jurisprudencia Civil* no. 35; 2 January 1914 *Colección Legislativa. Jurisprudencia Civil* no. 5; 13 June 1923 *Colección Legislativa. Jurisprudencia Civil* no. 92.

[16] STS 31 May 1910 *Colección Legislativa. Jurisprudencia Civil* no. 36, pp. 264–75: the obligations that flow from article 1902 CC must meet two necessary requirements: 'damage caused to another person, and an act or omission attributable to the tortfeasor due to his imprudence *or to the violation of regulations* enacted by public powers, of necessary observance' (emphasis added). On this evolution, see Cavanillas Múgica, *La transformación de la responsabilidad en la jurisprudencia*, pp. 42ff.

[17] *Colección Legislativa. Jurisprudencia Civil* 1930 no. 131.

[18] *Colección Legislativa. Jurisprudencia Civil* 1928 no. 63. The widow and children of one of the victims received 100,000 pesetas (approximately €600) plus damages for the loss of goods, which was a considerable sum at the time, taking into account that this was the average amount for death in the 1950s. The same idea is found in the STS 29 June 1932 *Colección Legislativa. Jurisprudencia Civil* no. 100, RJ 1932\1136, in a case of fire caused by a train and the destruction of crops on surrounding land: in spite of the 'formulary'

raising the standard of care, to be applied in many other fields: 'formulary' fulfilment of the indispensable regulations is not enough to elude liability. The defendant had tried to prove that the train crash that occurred on 22 January 1920 was fortuitous, bringing forth the briefs of 'official' inspectors, appointed by the public authorities, to sustain the evidence. According to the engineer's statements, the train was not overloaded and the mechanism of the locomotive was in good shape. The speed, however, was excessive and the bends of the railway line too sharp, but the night was cold and the frost had probably impaired the brakes. The engine driver could not have acted in any other way. The design of the line was known to have been the cause of previous accidents, and the line appeared to be cracked in some places; indeed, only a short time afterwards it had been improved. The court ruled that the accident was to be attributed to the negligence of the company, for not having taken whatever precautions seemed necessary in order to reduce the number of accidents, notwithstanding the strict observation of administrative regulations. Liability can derive from an omission: not having taken those precautionary measures that would have avoided the derailment.

It is difficult to say whether this decision can be related to the crisis the concessionaire railway system was manifesting, and to the fact that it coincided with a change in the attitude of public power towards the privileges and benefits awarded to private companies. Economic factors have been seen as the principal force of the discredit into which railway operations had fallen, notwithstanding the projects of reform and sterile 'patch measures' issued by successive *Ministros de Fomento* ever since the turn of the century. The path to wider public intervention and complete reform was initiated in 1922, with the creation of a public body (*Consejo Superior Ferroviario*), ancestor of RENFE (*Red Nacional de Ferrocarriles Españoles*) (1939 to 1940).[19] Rather, it seems to be an adequate and reasonable reaction to the deficiencies of safety prescriptions. Public supervision and official inspection were not enough to ensure the effectiveness of regulations. Some of them were not even considered to be appropriate or sufficient to attend to the increase of potential risk attached to activities that were becoming more prevalent in everyday life. In fact, a similar reasoning was being applied at the same time to accidents arising from

fulfilment of railway regulations, damage itself clearly demonstrates that the required security measures were imperfectly and negligently adopted. Reparation was absolutely necessary and unavoidable, on grounds of justice.

[19] The evolution is detailed by J. Bermejo Vera, *Régimen Jurídico del Ferrocarril en España (1844–1974), Estudio específico de Renfe* (Madrid: Tecnos, 1975), pp. 83, 94ff.

clearly unsatisfactory – but prior to this point 'approved' – electrical installations.[20]

Once the above-mentioned rule on 'formulary fulfilment' had been settled, it could easily be applied in lawsuits in which there did not really seem to be anything wrong or wanting in the measures that had, in fact, been taken. Courts, nevertheless, only had to leave out the word 'formulary' and conclude that damage itself is the best proof that sufficient care had not been exerted to avoid it; fulfilment of regulations does not mean adequate standard of care (*agotamiento de la diligencia*).[21] The rule has preserved its influence.

1.c Tort and contract

The previous existence of a contract has in no way hindered the recourse to tort actions, as far as personal injuries are concerned. Spanish case law does not apply a rule of *non cumul,* and claims framed in tort will not be rejected just because the damage has occurred when fulfilling contractual obligations. The case rules in this matter are far from clear, as they involve, among others, procedural questions. The so-called 'principle of unity of civil fault', however, allows the general provisions of the Código Civil on contractual liability, in particular those on standard of care (article 1104) or the extent of recoverable damages (articles 1106 and 1107), to be used when dealing with tort. Tort liability will not be excluded if the damage does not pertain to the 'rigorous scope of the agreement'; yet the boundaries are uncertain. Claimants may even present both actions alternately or as a subsidiary remedy.[22]

Recourse to contract could be thought of as advantageous, as the codified rules on liability of the carrier do, indeed, provide for quite strict liability, yet little attention is given to personal injuries. The carrier suffers

[20] A first step in this direction can be seen in the STS 21 December 1910: Cavanillas Múgica, *La transformación de la responsabilidad en la jurisprudencia*, p. 48; but decisive is the STS 24 February 1928 *Colección Legislativa. Jurisprudencia Civil* no. 114, pp. 686–703, taking into account that recent regulations had prescribed a higher standard by introducing further security duties.

[21] See SSTS 24 March 1953 (RJ 1953\913); 25 March 1954 (RJ 1954\1001).

[22] See M. Martín-Casals, J. Solé Feliú and J. Seuba Torreblanca, 'Compensation in the Spanish Health Care Sector', in J. Dute, M. Faure and H. Koziol (eds.), *No Fault Compensation in the Health Care Sector* (Wien and New York, NY: Springer, 2004), pp. 337ff. See also, for instance, R. De Ángel Yagüez, *Tratado de responsabilidad civil* (Madrid: Civitas, 1993), p. 13ff. A detailed analysis of case law on the subject is in S. Cavanillas Múgica and I. Tapia Fernández, *La concurrencia de responsabilidad contractual y extracontractual* (Madrid: Centro de Estudios Ramón Areces, 1992), pp. 87ff.

the burden of proof of *force majeure* (*caso fortuito o fuerza mayor*) in order to escape liability for the loss of, or damage to, carried goods.[23] Legal writing rejected analogous application of these prescriptions to the transportation of persons.[24] Physical damage is to be resolved by the general provisions on contractual liability based on fault. From this point of view, transportation is placed in the Código Civil as a variety of *locatio operis*, but none of the articles on the subject – of which there are only three – refers to the transportation of persons. The issue, *ergo*, is to be tackled by the general principles on contractual obligations. Fault, according to such criteria, is presumed (articles 1182 and 1184 CC) if the result at which the contract aims is not obtained by the debtor.[25] Exemption clauses, long before the legislation on abusive contract terms, were deemed immoral, and the TS declared them void even in the case of a freely provided transportation service.[26]

A detailed look at claims arising from road traffic accidents, however, shows that passengers seek to recover physical damage (only or alternately) in tort, whilst the codified rules on contractual liability of the carrier are called in aid alone or alongside tort rules, in the case of ruined goods.[27] The reasons for this appear to be numerous.

First, damage caused to persons, notwithstanding the contractual relationship, is one of the typical events to be excluded from the 'rigorous

[23] Article 1602 CC. Transportation contract is the third section of contracts on 'work and services' and includes three articles that only deal with goods. Public transportation falls under the provisions of the Commercial Code 1829 (article 208 Código de Comercio 1829 (CCM); articles 361–362 *CCm* 1885). This regulation is to be completed with the specific regulations on the activity concerned.

[24] Instead of many, see J. Garrigues, *Curso de Derecho mercantil* (Madrid: S. Aguirre Imprenta, 1940), vol. II, p. 332.

[25] SSTS 30 April 1959 (RJ 1959\1981); 31 May 1985 (RJ 1985\2835): an outstanding decision in which the TS declares the 'primary contractual obligation' to be the transportation of passengers 'safely' from the beginning to the end of the journey; the carrier is therefore liable (fault presumed) for any kind of bodily harm inflicted, unless he proves *caso fortuito* or *fuerza mayor*.

[26] STS 4 July 1953 *Colección Legislativa. Jurisprudencia Civil* no. 87. See T. Puente Muñoz, 'El transporte no oneroso de personas' (1965) *Revista de Derecho Español y Americano* 85; F. M. Sánchez Gamborino, *Doctrina Jurisprudencial sobre el contrato de transporte terrestre* (Madrid: Aguilar, 1957), p. 117.

[27] Under the Commercial Code 1829, damage to carried goods was to be compensated according to the provisions of the railway regulations (*Reglamento* 8 July 1859), with preference for the codified rules: SSTS 4 April 1873 *Colección Legislativa. Jurisprudencia Civil* no. 147; 24 October 1876 *Colección Legislativa. Jurisprudencia Civil* no. 313; 28 October 1876 *Colección Legislativa. Jurisprudencia Civil* no. 319; 11 December 1878 *Colección Legislativa. Jurisprudencia Civil* no. 334. The railway company is only exonerated if it can prove *casus*; compensation is not limited to the value of the deteriorated or

scope of the agreement'. It is frequently described as encompassing not only breach of contract, but at the same time transgression of the general duty *neminen laedere*.[28] The general evolution of tort in the 'strict' direction determines that the contract/tort dilemma is not decisive of the final outcome,[29] the basic difference being the wide range of limitation periods: fifteen years for contract versus one year for tort (articles 1964 and 1968.2° CC). The so-called *pro damnato* principle, liberally applied, means, in this context, that courts may be perfectly willing to apply the law of contract if it enables them to surmount an otherwise very short limitation period,[30] or on the contrary, they are not reluctant to resort to tort if the damage can be covered by insurance.[31]

Secondly, case law did not develop an extensive construction of 'security' contractual obligations, as far as passenger safety is concerned. It could be said that such duties were covertly taken into account under tort law, as courts were less inclined to admit the defence of a fortuitous event in a period when 'strict' decisions were still beginning to find their way. In fact, a difference can be traced in the treatment of passengers, as opposed to other claimants, received for harm suffered on the railway up to the 1930s (see below, Section 2.b). As for road traffic, the accident caused by the precarious state of a bus determined the liability of the owners, despite the employee having tried his best to make the defective brakes work in the STS 29 March 1933. The claim was based on the tort rules of liability for others that provide for a presumption of fault (article 1903 CC), and the driver had not even been sued. The court ruled the liability of the employer based not only on *culpa in eligendo* (fault in choosing its employees), but also on the duty of *vigilando*, now referred to

lost goods, but reaches loss of gain if proved. Since the coming into force of the current Commercial Code 1885, the 'police' railway law has complemented the prescriptions of the Commercial Code: SSTS 2 March 1892 *Colección Legislativa. Jurisprudencia Civil* no. 66. Proof of *casus* is rigorous; a fire on a train due to an unknown cause is not fortuitous: STS 26 March 1928 *Colección Legislativa. Jurisprudencia Civil* no. 103; 2 January 1945 *Colección Legislativa. Jurisprudencia Civil* no. 1. For the current doctrine, see STS 7 June 1991 (RJ 1991\4426), 12 September 2002 (RJ 2002\7828), among many others.

[28] See, on tort remedies for injury to passengers, F. Soto Nieto, 'Conjunción de responsabilidades contractual y aquiliana. Problemática frente al sistema objetivista incorporado a la Ley sobre uso y circulación de vehículos a motor' (1970) *Revista de Derecho de la Circulación* (RDCirculación) 16ff. For further references, see M. Yzquierdo Tolsada, *Sistema de responsabilidad civil contractual y extracontractual* (Madrid: Dykinson, 2001), pp. 95ff.

[29] See STS 19 February 1987 (RJ 1987\719).

[30] STS 31 May 1985 (RJ 1985\2835). For an opposing view: SSTS 18 October 1995 (RJ 1995\7544); 3 December 2001 (RJ 2001\9856).

[31] STS 10 June 1991 (RJ 1991\4434).

as supervising *cosas* (things): 'deficient vigilance or a bad choice can never be the rational justification to contend the right of another to not suffer any harm'.[32] In the following years, the accidental breakdown of a bus may not exclude liability,[33] albeit the defence was still admitted in damage caused to third persons until the 1960s (see below, Section 3.b).

Scholars, very critical of the courts' swinging between tort and contract, contend that security duties flow freely from article 1258 CC.[34] They are consistent with the 'nature' of the carrier's obligation as one of 'result', as opposed to one of 'means'.[35] This approach, of course, has not been totally neglected.[36] Indeed, recent decisions convey extensive judgments on the 'imperative contractual duty' to take care of passengers' bodily welfare, emphasising in particular that it is by no means to be limited to the period of effective transportation. Safety measures are to be taken not only with respect to the vehicle itself,[37] but on all the surrounding premises from the moment the claimant crosses the station's threshold, even before the purchase of the ticket, and certainly on his way to the train.[38]

[32] RJ 1933\1587. Another reason for deciding in tort refers to the assessment of damage. At this time, physical damage or death was fixed by taking into account the loss of future earnings. The amputation suffered by a young girl was to be compensated, as it was 'bound to reduce her capacity for all kinds of work and at the same time placed her in an inferior position to manage life's difficulties, in comparison with other women of her age, education and social standing'.

[33] It still does in the STS 3 May 1929 *Colección Legislativa. Jurisprudencia Civil* no. 10, but not if the bus driver's licence only enables him to drive smaller vehicles: STS 22 October 1948 *Colección Legislativa. Jurisprudencia Civil* no. 11; or even if there is no breach of regulations: STS 24 March 1953 *Colección Legislativa. Jurisprudencia Civil* no. 28.

[34] Contracts require not only what their terms express, but also all the consequences prescribed by law, usage or good faith. See the acute observations of Díez Picazo, *Derecho de daños*, pp. 262ff.

[35] Regarding the transportation of persons, see, extensively, T. Hualde Manso, *El transporte de viajeros por carretera* (Pamplona: Aranzadi, 1995), pp. 137ff.; N. Álvarez Lata, 'La responsabilidad civil por actividades empresariales en sectores de riesgo', in Reglero Campos (ed.), *Tratado de Responsabilidad Civil*, p. 1978.

[36] See, for instance, STS 30 April 1959 (RJ 1959\1981): a bus accident with multiple casualties.

[37] STS 6 November 2003 (RJ 2003\8270): a train's doors should not be able to be forced open by passengers when the train is in motion. As before, one of the reasons for the contractual approach was the time that had elapsed since the accident: seven years. On the other hand, although damages were reduced by 50 per cent for the contributory negligence of the victim, who had tried to board a moving train, the decision seems to imply that yesterday's deficiencies are to be judged by today's standards. See A. Fernández Crende, 'Pasajeros al tren' (2004) 3 *InDret* wp no. 240 (available at www.indret.com (last accessed 28 May 2009)).

[38] STS 23 December 2004 (RJ 2005\82): the escalator was not adequate for the handicapped passenger and the lift was out of order. Significant is STS 20 December 2004 (RJ 2004\8132): a young mother of two was assaulted and killed by a stranger in a tube station: "[*T*]*he*

Apart from these two reasons, compulsory insurance – indeed, a non-fault compensation scheme – had, quite early on, played an important part in damage recovery. In 1928, a first-party compulsory accident insurance for train passengers – by 1942 extended to public road transportation – was introduced to cover personal injuries, the premium being included in the price of the ticket.[39] A public body (*Comisaría del Seguro Obligatorio*) was in charge of awarding compensation for bodily harm according to a fixed valuation system, whatever the cause of the accident, though *force majeure*, such as war, riot or criminal attack, was expressly included. Fault of the victim was at first considered rather widely as a reason to reject the allowance, but this has gradually changed over time and, currently, compensation is denied only if the harmful event is due to the intent of the victim or his/her being under the influence of alcohol, drugs or similar. Courts first,[40] and legislature later, stipulate that the existence of this SOV, or the fact that the victim is entitled to or has already received pecuniary assistance from the *Comisaría*, does not interfere in the least with the eventual claim filed in tort. Nor do either of these lessen the indemnity due by whoever (employer/employee or third person) is held responsible.[41]

Since compulsory insurance for motor vehicles (including occupants) in respect of third-party risks was introduced (1962 to 1965), courts, notwithstanding contrary pronouncements, have clarified that the victim can obtain compensation from both sources simultaneously, if the event happens to fall under the respective requirements of each type of insurance. Of course, sometimes only one of them is available, so the judge may

indemnity of passengers must be preserved from the moment they enter the defendant's premises. Delinquency of this kind was increasing and the defendant knew it; the serious omission of safety measures is to be borne by the train company, *eius commoda*'.

[39] RD 13 October 1928, consolidated text 26 July 1929; amended by *Ley* 26 September 1941 (extending the *seguro obligatorio de viajeros* (SOV) to public transportation by road), *Decretos* 8 May 1942, 6 March 1969. Currently the RD 1575/1989, 22 December 1989, BOE no. 311, 28 December 1989, only denies compensation if the accident has been caused by the victim's intent or under the influence of alcohol, drugs or similar (article 9). Cover was at first limited to harm suffered inside the carriage, and currently includes entering or alighting and loading or unloading luggage directly from the vehicle.

[40] STS 19 February 1945 *Colección Legislativa. Jurisprudencia Civil* no. 69.

[41] *Decreto* 46/69, 6 March 1969, article 4. The *Comisaria* had no reimbursement actions against the responsible agent (article 5). Since the RD 22 December 1989, the SOV has been a private insurance 'for accidents'; the carrier is obliged to have a policy in which the passenger is the insured person. A public body (*Consorcio de compensacion de seguros*) will pay if the carrier does not have a policy in force. Article 2 still prescribes that the SOV should not absolve the transportation company, drivers or third persons of their own civil liability for the transportation, nor is the amount of their responsibility reduced by the SOV contribution.

deny SOV whilst admitting liability and coverage by the third-party compulsory insurance according to statute, or, vice versa, decline the latter and favour the former.[42]

2 Railway liability

2.a *The principles of railway liability*

Spanish tort law is divided into four different branches and corresponding jurisdictions.[43] Public bodies in particular are subject to strict liability, and the basic idea that harm suffered as a result of the 'normal or abnormal' performance of public services is to be compensated.[44]

Trains in Spain have not always been directly under public ownership. The first comprehensive train legislation of 3 June 1855 organised a concessionary system, granted by law, in which private companies, as 'concessionaries', were in charge under public supervision, and all premises were to revert to the state within ninety-nine years.[45] From 1924 onwards, however, the 'concessionaire system', with some exceptions, shifted to the procedure that was definitively established in 1941[46] with the creation

[42] See F. Reglero Campos, *Accidents de circulación: Responsabilidad civil y seguro* (Cizur Menor: Thomson Aranzadi, 2004), pp. 663ff. SAP Alava 15 March 2005 (JUR 2005/201150); SAP Granada 21 June 2005 (JUR 200/38740); SAP Zaragoza 5 September 2005 (JUR 2005/220190); SAP Santander 24 October 2005 (AC 2005/2059).

[43] For an overview, see P. Salvador and B. Arquillo 'El Derecho español de daños hoy: Características diferenciales', in J. M. Gonzalez Porras and F. P. Mendez (eds.), *Libro Homenaje al Prof. M. Albaladejo García* (Murcia: Colegio Oficial de Registradores de la Propiedad y Mercantiles de España, Servicio de Publicaciones de la Universidad de Murcia, 2004), pp. 4497ff.

[44] For a thorough, extensive and critical treatment of current thinking on the liability of public bodies, see O. Mir Puigpelat, *La responsabilidad patrimonial de la Admnistración. Hacia un nuevo sistema* (Madrid: Civitas, 2002), *passim*; J. M. Busto Lago, 'La responsabilidad civil de las Administraciones Públicas', in Reglero Campos (ed.), *Tratado de Responsabilidad Civil*, pp. 1710ff.

[45] The first line was opened on 23 August 1843. It was 28 km long, running between Barcelona and Mataró, and was not available for public use until 1848. The second line, 49 km long, running between Madrid and Aranjuez, was commissioned in 1845. The legislature was forced to enact railway activities. The network expanded and by 1908 more than 14,000 km had been built. See M. Gómez González, *s.v. Ferrocarriles*, in *Enciclopedia Jurídica Española*, (Barcelona: Seix, 1910), vol. XVI. For a description of the concessionary system and the privileges granted by statute for the benefit of private enterprises, assuming the reversion of all railways into public hands, see Bermejo Vera, *Régimen Jurídico del Ferrocarril en España (1844–1974)*, pp. 47, 66, 74ff.

[46] *Ley de Bases de Ordenación ferroviaria y de los Transportes por Carretera*, 24 January 1941. See the detailed treatment of the legal and economic grounds for the nationalisation of

of RENFE, the national public railway network. Things have recently changed, and the new legislation, in force since 1 January 2005, provides for a free competition system, in which the transportation company is obliged to have insurance covering its civil liability for personal and property damage to passengers or third parties.[47]

For as long as trains have been in private hands, liability has been decided, quite naturally, according to the codified rules on tortious conduct. Public ownership since 1941 has not changed this state of affairs. Notwithstanding the different rules and procedures (*jurisdicción contencioso-administrativa*) for public bodies, claims have continued to be filed before the civil jurisdiction, and civil judges will ignore the law on the tort liability of the public administration. This requires further explanation.

Statute described RENFE as a public body, but prescribed that it worked as a 'commercial company' and, in this respect, was subject to private law and civil jurisdiction.[48] Contractual relations regarding goods or persons were, beyond doubt, subject to private law.[49] Public lawyers and even the Council of State, however, contended that, at least since the law on strict liability for damage flowing from the 'normal or abnormal' performance of public services came into force,[50] tort claims addressed what is indisputably a public service and should therefore be governed by the corresponding norms. The rules on the liability of public bodies are supposed to have greater 'guarantee' capacity, as they provide for strict liability

the railways in Bermejo Vera, *Régimen jurídico del ferrocarril en España (1844–1874)*, pp. 160ff. The concessionaire system did not disappear entirely, as it was used for the exploitation of the so-called 'narrow' lines (*Ferrrocarril de Vía Estrecha* – FEVE).

47 Currently, *Ley del Sector Ferroviario*, *Ley* 39/2003, 17 November 2003 (BOE no. 276, 18 November 2003). *Reglamento del sector ferroviario*, RD 2387/2004, 30 December 2004 (BOE no. 315, 31 December 2004). A public body is in charge of the underlying structure, but private transportation companies may compete freely, subject to a previous licence and control of security standards, among other requirements. As for the compulsory insurance, see article 48 *Ley* 39/2003, article 63 RD 2387/2004. All Renfe's belongings have been transferred to the new, public state-owned company *Renfe-Operadora* (RD 2396/2004, 30 December 2004).

48 *Estatuto de la Red Nacional de Ferrocarriles Españoles*, D. 2170/1964, 23 July 1964. *Ley* 16/1987, 30 July 1987, *de Ordenación de los Transportes Terrestres*, article 175.1. According to the *Ley* 6/1997, 14 April 1997: 'state commercial societies are governed entirely … by private law, except in the areas related to budget, accounting or financial control'. 'They are subject to the jurisdiction of civil courts' (Additional Provision 12). See P. Salvador Coderch and C. Gómez Ligüerre, 'Trains' (2000) 1 *InDret* 7.

49 Bermejo Vera, *Régimen jurídico del ferrocarril en España (1844–1874)*, pp. 313ff.

50 *Ley de Expropiación forzosa*, 16 December 1954. Currently *Ley* 30/1992, 26 November 1992, *de Régimen Jurídico de las Administraciones Públicas y del Procedimiento Administrativo Cómun*, as amended by *Ley* 4/1999.

instead of fault, and are to be judged by administrative jurisdiction.[51] The civil courts, as in other fields, took little notice of the censure when a private person had been harmed; this may have been thought reasonable, taking into account the legal and academic uncertainties and the *vis attractiva* or, in other words, the legal competence of the civil jurisdiction to decide on whatever matters are not clearly attributed elsewhere.[52] Therefore, claims for damages have not been rejected on the grounds of the so-called *incompetencia de jurisdicción*. Even the administrative jurisdiction added to the confusion, as the STS 16 January 1991 (*Sala 3ª*) solemnly declared that train accidents (a level-crossing case) are to be brought before the 'civil jurisdiction'.[53] Public legal writers renewed their disagreement: understandable as it may be for civil courts to deny their own jurisdiction in such disputes, it is unjustifiable for administrative courts to relinquish it.[54]

Subsequent reform of the law (1992)[55] seemed to have settled the matter in favour of the administrative courts, and many decisions were issued accordingly. This did not prevent civil judges from ascertaining their own competence. Puzzled claimants were threatened by what has been described as 'trekking around' from one jurisdiction to another. The question was to be definitively answered by the specific Chamber of the Supreme Court in 2001:[56] the liability of RENFE, as an enterprise that belongs to the public administration, is to be submitted to the administrative courts (*jurisdicción contencioso-administrativa*), and the corresponding specific rules on strict liability are to be applied. Yet this was not the final decision, because the TS, at the same time, maintained that if

[51] The debate is summarised by F. Pantaleón, *Responsabilidad civil: conflictos de jurisdicción* (Madrid: Tecnos, 1985), pp. 80ff.; G. García Álvarez, 'Sobre la responsabilidad extracontractual de Renfe' (1999) 74 *Revista Española de Derecho Admnistrativo* 281.

[52] Pantaleon, *Responsabilidad civil*, p. 118, reports the STS 2 October 1969 (RJ 1949\4474) as being the first one of the civil chamber to decide and justify its own jurisdiction over a claim against the public administration after the new legislation; the defendant was a concessionaire (*Tranvías Eléctricos de Granada*). The main reasons are to avoid splitting facts between different jurisdictions and contradictory decisions.

[53] RJ 1991\397.

[54] García Álvarez, 'Sobre la responsabilidad extracontractual de Renfe', 281, at 294.

[55] *Ley* 30/1992, as amended by *Ley* 4/1999. As for the proceedings related to claims against the public administration: RD 429/1993, 26 March 1993. *Ley Orgánica del Poder Judicial* (LOPJ), as amended by *Ley Orgánica* 6/1998, 12 July 1998. *Ley de la Jurisdicción Contensioso-administrativa*, 13 July 1998. See Busto Lago, 'La responsabilidad civil de las Admnistraciones públicas', p. 1711.

[56] *Auto de la Sala Especial de Conflictos de Competencia del Tribunal Supremo*, 27 December 2001 (RJ 2002\4086); *Auto*, 21 October 2002.

the claimant sues 'RENFE and its (private) insurance company simultaneously', competence reverts to the civil courts.[57]

Criticisms poured in from all sides. Some writers argued in favour of the traditional application of private tort-law rules,[58] while administrative lawyers stressed that, in any case, the 'objective' rules of liability must be applied to the public administration. Furthermore, a law reform was suggested in order to provide for the possibility of suing a public body and its private insurance company together in the administrative courts.[59] The legislature, in yet a further reform, has paid heed to the latter.[60] So, by now, notwithstanding many questionable points, the liability of state-owned public transportation companies is definitely 'strict'.[61] Perhaps a little too late, RENFE's monopoly in the exploitation of the railways has come to an end.

Despite the important differences in procedural rules and material law, the switch towards a strict liability system will probably not result in a great difference from the victim's point of view and the probability of compensation.[62] Civil courts have been, and are, quite strict with damage flowing from railways at any rate. Recovery of damages does not depend on the fault of railway personnel directly involved in the accident; the 'objective' responsibility of the public administration, on the other hand, is developing, in legal writing and case law, its own ways of keeping the floodgates shut.[63]

[57] The general law on insurance contract, *Ley* 50/1980, 8 October 1980, *del Contrato de Seguro*, provides the victim with a direct action against the insurance company to recover damages: article 76.

[58] See C. Gómez Ligüerre, 'Cambio de vía' (2000) *InDret* wp no. 109; id., 'Dos veces en la misma piedra' (2003) 1 *InDret* wp no. 125; id., 'Paso a nivel' (2003) 3 *InDret* wp no. 152.

[59] O. Mir Puigpelat, 'La jurisdicción competente en materia de responsabilidad patrimonial de la Administración: una polémica que no cesa' (2003) 3 *InDret* wp no. 151; for further references on the discussion these decisions promoted, see Bustos Lago, 'La responsabilidad civil de las administraciones públicas', pp. 1788ff.

[60] *Ley Orgánica* 19/2003, 22 December 2003 amended the LOPJ (article 9.4º). See C. Gómez Ligüerre, S. Ramos González and A. Luna Yerga, 'Todos a una' (2004) 1 *InDret* wp no. 189; Busto Lago, 'La responsabilidad civil de las administraciones públicas', pp. 1786ff.

[61] It may be confusing, but the liability of 'concessionaires' of public services, including transportation, is currently subject to private law rules and civil jurisdiction, unless damage flows from requirements of the public administration: *Texto refundido Ley de Contratos de las Administraciones Públicas*, article 97. See, accurately, Bustos Lago, 'La responsabilidad civil de las administraciones públicas', pp. 1737ff.

[62] As Pantaleón foretold, considering the STS 3 December 1983. See *Responsabilidad civil: Conflictos de Jurisdicción*, p. 86.

[63] See Mir Puigpelat, *La responsabilidad patrimonial de la Administración*, pp. 153ff.; Bustos Lago, 'La responsabilidad civil de las administraciones públicas', pp. 1751ff.

2.b The evolution of the fault requirement

Case law suggests that fault liability rules were not applied or understood in the same way in claims by passengers and claims by those not on the trains. The gap, however, is far from being wide or deep. The issues, focusing on the concept and proof of fault and the causation link, will soon be treated in a similar way. Up until about 1930, passengers should have been well looked after, whether on the train or walking around the station, whereas pedestrians, carts or cars at level crossings were to take care of themselves. It may be, as suggested above (see Section 1.c), that the court was deciding the tort action with contract tools;[64] harm suffered by occupants could be clearly attributed to an infringement of duties imposed by railway regulations. The differences, however, blend into each other.

2.c Claims by passengers

As to the way rules were applied, it is quite obvious that anything to do with not meeting the legal technical requirements, the infringement of safety regulations, the lack of track repairs[65] or even the accidental failure of braking or steering devices[66] suffice to fulfil the 'fault' condition. One of the first decisions in this trend, STS 21 October 1882,[67] deals not with a train but a horse-drawn carriage: the brakes were just not strong enough to reduce the speed and that was the cause of the collision.

The defendant's contribution, it can be said, must be related to things that the train company itself could and should be keeping under control: engines, carriages, tracks or even the station premises, as when a passenger fell down on a pitch-dark platform and did not receive any help because there was nobody around to help him.[68] If the accident is

[64] Even if in STS 27 June 1894 *Colección Legislativa. Jurisprudencia Civil* no. 102, the court stresses that if the claimant is entitled to damages it is not as a consequence of a breach of the transportation contract, but probably because the train company had set up its defence on the basis that the claimant had not proven that he was in possession of a ticket.

[65] STS 27 June 1894 *Colección Legislativa. Jurisprudencia Civil* no. 102. STS 15 January 1902 *Colección Legislativa. Jurisprudencia Civil* no. 15: the train crash was deemed to have been caused by the poor state of the tracks, in spite of statements to the contrary from the inspectors and bad weather. There was negligence because there is a duty to keep the line in good condition in order to make transit easy and secure.

[66] STS 22 December 1902 *Colección Legislativa. Jurisprudencia Civil* no. 158: considering legal duties to supervise and exert constant control, repairing or replacing whatever is necessary.

[67] *Colección Legislativa. Jurisprudencia Civil* 1882 no. 316.

[68] STS 10 October 1889 *Colección Legislativa. Jurisprudencia Civil* no. 70. The STS 7 March 1871 (Criminal Chamber, JC no. 198) describes the omission of precautionary measures that could have prevented misfortune to passengers as 'reckless imprudence'.

caused by an external event, the claim is rejected.[69] On the other hand, passengers must also pay attention to safety regulations, and if they choose to ride on the open platform of a tram, they run the risk of falling off if they do not hang on tightly on a bend;[70] or are themselves to blame for injuries or death if they jump off a carriage while it is still in motion.[71] In all these cases, the victim has brought about his own injury, and the driver's behaviour is said to be 'irreproachable'. The standard of care of the former, however, does not mirror that imposed on *per se* dangerous activities, which is to be placed above the 'formulary' compliance with regulations.

2.d Other claims

Level-crossing cases provide many decisions in which the fault requirement is also shown by the infringement of security regulations or safety measures.[72] The STS 5 December 1927[73] is a good example: the guard had been on strike for a couple of days and the train was late. The company was held responsible, not only because its employee allowed the train to run outside official hours, but because it should also have supplied someone else to look after the chains. The claimant, therefore, will have to prove that the company did something wrong. Although judges tend to be stricter than official inspectors in deciding if compliance with regulations exists, there is no blame if the victim knew the existing crossing to be 'abusive', even if it was commonly used.[74] At the same time, breach is not decisive, and contrary proof is loosely admitted. As has been pointed out with reference to these decisions, courts used infringement as a prima facie presumption of negligence, subject to rebuttal.[75] Despite a lack of barriers, if the train was travelling very slowly[76] or could be seen straight

[69] STS 27 December 1923 *Colección Legislativa. Jurisprudencia Civil* no. 172.

[70] STS 22 December 1905 *Colección Legislativa. Jurisprudencia Civil* no. 157, 'a breach of statutory duties has not been proven', and perhaps, considering the circumstances, *volenti non fit iniuria*.

[71] STS 23 June 1924 *Colección Legislativa. Jurisprudencia Civil* no. 163.

[72] SSTS (Criminal Chamber) 3 May 1875, JC no. 2761; 22 March 1899, JC no. 62; 4 July 1900, JC No. 7; SSTS (Civil Chamber) 16 May 1893 *Colección Legislativa. Jurisprudencia Civil* no. 175; 21 October 1910 *Colección Legislativa. Jurisprudencia Civil* no. 1.

[73] *Colección Legislativa. Jurisprudencia Civil* 1927 no.14.

[74] STS 27 October 1931 *Colección Legislativa. Jurisprudencia Civil* no. 181.

[75] B. Perez González and J. Alguer, 'Anotaciones', in L. Enneccerus, T. Kipp and M. Wolff, *Tratado de Derecho Civil* (Barcelona: Bosch, 1935), p. vol. II, 625; yet case law, they add, has not established a clear rule on this matter.

[76] STS 12 June 1900 *Colección Legislativa. Jurisprudencia Civil* no. 14.

ahead from far away and heard whistling,[77] it could well have been the victim who did not stop and look carefully enough, even if the engine driver did not seem to be looking carefully either.

As for damage caused to surrounding land by fires caused by the engines, this seemed to receive a friendly start in STS 4 December 1858:[78] the train company was liable for negligent drivers who left the ashtrays open. Soon after, the STS 30 May 1865 would step back into the realms of fault: the claimant must prove the careless act of the engine driver, even if there is no doubt that the fire started as the train was travelling.[79] These decisions have been quoted to suggest that, in Spain, as in other countries, industrial and technical progress was being thus promoted, underlining the fact that locomotives could not work in any other way.[80] Whereas avoidable harm, such as the defective construction of the line, leading to the narrowing of the watercourse, is to be compensated and removed by the actual concessionaire, even if he did not build it himself; the subsequent flooding of adjacent estates as soon as it rained is to be imputed to fault when the 'proprietor of a defective thing allows it to be a source of damage to third persons, by omitting to repair it or to apply adequate measures in order to avoid harm'.[81] By 1932, however, the standard of care was also raised above regulation requirements; the standards on keeping the nearby surroundings free from dried-up vegetation in order to prevent fires were not really being observed, contrary to 'official' inspectors' reports.[82]

[77] SSTS 7 March 1902 *Colección Legislativa. Jurisprudencia Civil* no. 67; 6 January 1936 *Colección Legislativa. Jurisprudencia Civil* no. 18; or the tram was hooting: SSTS 23 December 1905 *Colección Legislativa. Jurisprudencia Civil* no. 159; 30 October 1909 *Colección Legislativa. Jurisprudencia Civil* no. 40.

[78] *Colección Legislativa. Jurisprudencia Civil* 1858 no. 31.

[79] *Colección Legislativa. Jurisprudencia Civil* 1865 no. 306. See also SSTS 15 March 1881 *Colección Legislativa. Jurisprudencia Civil* no. 136; 11 April 1889 *Colección Legislativa. Jurisprudencia Civil* no. 139; 9 January 1922 *Colección Legislativa. Jurisprudencia Civil* no. 8. On one occasion, it really seems that the claimant consented to assume the risk by stacking hay next to the tracks, on the company's premises; they were all aware that this was against the law: STS 3 June 1901 *Colección Legislativa. Jurisprudencia Civil* no. 147.

[80] F. Cabrillo, 'Industrialización y derecho de daños en la España del Siglo XIX' (1994) *Revista de Historia Económica* 591 at 601ff.

[81] STS 2 March 1904 *Colección Legislativa. Jurisprudencia Civil* no. 77.

[82] STS 29 June 1932 *Colección Legislativa. Jurisprudencia Civil* no. 100. The doctrine was repeated in SSTS 25 March 1954 *Colección Legislativa. Jurisprudencia Civil* no. 1001; 2 March 1956 *Colección Legislativa. Jurisprudencia Civil* no. 7.

2.e Further developments: contributory (comparative) negligence

Once it had been decided that the railways are to display whatever precautions are suitable to avoid harm, not only to passengers, but also to third persons,[83] defendants had to concentrate on proving an adequate standard of care. Even if, according to train regulations, some sort of signpost would suffice, courts thought otherwise. Bad visibility is to be taken into account, even if there was no legal obligation to have a barrier or a watchman; traffic signs could be rusty or invisible by night; the lie of the road or even trees may have impaired the view.[84] It is thus not only the fact that the crossing is dangerous for the purpose, but also *cuius commoda, eius incommoda*, that is the basis of compensation.[85]

Many railway decisions repeat, with minor variations, the same basic idea. The tort law system is fault-based. Dangerous activities, however, have given way to a 'moderately objective' trend in which the standard of care is higher; sticking to regulations will not be enough, and the defendant is burdened with the task of proving that all reasonable measures were adopted in order to prevent the damage, taking into account all the surrounding circumstances and every single situation. The railway company will not be liable if the accident has been caused by the sole fault of the victim or was not due to the operation of the railways.[86]

The victim's own imprudence, therefore, seems to be the central issue if the claim is to be rejected or reduced on the grounds of contributory negligence. The starting point is the STS 18 January 1936.[87] A car was hit at an unguarded level crossing, killing one of the occupants and causing injuries to the driver. The Court of Appeal sentenced both the train company and the car driver to pay half of the compensation to the widow. The TS reversed the verdict for the car driver. The importance of compulsory measures was emphasised; the rules are meant to prevent

[83] STS 2 October 1969 (RJ 1969\4474).

[84] SSTS 2 February 1940 (RJ 1940\89); 8 January 1946 *Colección Legislativa. Jurisprudencia Civil* no. 4; 21 November 1955 *Colección Legislativa. Jurisprudencia Civil* no. 43; 30 December 1967 *Colección Legislativa. Jurisprudencia Civil* no. 825; 3 July 1968 (RJ 1968\3610); 29 May 1972 (RJ 1972\2590); 22 January 1996 (RJ 1996\250); 7 October 1998 (RJ 1998\7388); 20 October 1998 (RJ 1998\8731).

[85] SSTS 11 January 1979 (RJ 1979\19); 3 December 1983 (RJ 1983\6817). The latter is, to some extent, an expression of a tendency that transpired through other cases, in which the standard of care has to be 'socially adequate', or inspired by 'principles of solidarity'. See Cavanillas Múgica, *La transformación de la responsabilidad en la jurisprudencia*, p. 65.

[86] SSTS 18 September 1984 (RJ 1984\4299); 12 December 1984 (RJ 1984\6039); 21 November 1985 (RJ 1985\5624); 4 February 1997 (RJ 1997\677); 17 February 1997 (RJ 1997\1426); 23 April 1998 (RJ 1998\2600).

[87] *Colección Legislativa. Jurisprudencia Civil* 1936 no. 60.

casualties and take into account that trains are very dangerous and must exercise 'extreme diligence'. Even if the Court of Appeal had admitted the existence of two negligent actions, they had to be of 'equal intensity and effectiveness' in their contribution. Imprudent as the car driver may have been, the railway's omission was of greater consequence, especially if the former was driving along a bumpy road and could not possibly have seen the train coming until he was on the tracks. The case was really a matter of contribution between tortfeasors, but the courts' wording can be found in many judgments deciding if the quantum of recovery is to be reduced to the extent that the claimant's fault contributed to it.

The aftermath can be summarised as follows: 'Level crossings are considered inherently dangerous in Spain. Many are neglected, poorly marked or situated in places of extremely poor visibility. There is almost always reason to condemn the railway, regardless of how imprudent the victim was.'[88] The train's contribution, indeed, will probably outweigh the imprudence of the victim, unless it is quite clear that the victim's intent has – as judges put it – 'broken the causation chain'.[89] Case law reveals that barriers or chains, lights and whistles, all working together, are security enough.[90] It really seems that nothing else could have been done.

In most cases, nevertheless, the contributory negligence of the victim will reduce, but not normally completely exclude, compensation.[91] Level crossings are dangerous, and it is up to the company to take whatever measures are necessary to close them down completely or adopt safer deterrent measures.[92]

[88] Salvador Coderch and Gómez Ligüerre, 'Trains', 3. The outcome, however, is not as advantageous as it may seem. Considering the period 1996 to 1998, the authors note that the victims or their relatives receive very low compensation for any type of damage. This would often then be reduced where the victim contributed to the injury.

[89] SSTS 8 June 1946 *Colección Legislativa. Jurisprudencia Civil* no. 12; 22 December 1954 *Colección Legislativa. Jurisprudencia Civil* no. 109; 10 May 1963 (RJ 1963\2510); 5 November 1964 (RJ 1964\4960); 12 December 1984 (RJ 1984\6039); 5 February 1992 (RJ 1992\828). According to SAN 7 June 2004 (JUR 2004/317349), it is not clear how the victim fell off the platform.

[90] SSTS 24 January 1992 (RJ 1992\207); 10 March 1993 (RJ 1993\1831); 20 September 1997 (RJ 1997\6608); 22 September 1997 (RJ 1997\6821); 3 April 1998 (RJ 1998\2312); 3 December 2001 (RJ 2001\9857). Even if the victim is only eight years old: SSTS 5 October 2000 (RJ 2000\8135); 24 July 2002 (RJ 2002\6490). It is certainly enough to exclude the strict liability of railways as public bodies: STSJ *Comunidad Valenciana* 2 January 2003 (RJCA 2003\318).

[91] SSTS 24 May 1963 (RJ 1963\2824); 15 December 1984 (RJ 1984\6118); 20 February 1998 (RJ 1998\1215); 8 May 1995 (RJ 1995\3626); 14 June 1996 (RJ 1996\4771); 22 January 1996 (RJ 1996\250); 5 November 1997 (RJ 1997\7884); 25 February 2000 (RJ 2000\1017); 8 February 2002 (RJ 2002\3279).

[92] STS 25 April 2002 (RJ 2002\5243).

2.f *Tracks and other forbidden places*

Since the 1970s, coinciding with the apogee of the 'objective' trend, many decisions have dealt with people who become injured while taking a short cut over tracks or walking far too near the tracks or over bridges that were only intended for trains. The claim is clearly dismissed on the basis of the sole fault or intent of the victim, as long as the train driver has been 'exquisitely diligent', as a 'minimum' of fault (*culpa levissima*) is necessary.[93] Not unusually, some compensation, even a very low sum, is granted on the grounds of contributory negligence. This can be explained either because the victim is a passenger[94] or because the track runs through a town. Thus, the engine driver must remain alert and look out for any not entirely unforeseeable obstacle,[95] and RENFE or the public authorities are liable for not having rebuilt or repaired a ruined wall or a hole in the fence, thus allowing people to cross the tracks, even if they are perfectly aware of the danger and a safe crossing was available somewhere nearby.[96] Sometimes it will be stressed that tracks should always be fenced off or enclosed when running through cities.[97] As for children, partial recovery is due for not having adopted whatever measures would have prevented them from approaching the tracks or entering the station premises.[98] In one outstanding decision (STS 31 December 1997), the harm could also have been described as foreseeable, considering what was by then the usual attitude of the courts. During the local *fiestas* at Manzanares, a city near Madrid, young boys were playing around, placing bets as to who

93 STS 18 February 1991 (RJ 1991\7231); 10 July 1992 (RJ 1992\6276); 15 July 1993 (RJ 1993\5810); 18 July 1996 (RJ 1996\5275); 24 April 1997 (RJ 1997\3399); 23 June 1998 (RJ 1998\5070); 28 November 1998 (RJ 1998\9242); 3 March 2000 (RJ 2000\2508); 12 June 2001 (RJ 2001\5680); 20 December 2001 (RJ 2001\10050).

94 STS 15 March 1989 (RJ 1989\2053): insufficient instructions as to how to find the right platform; STS 16 April 1968 (RJ 1968\2167): the station is too dark; STS 7 July 1997 (RJ 1997\5508): passengers were known to take the short cut out of the station, and no deterrent measures had been adopted.

95 STS 30 April 1974 (RJ 1974\1801); 17 May 2002 (RJ 2002\4974).

96 SSTS 30 December 1991 (RJ 1991\9608); 26 September 1997 (RJ 1997\6708). SAN 10 April 2002 (JUR 2003/60242): although the victim crossed the tracks in the wrong place, the nearest subway was not suitable for motorbikes and circumstances led to confusion.

97 STS 4 November 1999 (RJ 1999\8860). Same criteria according to SAN 23 April 2004 (JUR 2004/190405), in particular if the danger is evident due to prior accidents in the same place.

98 See 9 July 1988 (RJ 1988\5602); 24 February 1993 (RJ 1993\1251); 26 September 1997; 25 January 1997. Other decisions place all the fault on the child himself or on his or her custodian: see SSTS 21 November 1985 (RJ 1985\5624); 24 April 1997 (RJ 1997\3399); 2 December 2002 (RJ 2002\10405). As regards public authorities: STS (*Sala Contencioso-Administrativo*) 15 June 2005 (RJ 2005\9677).

could lie on the tracks the longest as the train approached. The company knew about this practice and had reported the events to the city council. Despite increased vigilance, two fifteen-year-olds were killed by a train travelling at 130 km/h. RENFE and the city council were held jointly and severally responsible. The company, said the TS, should have warned the train drivers and advised them to look out for the youths on that line, reduce their speed or even stop.[99]

Even though an area is not inhabited, the defendant can still be negligent, for example if there was time to reduce speed and even stop, or foresee the reaction of the victim, as in the case of a man who ran alongside the rails and jumped onto them to save a stray lamb.[100] If the tracks are near a beach where people often gather, especially in summer, even though there are overhead or subway crossings nearby, putting a fence up would have been a reasonable measure, enough to allow for some contribution to be paid.[101]

3 Road traffic liability

3.a *Legislation on civil liability and compulsory insurance*

The consolidated text of the law on civil liability and insurance in the use of motor vehicles (*Ley de Responsabilidad Civil y Seguro en la Circulación de Vehículos de Motor*, hereinafter 'LRCSCVM'), RD 8/2004, 29 October 2004 (BOE no. 267, 5 November 2004) is the last amendment of the specific legislation, which began with the approval of the Road Traffic Act of 24 December 1962 (consolidated text Decree 632/1968, 21 March 1968). The most important changes in between were made in 1986 (RD Legislativo 1301/1986, 28 June) and 1995 (*Ley* 30/1995, 8 October), as a result of the compliance with the European Directives relating to insurance against civil liability in respect of the use of motor vehicles,[102] but at the same time introducing, in 1995, a highly controversial binding valuation system for physical injuries.

[99] STS 31 December 1997 (RJ 1997\9145). Salvador Coderch and Gómez Ligüerre, 'Trains', 3 consider such cases as an illustration of the 'privilege of minors'.

[100] TS 24 December 1992 (RJ 1992\10956).

[101] STS 17 February 1997 (RJ 1997\1426), probably taking into account the fact that the two brothers aged ten and twelve who were run over were old enough to be playing on their own while their family was on the beach.

[102] Council Directive of 24 April 1972 (72/166/EEC), 2nd Council Directive of 30 December 1983 (90/232/EEC) and 3rd Council Directive of 14 May 1990 (90/232/EEC). As to the 4th and 5th Directives and their effect on Spanish law, see Reglero Campos, *Tratado de Responsabilidad Civil*, Ch. 9; id., 'La quinta Directiva CE sobre seguro de responsabilidad civil derivada de la circulación de vehículos automóviles' (2005) 11 *Revista de responsabilidad civil, circulación y seguro*, 4. The LRCSCVM has been further amended by *Ley* 21/2007, 11 July.

Currently, the Act provides for strict liability in the case of death and personal injuries suffered by anyone other than the driver. Damage to property, on the contrary, is subject to the general rules of the Código Civil (basically articles 1902–1904) and, therefore, undergoes the negligence test. Both are covered by compulsory insurance, with some exceptions.[103]

3.b The fault requirement up to 1962

The general rules on fault liability were applied by the civil chamber of the TS until the well-known judgment of 10 July 1943. In the preceding years, most traffic accidents were dealt with by the criminal division. However, a few milestones along the road towards a stricter approach in the civil chamber are worth noting.

Quite early on, case law made it clear that the risk involved in the use of motor vehicles was not to be treated in the same way as harm caused by animals out of control. This is already alluded to by the STS 27 October 1909,[104] where the victim was run over by a horse-drawn carriage as she unexpectedly stepped back into its path to avoid being crushed by a tram. The decisive pronouncement was to follow soon after. In the STS 2 January 1914,[105] the claim was filed before the civil court against the owner of the car because the chauffeur had died a few months earlier. The court declared that the plaintiff had not proved that the car had been driving very fast or that the tragedy had been caused by any kind of careless act or omission of the driver. Article 1905 CC provides for strict liability for animals, and only *force majeure* or sole fault of the victim exclude the keeper's responsibility. Even so, the court deemed that there are no analogies between the responsibility imposed upon the principal for the acts or omissions of his employees, who are expected to be capable of acting in a

[103] As to property damage, see article 5.2 LRCSCVM. Compulsory insurance does not cover damage to the insured vehicle, nor to goods carried, nor to property that belongs to the insurance holder, the insured person or the owner. This absence of cover is extended to goods that belong to the spouse or close relatives of any of the former. If the vehicle is not insured, has not been identified or has been stolen, recovery can be obtained from the *Consorcio de Compensación de Seguros* (article 11), subject to exceptions. On the other hand, medical, pharmaceutical and hospital expenses, as well as burial and funeral costs (according to custom), are included in the insurance cover for personal injury, according to article 10.2 Regolamento del seguro obligatorio de responsabilidad civil en la circulación de vehículos de motor, RD 1507/2008, 12 September 2008.

[104] *Colección Legislativa. Jurisprudencia Civil* 1909 no. 35.

[105] *Colección Legislativa. Jurisprudencia Civil* 1914 no. 5.

conscientious and reasonable way, and the provision that holds him liable for not keeping harmful animals under control.

Car accidents, therefore, were definitively to be considered as being ruled by the general negligence principle of article 1902 CC. Suggestions to reverse the burden of proof were rejected.[106] The predominant ideas are clearly expressed in the STS 31 October 1931: the codified rules cannot be construed in such a way as to allow any place for 'modern theories on civil liability without fault of those who create a risk for third parties, as is the case in road traffic'. Such theories will find their way, but the court hints that the task falls upon the legislature.[107]

The first decisive step seems to have been taken by the STS 10 July 1943, usually quoted as being the first one that gave way to the reversal of the burden of proof of fault, 'despite the fact that the principles of strict liability for car accidents are not acknowledged by the law'. It is for the agent to prove that he was as careful as circumstances required. If the victim has contributed to the accident, it will be necessary to determine whose role was more important, even if both have infringed a relevant regulation.[108]

By the 1950s, the TS assumes that an 'objective tinge' has already been cast by the judiciary. 'Rigorous proof' is necessary to refute the presumption of negligence: 'the court will not be satisfied with just a formulary compliance with administrative regulations intended to prevent accidents'.[109] In the following years, the grounds on which the claim was rejected were nearly always the same as those that the 1962 Act would be prepared to accept: sole fault of the victim and *force majeure* – still wide enough to include accidental car failure.[110]

[106] STS 13 June 1923 *Colección Legislativa. Jurisprudencia Civil* no. 92. If there is fault, despite defences of absence of damage, compensation for pain and suffering (*daño moral*) will be granted to close relatives, especially if the victim is a child: STS 24 February 1928 *Colección Legislativa. Jurisprudencia Civil* no. 114.

[107] *Colección Legislativa. Jurisprudencia Civil* 1931 no. 186. See Cavanillas Múgica, *La transformación de la responsabilidad civil en la Jurisprudencia*, p. 22. See also SSTS 29 February 1936 *Colección Legislativa. Jurisprudencia Civil* no. 152; 16 March 1936 (RJ 1936\548).

[108] RJ 1943\856. Similarly, as regards the victim's contribution, STS 12 February 1932 *Colección Legislativa. Jurisprudencia Civil* no. 61; but it can reduce compensation: SSTS 24 May 1947 *Colección Legislativa. Jurisprudencia Civil* no. 95; 19 June 1957 (RJ 1957\2209). As for the importance of this sentence in courts' attitude, see Reglero Campos, *Accidents*, pp. 181ff.

[109] STS 24 March 1953 *Colección Legislativa. Jurisprudencia Civil* 1953 no. 28.

[110] As in SSTS 20 October 1950 *Colección Legislativa. Jurisprudencia Civil* no. 8; 30 January 1951 *Colección Legislativa. Jurisprudencia Civil* no. 37; 28 May 1960 (RJ 1960\263); 28 June 1961 (RJ 1961\2868).

In the 1960s, the 1962 statute was applied to decide cases that had taken place before it actually came into force (June 1965). The most famous and quoted decision of this period is the STS 9 April 1963.[111] The court summarised case law development since 1943 and the technical devices applied in order to achieve nearly strict liability results within the domains of fault: the burden of proof is reversed and the standard of care and the concept of fault itself has become wide enough so as to consider perfectly legal acts as negligence. In this case, the claim filed, as was then still the norm, was against the driver and his employer. An occupant had been killed, and his two young orphan daughters sought to recover damages. The inferior courts had dismissed the claim: the car was not going faster than regulations prescribed and the accident could have been caused by a slippery road, wet with rain and snow. But the TS decided that the speed was not appropriate, considering the weather and the state of the road. It did not ensure full control over the vehicle, as was shown by the way the accident happened: the car skidded off the road for 300 metres and crashed into a tree. As to liability for road traffic, the decision explains the following points, which were to be recalled constantly in the years thereafter.

Traffic responsibility derives from the fact that driving a car is a dangerous activity, and this could be enough to attach liability to the car owner, as long as the general requirements concur: a voluntary act or omission, harm or damage and a causation link between the two. The accident must not have been caused by *force majeure* or an inevitable event, and a car breakdown will not be considered as such. The participants in any kind of traffic situation cannot expect anything other than normal behaviour from others in similar circumstances. The duty of care of the driver, however, is to foresee obstacles or sudden dangers. It is his task to be the absolute master of the car for security's sake.

3.c The 1962 Road Traffic Act:the mutual influence of new law and old rules

Legal writing had, for quite a long time, been urging the legislature to adopt a no-fault system and compulsory insurance for traffic accidents. A variety of reasons, including the well-known *cuius commoda, eius incommoda*, were put forward to sustain the claim that driving was a dangerous but convenient and necessary activity. Foreign systems, especially French,

[111] *Colección Legislativa. Jurisprudencia Civil* no. 354, followed by 15 April 1964 (RJ 1964\1889).

German and Italian systems, were quite well known, and some authors suggested following their example. Up until about 1925, the trend was still moving slowly.[112] By 1934, traffic accidents were looked upon as a major tragedy, as 'it used to take a year to shed all the blood that is now spilled every day', while courts were wasting their time discussing whether the negligence cap fitted or not.[113] In the 1940s, legal writers predicted that a strict liability future was imminent, because in 1943 the Supreme Court had decided to reverse the burden of proof of fault. Over the next years, the standard of care progressively escalated to *culpa levissima*.[114]

The proximate inspiration for the wording of the new law seems to have been, on the one hand, international proposals[115] and, on the other, national regulation, especially regarding work accidents,[116] albeit with important differences. The best explanation is found in the explanatory memorandum (*Exposición de Motivos*) of the law itself:

The ever-increasing road traffic and use of motor vehicles, the constant development of technique and the necessities of modern life have given way to a serious situation, causing major concern in view of the number of victims and damage to property it causes in steady progression,

[112] See R. Gay de Montellá, 'El problema de la responsabilidad civil resultante de los accidentes de automóvil' (1909) *Revista Jurídica de Cataluña* 103; F. Castejón Martínez, 'Ensayo sobre las notas de diferenciación e integración de los derechos penal y civil' (1912) 121 *Revista General de Legislación y Jurisprudencia* (RGLJ) 447; J. Mª. Manresa y Navarro, *Comentarios al Código civil español* (Madrid: Imprenta de la Revista de Legislación, 1911), vol. XII, p. 626; E. Miñana, 'La responsabilidad sin culpa' (1919) *Revista de Ciencias Jurídicas y Sociales* 209; M. Traviesas, 'La culpa' (1926) *Revista de Derecho Privado* (RDP) 273; F. Clemente de Diego, *Curso elemental de Derecho civil español, común y foral* (Madrid: Librería General de Victoriano Suárez, 1926), vol. VI, p. 321; ibid., *Instituciones de Derecho civil español* (Madrid: Imprenta de Juan Pueyo, 1930), vol. II, pp. 310ff.

[113] A. Ossorio Gallardo, 'El hecho, generador de obligaciones (Contribución al estudio de la responsabilidad sin culpa)' (1934) 164 RGLJ 247 at 260 and 272; S. Gubern Salisachs, 'La responsabilidad sin culpa en España' (1945) 177 RGLJ 558.

[114] Borrell Maciá, *Responsabilidades derivadas de culpa extracontractual civil*, pp. 14ff.; 2nd edn (Barcelona: Bosch, 1958); J. Bonet Correa, 'La responsabilidad objetiva' (1960) *Revista de Derecho Notarial* (RDN) 209; F. Fernández de Villavicencio, 'Responsabilidad sin culpa y responsabilidad objetiva' (1962) 13 *Anales de la Academia Matritense del Notariado* (AAMN) 27 at 43.

[115] Reglero Campos, *Accidents*, p. 178 reports the Avant project 1948 of the Institute pour l'unification du droit. As regards compulsory insurance and direct action, the European Convention on Compulsory Insurance against Civil Liability in respect of Motor Vehicles, 20 April 1959, was quoted by the Minister of Justice, D. A. Iturmendi, when introducing the law, in 'Discurso' (1963) *Pretor* 152. See J. Baillo y Morales Arce, *La accion directa en el seguro obligatorio de responsabilidad civil automovilística* (Bolonia: Publicaciones del Real Colegio de España, Studia Albornotiana, 2000), p. 30.

[116] See Reglero Campos, *Accidents*, p. 180.

with severe impairment of personal security and the nation's economy. The immediate compensation of damage suffered by the victim is to be provided for at all costs (*a ultranza*), and the law is to be the source of such an obligation, taking into account the risk involved in the use and circulation of motor vehicles.

Thus, advantages on the one side and risk on the other justified the welcomed new rules. The president of the Law Commission put forth yet another reason: compensation of the faultless victim is 'a question of justice'.[117]

The 1962 Act had been designed to introduce a comprehensive set of measures that would meet the requirements long insisted upon by legal writing, the main tools being a strict liability system and compulsory third-party insurance, drawn together in what has been called an 'indissoluble equation'. Thus, two objectives were achieved. On the one hand, the new rules on civil liability diverted from the traditional fault system, ensuring compensation even when negligent driving has not been proven. On the other hand, compulsory insurance guaranteed that the victim would recover damages, despite the defendant's lack of financial resources. Apart from criminal provisions, later to be included in the Criminal Code, the main interest of the new law and further complementary regulation is against whom, and by what procedure, the victim is entitled to claim compensation.[118] Once it is set out, in only one article, that this does not depend on the fault of the driver, the rest of the Act is primarily concerned with the victim's loss. The use of uninsured vehicles is forbidden, and the obligation to buy insurance is imposed upon the owner, who is only mentioned in this regard. A public body (*Fondo Nacional de Garantía de Riesgos de la Circulación*),[119] sustained by insurance premiums, was created in order to cover events excluded from the mandatory policy (such as uninsured, stolen or unidentified cars). The aggrieved party (or its heirs) was to be granted direct action against the insurance company (or public body), without having to try to obtain payment from the tortfeasor in

117 G. de Aranda, 'Defensa del Dictamen de la Comisión' (1963) *Pretor* 136. Since 1953, casualties have increased by 175% and deaths by 376%.

118 The new rules received intensive attention from all parties involved. Scholars, judges and the legal profession dealing with insurance companies provided all kinds of interpretations on the many uncertainties the law had created. For the early reactions and variety of opinions, see R. Uría, *Actas del coloquio sobre el seguro de responsabilidad civil en la ley del automóvil* (Bilbao: Imprenta Editorial Moderna, 1963).

119 Currently *Consorcio de Compensación de Seguros*. The risk is thus socialised as to burden car owners who have to pay for the insurance, being at the same time potential victims. See Reglero Campos, *Accidents*, p. 191.

the first place. In addition, specific measures were introduced to guarantee a swift procedure of an executive nature, which at the same time was intended exclusively for direct action against the insurance company – the only body that can be sued according to such rules. Defences against this so-called '*acción ejecutiva*' are limited to the same ones that exclude the driver's liability (*force majeure* and sole fault of the victim), leaving other defences to be dealt with by reimbursement actions.

It is not surprising, therefore, that scholars debate extensively on the nature of compulsory insurance (*seguro obligatorio de automóviles*) and the character and meaning of direct action.[120] Despite its not being the opinion of the majority, mandatory insurance seems to work more as an 'autonomous criterion of imputation of responsibility'; it is really 'external to the conflict between tortfeasor and victim'. Indeed, it does not require a previous statement of the insured person's liability; and if driver and insurance company are sued together in the ordinary civil proceedings, the TS, on some occasions, has only condemned the latter within the quantitative limits of the compulsory insurance.[121]

The new law, however, whilst procuring relatively expeditious attention by way of direct action and executive procedure, was ineffective in its aim to compensate victims adequately. The main reason seems to have been the very low compensation amount covered by compulsory insurance until 1986, when compliance with European directives forced the change.[122] The victim, therefore, may not even take advantage of the specific procedure against the insurance company. The claim would be filed against all three potential payers – the driver, the owner and the insurance

[120] For a detailed overview, see Mª. J. Morillas Jarillo, *El seguro del automóvil: El aseguramiento obligatorio de la responsabilidad civil automovilística* (Barcelona: J. M. Bosch, 1992), pp. 83ff.; Baillo y Morales Arce, *La acción directa en el seguro obligatorio de responsabilidad civil automovilística*, pp. 41ff. Courts, in any case, had, since the 1930s, been admitting the claims of victims directly against the insurance company, pleading a subsidiary verdict against the insurer; for what was justified using a mixture of theoretical and practical arguments, see Baillo y Morales Arce, *La acción directa*, pp. 107ff. and STS 26 March 1977 (RJ 1977\1354).

[121] F. Pantaleón, 'Comentario a la STS 27 enero 1983' (1983) *Cuadernos Cívitas de Jurisprudencia Civil* (CCJC) 99. See SSTS 30 April 1969 *Colección Legislativa. Jurisprudencia Civil* no. 291; 4 July 1970 (RJ 1970\3656); 20 March 1971 (RJ 1971\1445); 30 March 1974 (RJ 1974\1211); 7 February 1980 (RJ 1980\514).

[122] By RD 19 November 1964, the maximum amount was 300,000 pesetas (approximately €1,800) in the case of death or severe invalidity. In 1980, the maximum was raised to 1,000,000 pesetas (approximately €6,000) and, in 1986, to 8,000,000 pesetas. As to the effect this had on the system, see M. Medina Crespo, *El seguro obligatorio de automóviles* (Madrid: M. Medina Crespo, 1994), pp. 113ff.

company – in ordinary proceedings, in order to obtain not only the compulsory limited amount, but also full recovery at the same time. As noted earlier, on these occasions it has sometimes been the case that only the insurance company is condemned within the mandatory limits. On the other hand, many of the decisions of the TS on traffic liability deal with claims that are filed once the compulsory amount has been satisfied. In such cases, the defendant's liability is decided according to the codified rules, as the courts contend that the claimant has filed the common 'tort action' based on fault. Hence, the predominant opinion of legal writers and court decisions ascertained the interdependency between strict liability and compulsory insurance; beyond its boundaries and, in particular, in order to reach the keeper/owner behind the driver, the specific liability rules of the Traffic Act do not apply.

That said, it must be noted that the TS has not developed a sharp difference in this field between the strict rules of the Traffic Act and the codified rule of negligence.

As to the construction of the statute, the path is far from straight. Case law is frequently confusing and difficult to summarise in a few statements.[123] On the whole, it can be said that the system of traffic liability is not construed as a separate body completely displacing the negligence rule.[124] The specific regulation is described as 'quasi-strict' or as the legal sanction of the reversal of the burden of proof with limited defences. Furthermore, the law has been conceived chiefly to ensure recovery for pedestrians and occupants who create no risk, and does not apply automatically to collisions between moving vehicles, as both drivers partake in the peril. If no clear line can be drawn between wrongdoer and victim, judges tend to dismiss the reversal of the burden of proof, and recovery depends on the contribution of each to the damage suffered by the other.[125]

On the other hand, the rules on traffic liability have influenced the understanding of the codified negligence rule, when deciding on the driver's or owner's liability above the limits of compulsory insurance. The

[123] For a clear description of traffic liability as 'objective' and covered by compulsory insurance and ordinary tort liability based on fault, see SSTS 22 October 1981 (RJ 1981\3952); 1 March 1982 (RJ 1982\1277).

[124] See G. Pomar, 'Cars and accidents (I) The position of the Supreme Court' (2000) 2 *InDret* 8: 'According to First Chamber criteria, it is, at most, an additional factor with some influence in the moderate but still appreciable process of making the rule of negligence more objective, in virtue of hazard liability.'

[125] The matter is very controversial. See E. Monterroso Casado, *Responsabilidad civil por accidentes de circulación. La concurrencia de causas* (Cizur Menor: Aranzadi, 2001), pp. 123ff; Reglero Campos, *Accidents*, pp. 206ff.

wide use of optional insurance seems to have favoured this inclination, although courts will not explicitly own up to it. The TS, probably reacting to the increasing insufficiency of the compulsory amount, found yet another argument to forsake the 'traditionally subjective' approach to tort: the analogous application of the specific statute.[126] It has gone as far as to declare that the optional third-party insurance covers the same sort of responsibility as the compulsory one: insurance exists on account of liability, not liability on account of insurance.[127]

3.d *Evolution of the rules on strict liability*

The basic liability rules laid out in 1962 have not undergone many substantial changes. Most of the additions have been introduced from 1995 onwards. Some of them are aimed at settling controversial issues in case law and legal writing, such as the role of contributory negligence within the limits of compulsory insurance and the part played by victims incapable of civil fault (see 3.d.iii, below). Equally, the express indication that the scope of the law and the cover of mandatory insurance, enclosed in the words *hecho de la circulación* (a traffic event), are not intended to include events in which a vehicle has been used as the precise instrument for committing a crime.[128] By far the most important and polemical innovation has been the binding valuation system for personal injuries.

3.d.i Coexistence with a fault-based scheme

The original idea, as reflected in the 1962 Act (articles 39 and 40), was to introduce strict liability and compulsory insurance for both personal injuries and property damage. However, it seemed to be going

[126] SSTS 9 July 1987 (RJ 1987\5213); 29 October 1987 (RJ 1987\7483);19 October 1988 *Colección Legislativa. Jurisprudencia Civil* no. 759. On the approximation of both kinds of liability, see STS 3 October 1996 (RJ 1996\7009).

[127] STS 21 July 1989 (RJ 1989\5772). See Reglero Campos, *Accidents*, p. 204.

[128] Case law had been very generous in compensating third parties within the limits of compulsory insurance when the car had been used as a weapon or instrument to cause harm, notwithstanding the subsequent right of return against the intentional agent, normally the driver. The matter has been widely discussed. See F. Gómez and B. Arquillo, 'Intentional harm and insurance' (2000) 3 *InDret* 9. Currently, article 1.4 LRCSCVM expressly states that a vehicle used as an instrument of intentional criminal offence against people or property is not to be considered *hecho de la circulación*. The point is still controversial, as the wording of the law and the regulation of recovery action is misleading. See Reglero Campos, *Accidents*, pp. 146ff.; M. Yzquierdo Tolsada, 'Apuntes en torno al RRCSCVM aprobado por RD 7/2001, de 12 enero' (2001) 7 *Revista de Derecho Patrimonial* 89.

too far. Car ownership was growing rather fast, in chorus with payment by instalments. The economic means of most people could hardly meet the monthly payments; as such, it was probably unwise to establish an expensive mandatory insurance. Public opinion was outraged by the announced drastic growth of insurance premiums in comparison to what had been, up until then, the norm for optional cover.[129] So even before the Act came into force,[130] the application of the new type of responsibility was limited to the recovery of damages in respect of death or bodily injury (of 'greater social interest') and within the limits of compulsory insurance, alleviating in this way the economic burden of insurance premiums.

In 1995, this duality concerning personal injury was repealed. The current system now prescribes strict liability for bodily injuries, regardless of the higher compulsory insurance limits. Pursuant to article 4.3.II LRCSCVM, if the amount of damages fixed by the binding schedule is not covered by mandatory insurance, the remainder shall fall on the optional insurer or on the person who is liable. The importance of this reform is lessened if one bears in mind the influence of the specific traffic criteria on the negligent rule. The change, therefore, is not quite as innovative as it may seem.

Property damage is ruled by the general codified fault provisions. The differences between property damage and personal harm were definitively established in 1986. Nevertheless, it is also mentioned in article 1.1 LRCSCVM in the overall description of road traffic liability as stemming from the risk created by motor vehicles – which could be used as an excuse to achieve 'quasi-strict' solutions.[131]

3.d.ii The defences: *force majeure* and the victim's sole negligence

The law provides for two possible defences: *force majeure* (*fuerza mayor*) and sole fault of the victim. These defences specifically explain why courts consider that traffic liability is not to be described as a totally no-fault scheme. Perhaps it is simply the natural aftermath of the way in which

[129] See M. Olivencia Ruiz, 'Problemática que plantea la introducción del seguro obligatorio de automóviles en España' (1965) RDCirculación 297.

[130] The 1962 Act did not come into force until 1 June 1965: *Decreto-Ley* 4/65. The provisions on compulsory insurance were detailed in the *Reglamento del Seguro obligatorio* 19 November 1964. Currently, *Reglamento del seguro obligatorio de responsabilidad civil en la circulación de vehículos de motor* RD 1507/2008, 12 September 2008.

[131] See Reglero Campos, *Accidents*, pp. 203.

both have been handled. In other words, to assess whether an external event is the sole cause of the accident, or whether the victim's harm has been entirely brought about by his or her own carelessness, courts find it necessary to determine if the event in itself, or the victim's behaviour, was or was not foreseeable or avoidable by a driver, whose duty of care had been placed on a very high level long before the Traffic Act had even been thought of.

Fuerza mayor was and still is described[132] as 'an event external to the driving or performance (or working) of the vehicle'. In particular, it does not encompass the vehicle's defects, or the unforeseeable breakdown or any kind of failure of its parts or mechanism. Case law and doctrinal writing construe this provision rather widely as only excluding responsibility when some sort of contingency alien to the car, to the driver or to the state of the road is the cause of the accident. Attention is focused on the fact that it has to be an independent event that typically has nothing to do with the risks involved in using motor vehicles. Brake failures or tyre bursts, albeit inevitable or in no way attributable to anybody's lack of care, will not suffice to escape liability. Natural events, such as bad weather, unexpected animal intrusions, unforeseeable obstacles on the road or poor traffic signs, external as they may be to the vehicle itself, will not be considered an independent event, unless they have 'interrupted completely the chain of causation'. That will not be the case if the court ascertains the slightest negligence of the driver, who should have done better and should be as careful as the surrounding circumstances demand.[133] The final outcome depends very much on the individual case, and, sometimes, the wording

[132] Article 39 *Ley* 122/62; article 1 *Decreto* 21 March 1968, *Texto Refundido Ley sobre uso y circulación de vehículos de motor.* Currently, article 1.1.II LRCSCVM.

[133] See F. Soto Nieto, *La responsabilidad civil en el accidente automovilístico. Responsabilidad objetiva*, 2nd edn (Madrid: Editorial Revista de Derecho Judicial, 1972), pp. 198, 201ff.; Morilla Jarillo, *El seguro del automóvil. El aseguramiento obligatorio de la responsabilidad civil automovilística*, pp. 434ff.; E. Monterroso Casado, *Responsabilidad civil por accidentes de circulación*, pp. 292ff.; STS 11 May 1983 (RJ 1983\2683): a pothole could have been avoided if the driver had been sufficiently attentive. In the STS 13 April 1982 (RJ 1982\1946), the improper signing of roadworks permits the reduction of compensation on the grounds of contributory negligence. In the STS 22 December 1992 (RJ 1992\10639), strong wind had pushed the motorbike against the rear of the lorry that was overtaking it; the courts decided compensation on account of compulsory insurance, the wind being a 'fortuitous case', but not *force majeure.* As to accidents caused by animals unexpectedly running across the road, courts will usually consider it defence enough. A very recent statute reform, not of the Traffic Liability Act but of the Law of traffic, circulation of motor vehicles and road security (*Ley sobre tráfico, circulación de vehículos a motor y seguridad vial, Real Decreto legislativo 339/1990,* 2 March), has introduced a provision (*Disposición*

of court decisions is misleading. For instance, in the STS 17 November 1989, the TS sustained the decision that a pedestrian who unexpectedly stepped into the road was an external event (*force majeure*) completely alien to the driving. Hence the driver, who, in order to avoid running him over, swerved onto the wrong side of the road, colliding with another car and killing one of his own passengers, could not possibly have reacted otherwise and is not responsible, pursuant to the Act. However, a closer look at the facts shows that the maximum amount covered by the compulsory insurance had been already granted. So the act of a third person, in this case, had not impeded compensation by the insurance company within the limits of the obligatory cover.[134]

As to the 'fault of the victim', academic writing and case law stress that it only works as a complete defence if and when it is the only cause of damage. It is true that, in a strict liability system, the victim's fault may be thought irrelevant to his recovery. In addition, this defence will inevitably force a closer look at the care displayed by the driver, which is precisely not what is supposed to be at stake. Yet again it is quite usual to read that the specific rules on traffic liability do not provide for strict liability to be equal to responsibility for purely factual causation. Therefore the victim's own carelessness will very frequently be discussed, turning the scenario into an analysis of the acts of everyone involved in the accident. The duty of care of the driver – compared with a pedestrian or a cyclist – is stricter; maximum care is required in his or her own behaviour and the victim's actions must have been totally unforeseeable.[135]

According to some legal authors, the 1962 Act, in using the word 'fault', meant that only the behaviour of a sound and mature victim would be taken into account. Hence, children or insane people who themselves lack tortious capacity would or should be entitled to recover full damages. However, case law took another turn, as did the prevailing opinion. Minors must also abide by what is usually called 'objective norms of conduct' and must, of course, adhere to the 'Circulation Code' rules, impossible or improbable as it might be for them to reach that standard. Since 1995, the new wording of this defence has left no doubt that victims who

adicional 9ª) on civil liability in traffic accidents caused by the running over of wild animals (*Ley* 17/2005, of 19 July, BOE no. 172, 20 July 2005). The driver is liable in cases where an infringement of traffic regulations can be imputed to him.

134 See F. Reglero Campos, 'Comentario a la STS 17.11.1989' (1989) 21 CCJC 1061.

135 Despite the irregular behaviour of the victim, courts emphasise the liability of the driver if he or she had the last best choice to avoid the accident, alluding to reasons of 'social solidarity' and 'adequate distribution of risk': SSTS 10 July 1969 (RJ 1969\3859); 13 February 1973 (RJ 1973\3203).

are 'inimputables', those who lack understanding and are not capable of being negligent, can be deemed to be the sole cause of the harm they have suffered. This amendment has been very much criticised.[136]

3.d.iii Contributory negligence

From the very beginning, general opinion held that the 1962 Act was to be construed as excluding compensation only in cases in which the accident is entirely the victim's fault. It was supposed to be an 'either or' matter as far as compulsory insurance was concerned; reduction beneath this limit was rejected. Only if the plaintiff was pleading for more money, over the obligatory limits, could the court reduce damages by the amount of his own contribution to the harm.[137] Case law seemed to follow the majority's opinion, yet with contradictory decisions. The controversy was settled by the 1995 amendment. Currently, article 1.1.IV LRCSCVM states that the concurring negligence of the driver and the aggrieved party determines the equitable moderation of responsibility; recovery of damages is apportioned, taking into account the *entidad* (importance or magnitude) of 'concurring faults'.

Courts may find a way to declare that the driver was not as careful as he could have been, or that he should have expected the careless or absent-minded behaviour. However, if the victim has indeed conducted himself in an unexpected or unlawful way, judges are quite prone to declare contributory negligence. This also applies, very frequently, when children, as pedestrians or cyclists, are knocked down. Spanish courts identify the fault of the parent or guardian with that of the child, in order to reduce damages due.

3.d.iv Liability of the owner

The 1962 Act only mentioned the driver's liability. It was surprising, and had earlier been criticised,[138] that a specific provision on owner responsibility was not included at all until 1995, nor was it covered by compulsory insurance. The legislature considered that the codified rules on responsibility for the wrongful acts of others would be enough. Responsibility,

[136] Section 1.1.II LRCSCVM now uses the words 'conduct or negligence' of the aggrieved party. Rule 1.2. of the Annex of the Act states that a victim lacking tortious capacity who has caused or contributed to the causation of the accident will be deemed to be at 'fault'.

[137] Accurate information on different opinions is given by Medina Crespo, *El seguro obligatorio de automóviles*, pp. 213ff.

[138] It was, however, a conscious decision of the legislator. See Reglero Campos, *Accidents*, p. 209.

therefore, was not fastened upon the owner for the sole reason of ownership. Courts proved this omission to be of little consequence and found a way to reach the owner, who was likely to have optional third-party insurance or, in any case, would be an employer or a parent, with enough means to absorb the loss if the insurance company did not. If liable, the owner could also be the target of a reimbursement action from the Insurance Compensation Consortium, who had already paid the victim of an uninsured car.

According to the provision introduced in 1995, the owner of the car who was not driving it when the accident happened can be held liable if his or her relationship to the driver falls under the provisions of the Código Civil (article 1903) or the Criminal Code (article 120.5°) that establish liability for the actions of others (section 1.1.V LRCSCVM). Following these rules, the owner could earlier, and can still, incur liability pursuant to article 1903 CC as a parent/guardian (in the case of a minor) or as the employer of the driver. The Código Civil provides in such cases for direct liability based on fault, with a reversal of the burden of proof, as stated in article 1903.IV (*culpa in vigilando, culpa in eligendo*). Those who are considered responsible for the acts of another, therefore, are held jointly and severally liable with the direct wrongdoer. The victim can file his claim against the latter, the person vicariously responsible, or both at the same time. Article 1.1.V LRCSCVM, picking up the same rule as in article 1903.IV CC, allows the car owner to avoid paying compensation when he proves that all the duty of care of the reasonable person (*buen padre de familia*) was taken to prevent the damage. In addition, the relationship between the car owner (guardian or principal) and the driver has to match the specific legal conditions.

The judicial trend has nevertheless steadily increased the liability of the former, using a number of devices. To begin with, case law has made it rather difficult to prove adequate and sufficient care.[139] On the other hand, the master/servant relationship has been broadly interpreted, in the same way as the meaning of the 'employer/principal' and 'dependant' requirements of article 1903 CC have been considerably expanded,

[139] A trend that probably started with STS 24 March 1953 (RJ 1953\913). The overturning of a bus caused severe injuries to a passenger who leapt out of the bus window to avoid being crushed. The bus company sought to prove that reasonable steps had been taken to avoid accidents. The driver was sufficiently experienced and all legal requirements had been fulfilled. The Supreme Court, nevertheless, recalled the shade of objectiveness cast by case law on civil liability by way of demanding vigorous proof in order to rebut the legal presumption of negligence: 'and in this tendency we must persist, for social convenience'.

so as to include cases in which the car is seen to be driven, in some way or another, for the owner's purposes or convenience. Liability has even been flatly pinned on the premises of article 1902 CC, in cases where the car had been lent to someone who turned out to be a careless driver, as long as it could be said that the owner retained control of the usage of the car.[140] Thus, if control has been transferred, in a more or less definite way, to somebody else, such as would happen in a leasing contract, the owner cannot be held responsible.

Article 120.5° Criminal Code 1995, unlike its predecessor, has gone even further, as it states subsidiary and, it seems, strict liability of the *titular* (meaning the owner or the person, individual or organisation who is the holder and controls the usage) of a 'vehicle that is likely to create risk for others' in the case of crimes or misdemeanours perpetrated while being used by dependants or representatives or authorised persons ('*dependientes, representantes o personas autorizadas*'). Authorisation can be tacit.[141] This new rule has been welcomed by some and feared by others. It supplies a firm ground on which the vehicle holder's liability can be built. The need to establish any sort of 'dependence' relationship, or similar, has quite disappeared. The final words are eloquent enough: the owner must respond, unless the car was being used without, or against, his will.[142]

Finally, scholars and courts have pointed out the inescapable liability of the owner pursuant to article 1902 CC – albeit the silence of the LRCSCVM – if he neglected the car and the lack of repair gave rise to the accident.[143]

[140] STS 23 February 1976 (RJ 1976\880) became famous, as it imposes liability upon the owner of the car: a young woman who lent her car to her boyfriend, who subsequently died in a crash that inflicted injuries on the plaintiff.

[141] For an overview of case law from both the civil and the criminal chambers as to liability for others and car accidents, see Reglero Campos, *Accidents*, pp. 212–25; J. J. Barceló Domenech, *Responsabilidad extracontractual del empresario por hechos de sus dependientes* (Madrid: Civitas, 1995), pp. 185, 232ff., 318ff.

[142] Case law, esp. that of the criminal chamber of the Supreme Court, has been forcing the law in this very direction for the last thirty years in its desire to find solvent liable persons and compensate the victims of traffic accidents. See C. García Pérez, 'Articulo 120', in Cobo del Rosal (ed.), *Comentarios al Código penal*, (Madrid: Edersa, 2000), vol. IV, pp. 790 ff.

[143] In the STS 6 May 1983 (RJ 1983\2670), a widow and three daughters had been granted the amount covered by compulsory insurance. The victim was run over while walking on the pavement, on his way to work. The driver had lost control because part of the steering column had broken in two. The claim, intended to recover more damages (up to 1,700,000 pesetas, approximately €10,000) was filed against the driver, the owner, who had optional insurance, and the insurance company. The driver was acquitted, because he could not possibly have noticed the crack and was driving carefully. For the owner, it was a different story. The TS followed the doctrine of the STS 9 April 1963 (RJ 1963\1954) and

3.d.v The importance of being faultless

Traffic law has shifted liability towards a victim's-loss approach. Compensation does not require any kind of moral reproach or unlawful behaviour. The (at present) broad insurance cover and the limited defences do the rest. Nonetheless, case law treatment of traffic issues is plain evidence of what has been called the 'vanishing distinction between negligence and strict liability' and of the 'continuum between pure subjective liability for breach of duty of care and strict liability for unforeseeable harm'. As pointed out earlier, the defence of the victim's conduct and the legal sanction of contributory negligence highlight the role of so-called 'bilateral care'.[144] Courts have been reluctant to forsake 'negligence' entirely, and the latest law reforms seem to follow the same trend.

Fault, indeed, will not lose sway. It emerges from the background to decide the direction of recovery actions, for example against a negligent driver who causes the accident that leads a careful driver to run over and subsequently have to compensate an innocent pedestrian.[145] Apportionment between insurers of multiple wrongdoers – jointly and severally responsible towards the injured – is naturally settled, if possible, attending to the 'entity of the concurring faults'.[146]

Perhaps the most outstanding importance of fault is its significance in overcoming the limits of the binding valuation system. The schedule was approved in 1995 and is currently included in the schedule (*Anexo*) to the Traffic Act. The intention of the legislature, following instructions from the insurance lobby,[147] was that any kind of personal damage in traffic accidents, including *damnum emergens*, loss of earnings and pain and suffering, is to be assessed in accordance with the criteria and limits of the *Anexo*, regardless of the insurance coverage.[148] Such is the provision of article 1.2 LRCSCVM.

decided that the owner was at fault, tenuous (*tenue*) but nevertheless real, as the steering mechanism had not been in perfect condition for quite a while. Other decisions in this trend: SSTS 26 December 1969 (RJ 1969\6210); 27 May 1983 (RJ 1983\2916); 14 December 1984 (RJ 1984\6029); 23 March 1997 (RJ 1997\1864); 14 June 1997 (RJ 1997\2888).

144 P. Salvador Coderch and A. Rubi-Puig, 'El círculo de responsables. La evanescente distinción entre responsabilidad por culpa y objetiva' (2005) 4 *InDret* 1 at 23: 'The duty of care is expelled from the defendant's sphere of influence, only to re-enter the victim's house.'

145 Articles 10 and 11.3 LRCSCVM. See STS 7 February 1980 (RJ 1980\514).

146 Article 19.2 Regolamento del seguro obligatorio RD 1507/2008.

147 This seems to be indisputable. See F. Pantaleón, 'Los baremos indemnizatorios en la valoracion de los daños a las personas' (1995) 81 *Documentación jurídica* 171; J. Pintos Ager, *Baremos, seguros y Derecho de daños* (Madrid: Civitas, 2000), p. 365.

148 Medical, pharmaceutical and hospital expenses (as long as they have been 'justified'), as well as burial and funeral costs (according to usage) are to be paid in addition to the

This system has produced streams of legal writing. The reasons put forth to sustain it have been criticised as being inconsistent or, at least, insufficient.[149] Despite undeniable advantages, such as facilitating the valuation of damages – in particular pain and suffering – and the expected beneficial effect on litigation rates,[150] the many deficiencies and uncertainties have led to various pronouncements by the Constitutional Court. The STC 181/2000, 29 June[151] has afforded some relief to critics: recovery of damages, in particular loss of earnings, is not to be limited by the schedule, but rather be fully granted according to the extent of proof given, as long as the judge appreciates '*culpa exclusiva del conductor causante del accidente, relevante y judicialmente declarada*'. That is, fault.

indemnity due according to the schedule (Annex 1, no. 6). Payment of medical expenses usually takes place according to the agreements between the *Consorcio de Compensación de Seguros*, the Spanish Union of Insurance Companies (*Unión Española de Entidades Aseguradoras y Reaseguradoras* – UNESPA) and public and private health institutions (*Convenios de Asistencia sanitaria*). See Reglero Campos, *Accidents*, pp. 526ff.

149 See Pantaleón, 'Los baremos indemnizatorios en la valoración de los daños a las personas', 171ff.; Pintos Ager, *Baremos, seguros y Derecho de daños*, pp. 121, 162ff.

150 It appears, however, to be dubious. See J. Pintos Ager, 'Damage schedules and tort litigation in Spain' (2003) 2 *InDret* 2.

151 See J. Ribot Igualada, 'La culpa "relevante" como culpa "adicional": La STC 181/2000 a la luz de la interacción entre responsabilidad objetiva y culpa', in A. Cabanillas Sánchez (ed.), *Estudios Jurídicos en Homenaje al profesor Luis Díez-Picazo* (Madrid: Civitas, 2003), vol. II, p. 2869. For extensive information on the consequences of the various verdicts of the Constitutional Court as to the 'baremo', see Reglero Campos, *Accidents*, pp. 290ff.

7

The development of traffic liability in Sweden

SANDRA FRIBERG AND BILL W. DUFWA

This chapter examines the development of liability for traffic accidents in Sweden and, where possible, in other Scandinavian countries. Section 1 (liability for railway accidents) has been written by Sandra Friberg; Section 2 (liability for road traffic accidents) has been written by Bill W. Dufwa.

1 Liability for personal injuries resulting from rail operations

In the Nordic countries, legislation is very similar regarding liability for personal injuries as a result of rail operations, and it is generally based on purely objective grounds. More often than not, objective responsibility has been justified by the special dangers or risks connected with rail operations. In some Nordic countries, these dangers or risks have been conditions precedent to impose liability upon rail operators without legislative support. Also, in most Nordic countries, the development of general tort law has occurred at a later stage than when the railways came into operation. The provisions that did exist in the late 1800s and the early 1900s were not sufficient to meet the needs that this new mode of transportation brought about.

1.a Sweden

The first Swedish steam railways operated from 1856. Shortly thereafter, it became clear that the ordinary rules on tort liability were not sufficient to deal with matters of compensation for personal injuries, loss or damage as a result of rail operations. In late December 1864, a serious rail accident at Sandesjö caused the death of seven people, and eleven people were seriously injured. The only way the injured could claim damages was to bring an action against the train driver, who was held to have been negligent.[1] The train driver had nowhere near the funds needed to satisfy such a claim, so a petition was put forward to the Swedish parliament that the State should finance the train driver's liability. The accident made it clear that there was a pressing need for legislation suited to the special needs that railway operations involved.[2]

1.a.i The 1886 Railway Liability Act

In 1886, the first legislation concerning rail operation was passed: the 1886 Railway Liability Act. It was drawn up on the pattern of legislation in England, France, Belgium and Italy.[3] According to section 2 of the Act, the railway was liable in damages if someone died or suffered bodily harm as a result of rail operations, when death or bodily harm was caused by someone employed by the railway.[4] The main difference regarding liability for personal injuries between the ordinary tort provisions and the new Act was that the railway now became liable for acts or omissions of its staff committed in the course of rail operations.[5] (If the Act had been in effect when the accident at Sandesjö took place, the injured people would have been compensated by the railway company since the train driver had been found negligent.) For liability, it was of no matter if the injured was a passenger, a member of the staff or a non-passenger.[6] However, except in

[1] Provisions concerning tort liability were regulated in chapter 6 former Penal Code (the 1864 Penal Code, in effect from 1864 to 1965). According to chapter 6, section 1, someone who caused damage to someone else through a criminal act was to compensate the damage, not considering if the criminal act was committed by fault or negligence. If the injured person had contributed to the damage by his own actions, the damage could be adjusted accordingly. This provision had, through a number of court rulings, been found to be applicable beyond the scope of criminal acts, and included other non-criminal actions that caused damage, i.e. if someone by negligence caused personal or material damage, he or she was to compensate the damage, even though he had not committed an offence. See the 1972 Governmental Bill no. 5 regarding a new Tort Law (p. 19).

[2] See *Nytt Juridiskt Arkiv* (NJA) II 1886 no. 4, pp. 1–10 and K. Grönfors, *Om trafikskadeansvar utanför kontraktsförhållanden* (Uppsala: Almqvist & Wiksell, 1952), pp. 25–6.

[3] The 1974 Swedish Government Official Reports (SOU), no. 89, p. 34.

[4] Regarding the question of who was to be liable, 'the Railway' was interpreted as the one who possessed the railway in its own name and in its own account, even if the execution had been assigned to someone else. See E. Herslow, *Om ansvarighet för skada i följd av jernvägs drift* (Stockholm: Norstedt & Söner, 1887), p. 20, and J. Hellner and M. Radetzki, *Skadeståndsrätt* (Stockholm: Norstedts Juridik AB, 2006), p. 179. See also NJA 1949 p. 544.

[5] See, for example, Hellner and Radetzki, *Skadeståndsrätt*, p. 34; Herslow, *Om ansvarighet för skada i följd av jernvägs drift*, p. 11; Grönfors, *Om trafikskadeansvar utanför kontraktsförhållanden*, p. 26.

[6] See Grönfors, *Om trafikskadeansvar utanför kontraktsförhållanden*, p. 202 and Herslow, *Om ansvarighet för skada i följd av jernvägs drift*, p. 39.

certain cases, a railway was not liable for personal injuries, loss or damages that were not the result of someone's fault or negligence. Which kind of damages could be compensated and how the damages should be calculated were determined by the ordinary tort provisions.

The definition of 'railway' was: 'railway on which conveyance of people and goods are carried by steam power' (section 1 1886 Act). The word 'railway' indicated that it concerned a track along railway lines.[7] The definition of railway has extended through legislation include railways run by locomotive,[8] and has extended further through case law. For example, the Supreme Court considered tramways under the Railway Liability Act in a case from 1921,[9] and in 1963 the Supreme Court determined that damage caused by a diesel-powered railway vehicle should come under the 1886 Act.[10]

Parallel to the 1886 Act, the Regulation on Carriage by Rail (originating from 1914, amended in 1925 and in 1966) and other traffic regulations were in effect, containing, among other things, provisions about railway liability for conveyance of goods. These regulations were not intended to be exhaustive, but further provisions could be included in the standard stipulations that applied for every rail operator who carried out a general traffic service. Freedom of contract prevailed, but not to such extent that the rights a passenger was assured according to the 1886 Act and the Regulation on Carriage by Rail could be made invalid.[11]

The railway's liability for personal injuries, as mentioned above, required someone's fault or negligence. Another prerequisite of liability was that the accident was a result of rail operations.[12] It was therefore necessary to identify the activities that fell into this category. Despite this, the 1886 Act gave no further information about how to determine what was to be considered actions pertaining to rail operations. There is probably a

[7] See Grönfors, *Om trafikskadeansvar utanför kontraktsförhållanden*, pp. 191–2; Herslow, *Om ansvarighet för skada i följd av jernvägs drift*, pp. 14–18; A. O. Winroth, *Strödda uppsatser Om skadestånd* (Uppsala: Norstedt, 1907), vol. IV p. 247.

[8] Through the 1904 Act (and later the Act of 1916) concerning the 1886 Railway Liability Act's application to Electrical Railway. See Grönfors, *Om trafikskadeansvar utanför kontraktsförhållanden*, pp. 26 and 193.

[9] NJA 1921 p. 362. See also the 1974 SOU, no. 89, p. 39 and Grönfors, *Om trafikskadeansvar utanför kontraktsförhållanden*, pp. 194–5.

[10] NJA 1963 p. 28.

[11] The 1974 SOU, no. 89, p. 35 and the 1975/76 Governmental Bill, no. 7, concerning Railway Liability for Passenger Conveyance, pp. 38–9.

[12] See the 1974 SOU, no. 89, p. 40; Grönfors, *Om trafikskadeansvar utanför kontraktsförhållanden*, pp. 196–201; Herslow, *Om ansvarighet för skada i följd av jernvägs drift*, pp. 25–34.

simple enough reason for this: it is difficult, if not impossible, to express a satisfactory definition of 'rail operation' in a provision that at the same time should be concise and explicit. Regardless of this lack of definition, it was considered clear that the transportation of railway vehicles on railway tracks, preparations for such transportation and maintenance of vehicles while located on the tracks were actions pertaining to rail operations.[13] Any damages that someone sustained while staying in railway workshops, waiting rooms and similar spaces was not considered the result of rail operations and the railway should therefore not be held liable.[14]

Beside the general provision (section 2) in the 1886 Act regarding liability for personal injuries, the railway had a special responsibility for its employees. According to section 3, the railway was held liable if an employee, while performing his or her duties, died or suffered an injury as a result of rail operations, even if the cause of the accident could not be attributed to another employee. An exception was made if the deceased or injured employee could be said to have caused the accident himself by transgressing relevant rules of conduct or by gross negligence.[15] With the development of a general compulsory insurance for work accidents, section 3 1886 Act decreased in significance and was subsequently abolished when the 1954 Act on Insurance for Occupational Injuries came into effect.

The regulation of liability for personal injuries as a result of rail operations that came into effect with the 1886 Act did not affect the general tort law provisions regarding liability for personal injuries.[16] Consequently, the injured person could, instead of suing the railway, choose to claim damages from the railway employee who caused the damage.[17] But since the railway was held liable for personal injuries according to the 1886 Act, the employee who caused the damage had a right of recourse against the employer for compensating the injured person.

[13] See Grönfors, *Om trafikskadeansvar utanför kontraktsförhållanden*, pp. 198–9; Herslow, *Om ansvarighet för skada i följd av jernvägs drift*, pp. 30–2; NJA 1902 p. 502; NJA 1903 p. 37; NJA 1904 p. 434; NJA 1906 p. 239; NJA 1906 p. 572; 1930 A 35; 1944 B 208; NJA 1945 p. 55.

[14] See Grönfors, *Om trafikskadeansvar utanför kontraktsförhållanden*, p. 200; Herslow, *Om ansvarighet för skada i följd av jernvägs drift*, pp. 28–30; Winroth, *Strödda uppsatser*, p. 181; NJA 1909 p. 248 and NJA 1934 p. 371.

[15] See Grönfors, *Om trafikskadeansvar utanför kontraktsförhållanden*, pp. 213–14; Herslow, *Om ansvarighet för skada i följd av jernvägs drift*, pp. 50–2.

[16] Provisions concerning tort liability were regulated in chapter 6 of the former Penal Code (the 1864 Penal Code) and the 1965 Penal Code, up until 1972 when the Swedish Tort Law was promulgated.

[17] See the 1974 SOU, no. 89, p. 45.

1.a.ii The 1976 Act on the Liability of the Railway when carrying Passengers

In 1973, the Additional Convention to the International Convention on the Carriage of Passengers and Luggage by Rail (CIV) came into force, and Sweden acceded to it in 1976.[18] Consequently, the rules concerning liability of the railway for damage caused as a result of rail operations to a passenger or property in his possession in the course of passenger transportation were removed from the 1886 Act, and became governed by an Act on the Liability of the Railway when Carrying Passengers (1976 Act), which was applicable to both domestic and international passenger transportation by railway, underground or tramway.[19] Under this Act, the railway was liable in most cases on essentially objective grounds. The railway was held liable, regardless of proven fault or negligence, when a passenger sustained an injury as a result of an action pertaining to rail operations. The only exceptions where the railway could escape liability were if the damage was the result of an action not considered pertaining to rail operations, if the interference in rail operations which caused the accident was due to some outside force – such as a natural event – or the act of a third party. Even then, the railway had to show that it would have been impossible to avoid the outside force from affecting the operations of the railway, or to prevent the injurious consequences thereof, even if the railway had taken the care required in the particular circumstances of the case. The railway was also relieved of liability in so far as it proved that the passenger himself caused the injury.[20] It should be observed that injury caused as a result of rail operations to someone who was *not a passenger*, was still regulated by the 1886 Act, which meant that a person (e.g. a road-user at a railway crossing who sustained an injury) still generally had to show that the personal injury, loss or damage concerned was due to fault or negligence on the railway's part.

Another situation where the stricter liability in the 1976 Act was applicable was when the railway, due to a temporary interference in rail operations, carried the passengers with some other means of transportation than a railway vehicle (e.g. by bus or by car). In those cases, the railway was liable for any injuries a passenger sustained as a result of this conveyance, regardless of fault or negligence in the substitute transportation.[21] The passenger could then be entitled to compensation from the railway as well as

[18] See the 1974 SOU, no. 89, pp. 72–3 and the 1975/76 Governmental Bill, no. 7, p. 38.

[19] See the 1974 SOU, no. 89, pp. 95, 97–100 and the 1975/76 Governmental Bill, no. 7, p. 39.

[20] See the 1974 SOU, no. 89, pp. 74–6, 104–10 and the 1975/76 Government Bill, no. 7, pp. 41–2.

[21] See the 1974 SOU, no. 89, pp. 113–14 and the 1975/76 Government Bill, no. 7, pp. 71–4.

from the motor vehicle's insurance, according to the 1975 Traffic Damage Act. Another situation regarding motor vehicles was when personal injury was caused by a collision between a rail and a motor vehicle. The rail-transportation operator was then liable for damage caused to the latter only if it was shown that this was caused by fault or negligence in the rail operations, while the motor vehicle's insurance was required to pay traffic damage on purely objective grounds for any damage caused in respect of the rail vehicle, including the railway passengers.[22] In these cases, quite difficult issues could arise regarding right to recovery of such payments for damage between the rail operator and the traffic insurance companies.

The 1976 Act did not provide a definition of who was to be considered a 'passenger', but it was supposed that a person should be considered a passenger if he was entitled to the conveyance in question due to an agreement between the railway and himself entered into, or an agreement that he could be assumed to be entering into. The passenger's right to damage was, however, only in effect during the period of time when staying in the railway vehicle or while entering or alighting from such a vehicle.[23] Since the railway liability for personal injuries was objective regarding passengers but based on fault or negligence regarding non-passengers, the definition of passenger turned out to be essential. For the railway employees, the 1954 Act on Insurance for Occupational Injuries had already received a satisfactory solution for personal injuries sustained from an action pertaining to rail operations.

1.a.iii The 1985 Act on Carriage by Rail

In 1980, the Committee on New Legislation for Carriage by Rail delivered a report including a bill addressing these above-mentioned issues. In 1985, the Act on Carriage by Rail (the 1985 Act) and the Act on International Carriage by Rail came into effect, and that Act repealed the 1886 and 1976 Acts, as well as the 1966 Regulation on Carriage by Rail. From having sets of regulations concerning liability for personal injuries, loss or damage, the different provisions were now collected into one Act – one Act which governed the liability of the railway authority and the train operators towards customers and others injured as a result of rail operations.[24] The Act included not only transportation by railway, but to some extent also transportation by underground and by tram. The main change of

[22] See the 1980 SOU, no. 37, p. 77.

[23] See the 1974 SOU, no. 89, pp. 97–9 and the 1975/76 Government Bill, no. 7, pp. 54–7.

[24] See the 1980 SOU, no. 37, pp. 58–60 and the 1983/84 Government Bill, no. 117, pp. 31–2.

importance concerned railway liability for personal injuries to non-passengers, while the provisions concerning the carrying of passengers were substantially the same as those of the 1976 Act.[25]

The basic principle underlying the rules governing liability for personal injury or damage to property sustained by a third party as the result of operations of a railway, underground or tramway were that liability for damage caused by rail should – as in the case of motor-vehicle traffic – generally be based on purely objective grounds.[26] However, one of the distinctions between carriage by rail and motor-vehicle traffic is that railways largely operate within an area that is carefully divided off from areas used for other kinds of traffic. The committee proposing the legislation took this factor into account, in that objective liability did not apply in the case of damage occurring in a part of track area that was forbidden to the public, provided that the person who sustained injury was there without authorisation. Even so, the 1985 Act would, according to the committee, increase the railway operator's liability compared to the rules in the 1976 Act, since the injured person was considered entitled to damages from the operator not only if the damage had been caused by fault or negligence during rail operations, but also if it occurred due to a defect in equipment essential to these operations.[27] These changes made it more or less unnecessary to differentiate between passengers, railway employees and persons who were not passengers since the basis for damage were purely objective in all cases.

Once again, the definition of 'railway' was discussed. The committee pointed out that the question of whether a rail construction should be considered as a railway had not come up in a long time, and that it did not seem to be a problem in practical life. It was also pointed out that the conception of the railway had been used in legislation not only concerning the rail construction but also the legal entity that is in possession of the railway and which is entitled to use the construction for its own interest and assimilate the profits.[28] The legislator considered a provision defining 'railway' unnecessary, since the conception used seemed natural and a statutory definition could not bring further clarity to the issue.[29] The legal body liable in damages should also henceforth be the one in possession

[25] See the 1980 SOU, no. 37, pp. 174–8 and the 1983/84 Government Bill, no. 117, pp. 78–86.

[26] See the 1980 SOU, no. 37, pp. 174–6; the 1983/84 Government Bill, no. 117, pp. 82–4; Hellner and Radetzki, *Skadeståndsrätt*, pp. 175, 275 and 285.

[27] See the 1980 SOU, no. 37, p. 178.

[28] See the 1980 SOU, no. 37, pp. 62–7.

[29] See the 1983/84 Government Bill, no. 117, p. 33.

of the railway and the one that is entitled to use the construction for its own interest and assimilate the profits. Even if the possessor commissions another legal entity to operate the rail traffic, it would not affect his status as possessor. If the damage ensued from negligence with the operating company, the railway should be able to recover the paid damage according to general rules of right to recourse. Since the 1985 Act, the definition of railway is considered as having a generally accepted meaning.[30]

The definition of 'passenger' remained the same as before; that is to say, a person who is located in, embarking or alighting from a rail vehicle is considered to be a passenger.[31] Since the rules governing liability for damage to other persons than passengers changed, there was considered no need to alter the conception of passenger. There has been some disagreement concerning whether 'stowaways' should be considered as passengers or as third parties. The Supreme Court ruled in a case from 1981 that free-riders should not be considered as passengers,[32] but since all personal injuries caused by rail operations are compensated on purely objective grounds according to the 1985 Act, there is nowadays hardly any reason to differentiate between passengers and non-passengers.

The main change of importance concerned, as mentioned, the railway liability for personal injuries to non-passengers. Under the 1976 Act, the railway became liable on purely objective grounds for personal injuries to passengers, but liability for damage to persons other than passengers remained to be governed by the 1886 Act, which stipulated a prerequisite of fault or negligence for railway liability. During the years since the 1886 Act came into effect, other legislation governing non-contractual liability for other forms of transportation was passed. When it comes to motor-vehicle traffic and air traffic, the legislation has involved a considerably stricter liability of the transporter than was provided either in the 1886 Act or in general tort law. These differences between various kinds of transport were considered unjustified. The railway should therefore be held liable for personal injuries as a result of rail operations on purely objective grounds. No such exception as the committee had proposed was made from this objective liability regarding persons who sustained injuries in a part of track area that was forbidden to the public.[33] Instead,

[30] See the 2003/04 Government Bill, no. 123, pp. 66–7 and Hellner and Radetzki, *Skadeståndsrätt*, pp. 179 and 285.

[31] See the 1980 SOU, no. 37, pp. 78–9 and the 1983/84 Government Bill, no. 117, pp. 46–8.

[32] NJA 1981 section 412. See also the 1983/84 Government Bill, no. 117, pp. 47–8 and 120–1 and Hellner and Radetzki, *Skadeståndsrätt*, p. 286.

[33] See the 1980 SOU, no. 37, p. 176.

such circumstances could be taken into consideration when determining the amount of damages. If the injured person had contributed to his own injury by intent or by gross negligence, the amount of damages should be adjusted accordingly. Practically the same should apply if someone died as a result of rail operations. The damages to the deceased's family should be able to be adjusted if the deceased had contributed to the damage intentionally.[34]

Another issue of great importance was how to distribute responsibility amongst railway and motor-vehicle insurance. In a collision or a near collision between a train and a motor vehicle that are both in operation, the injured persons should, according to the 1985 Act, no longer be able to claim compensation from the railway company and the motor-vehicle insurer at the same time. Instead, the claim ought to be channelled through the transporter with whom the victim was travelling.[35] That is, in the first instance, railway passengers and others on board the train should direct their claims for damage to the railway, while injuries to the driver and passengers in the motor vehicle should claim damages from the motor-vehicle insurance. In both cases, liability is based on purely objective grounds. The only exception to this type of channelling should be if it can be determined that the damage was caused by fault or negligence on either side in the collision or as a result of defectiveness of either vehicle. In the final settlement between railway and motor-vehicle insurance, the question of fault or negligence and potential defectiveness will be decisive for the distribution of damage.[36]

When it comes to assessing which types of injury should be compensated and how to determine what amount of damage should be paid, neither the 1985 Act nor any of the preceding Acts have offered any guidance. Instead, the general tort law provisions in the 1972 Act of Tort Law governing assessment of damage have been – and are still being – used.[37]

1.b Norway

In the same way as in Sweden, it became clear in the 1860s that more objective responsibility for certain actions was needed, since the ordinary rules on tort liability were not sufficient to deal with matters of compensation for

[34] See the 1983/84 Government Bill, no. 117, pp. 85–6.

[35] See the 1980 SOU, no. 37, pp. 182–6 and the 1983/84 Government Bill, no. 117, pp. 89–93.

[36] See the 1983/84 Government Bill, no. 117, pp. 83 and 85 and Hellner and Radetzki, *Skadeståndsrätt*, pp. 253, 280 and 285.

[37] See Hellner and Radetzki, *Skadeståndsrätt*, p. 275.

personal injuries, loss or damage as a result of rail operations. The question of fault as a prerequisite for liability had developed and gained ground in the Nordic countries, but the legal community faced new challenges with industrialised and technical progress, in which the growth of the railways was an important component.[38] A new form of liability was pushed, which had great similarities to previous case law, but was not exactly the same.

The first ruling from the Supreme Court that held someone liable on purely objective grounds without legislative support came in 1866 (Rt. 1866 p. 735). The ruling concerned railway responsibility for damage through soot (from trains) and noise on a house situated near the railway tracks. Thereafter, several rulings followed during the 1870s and onwards.[39] In actual fact, it was the fault principle that applied, but the demand for caution was very strict. In a dissertation from 1897, the writer deemed that the verdicts expressed an objective liability regardless of the awareness of fault by the person causing the injury.[40] Through a series of rulings, a base was founded regarding which requirements an objective liability that was not regulated by law had to meet.[41] In some areas, this objective liability came to be confirmed by law, and the responsibility for the Norwegian railway was one of these, but the development came first and foremost through court rulings.[42]

Norway has, as well as Sweden, acceded to the Additional Convention to the CIV from 1973, although Norway at that time did not have legislation regarding national conveyance of passengers by railway. Up until 1977, liability was dependant on stated technical deficiencies or indefensible arrangements, but since then, railway and tramway has, according to the Railway Act, an objective liability for passenger injuries.[43] Although Norwegian legislation has been strongly influenced by international conventions, the Railway Liability Act's provisions concerning personal injuries are only applicable to national transportation.[44] From 1999, the objective liability has expanded from only including passenger damages

[38] See Hellner and Radetzki, *Skadeståndsrätt*, pp. 32–4; N. Nygaard, *Skade og Ansvar* (Bergen: Universitetsforlaget, 2000), pp. 248–50.

[39] See, for example, Rt. 1874 p. 145; Rt. 1875 p. 330; Rt. 1889 p. 642.

[40] N. Gjelsvik, *Om skadeserstatning for retmæssige Handlinger efter norsk Ret* (Kristiania: W.C. Fabritius & sønners bogtrykkeri, 1897).

[41] See, for example Rt. 1905 p. 715; Rt. 1909 p. 851; P. Lødrup, *Lærebok i Erstatningsrett*, 4th ed (Oslo: Gyldendal, 1999), pp. 109–18 and Nygaard, *Skade og Ansvar*, pp. 249–67.

[42] See Lødrup, *Lærebok i Erstatningsrett*, p. 195.

[43] LOV-1977-06-10-73. See also Rt. 1964 p. 272; Rt. 1975 p. 710; Nygaard, *Skade og Ansvar*, p. 270.

[44] Sections 1 and 2 Railway Liability Act. See Lødrup, *Lærebok i Erstatningsrett*, p. 209.

to comprise cases of non-passenger injuries. When children under the age of fifteen are run over by train or tram, and in other cases of collisions (without the limitation to children under the age of fifteen), the railway is held responsible on objective grounds, according to section 9. Apart from that, liability is still dependent on fault by the person causing the injury, technical deficiencies or indefensible arrangements. The only exception is responsibility for fire caused by sparks.[45]

The definitions of 'railway' and 'passenger' is the same as in Swedish legislation and, when it comes to determining which actions should be considered pertaining to rail operations, the Norwegian Railway Liability Act takes a rather liberal position. The manner in which liability is limited is to require causality between the action and the damage. If the damage can be said to be a result from other causes, the railway is not liable, even if the damaging action takes place during rail operations.[46]

In situations of collision or near collision between a railway vehicle and a motor vehicle, the Norwegian Railway Liability Act stipulates the same conditions as in Swedish law. The claim for damage is channelled to the transporter that the injured person was travelling with (section 1 Railway Liability Act and section 3 Railway Act). Between the operators, there is a general right of recourse that can be affected if one of the operators has been negligent.

1.c Denmark

In Denmark, an objective liability was introduced at an early stage. The first Act on responsibility for railway actions came into effect in 1898, followed by the 1921 Act, and in 2003 the Act was updated (the Railway Transport Act of 28 March 2003). Denmark acceded to the Additional Convention to the CIV in 1973, and it was incorporated into the national legal system (without any transformation into national legislation). Liability is imposed on the operator of the activity, but if more than one person is found liable on objective grounds, and none has been at fault, the court can decide the appropriate right of recourse on the basis of what is fair.[47] If, however, one of the responsible parties has acted with fault or negligence, it is considered

[45] LOV-1999-05-21-31. See RG 1998 p. 1223; Rt. 1948 p. 439; Rt. 1955 p. 46; V. Hagstrøm, *Offentligrettslig erstatningsansvar, Studier i spesiell og alminnelig erstatningsret* (Oslo: Tano, 1987), p. 200 and Lødrup, *Lærebok i Erstatningsrett*, pp. 211–12.

[46] See Lødrup, *Lærebok i Erstatningsrett*, p. 210.

[47] See the 1980 SOU, no. 37, p. 58 and H. Ussing, *Erstatningsret* (Copenhagen: Gad, 1962), pp. 132–3.

as a key rule that the operator who is only liable due to objective grounds has a right to full recovery from the guilty operator.

The provision of paramount importance in the Act is section 13, paragraph 1, which states that: 'Rail operations are to compensate damages to passengers, for whom no special rules are applicable due to a service relationship to the railway or the possessor of the rail infrastructure, where the harm results from an act relating to railway transportation during which the passenger is seated in, entering or alighting from the railway vehicle.' The provision clearly provides for liability on purely objective grounds.

According to section 15, the railway company is to compensate for harms to persons or goods that are not being transported where this results in a collision. The amount of damages can, according to section 14, paragraph 1, be adjusted or be reduced to nothing if the injured person has contributed to his own injury by intent or by gross negligence.[48] Claims for damages caused by the railway must be covered by liability insurance (i.e. there is an obligation to hold liability insurance dedicated to rail operations).[49]

1.d Finland

The Finnish way of regulating railway operations has great similarities with the Swedish legislation. Finland acceded to the Additional Convention to the CIV in 1973 and it has been incorporated, just as in Denmark and Sweden, into the national legal system.[50] The railway transporter is liable on purely objective grounds for damage resulting from railway operations. The railway can escape liability when the damage is the result of an action not considered pertaining to rail operations, if the interference in rail operations that caused the accident is due to some outside force – such as a natural event – or the act of a third party. Only the acts of those who are employed under a contract in the railway service can give rise to liability on the part of the railway.[51]

Since responsibility requires that the damage has been a result of rail operations there are two requirements.[52] Firstly, one has to decide which actions should be considered as pertaining to rail operations. Secondly,

[48] See FED 2001.2255 V. See also Ussing, *Erstatningsret*, 183–91.

[49] Section 17, paragraph 1. See B. von Eyben and H. Isager, *Lærebog i erstatningsret* (Copenhagen: Jurist- og Økonomforbundets Forlag, 2004), pp. 205–6.

[50] See the 1980 SOU, no. 37, p. 58.

[51] See H. Saxén, *Adekvans och skada* (Åbo (Turku): Åbo Akademi, 1962), pp. 150–1.

[52] See Grönfors, *Om trafikskadeansvar utanför kontraktsförhållanden*, pp. 196–201.

one has to conclude that there is a causal link between the rail operation and the damage. It is certain that 'actions resulting from rail operations' not only consists of situations in which a specific risk of damage is involved which has justified the objective ground for liability. Even damage originating from a motionless train can be governed by the Railway Act. On the other hand, damage that has occurred in the railway administration offices or waiting areas can be something that will be compensated.[53] According to the preparatory works of the Railway Act, it has been stated that the activity that has caused the damage should have an immediate linkage to the transportation itself, and as a result of this should have been affected by the danger associated with the transportation.[54]

1.e Conclusion

Scandinavian countries have reacted with a similar methodology to the changing transportation technologies that might generate tort liability, and this is particularly evident in Sweden. It needed a disaster to trigger railway regulation , but once this happened, the legislative response grew in space, covering ever more potential claimants over about a century. The pattern of regulation was broadly similar in road accidents, though without such an obvious trigger. Arguably, there was a more direct point of comparison between cars and other forms of road transportation, such as horse-drawn carriages, so lessons could be learnt earlier. And yet there were large periods of inactivity between when reform proposals were first discussed and when they were enacted. Here we find one difference between road and rail: rail legislation did not wait for a general reform of tort law, as road regulation did. It should, of course, be noted that rail regulation was taking place much before such moves for a general reform of tort law. At the same time, the recognition that one area of tort law could not cope with new transportation technology could easily have triggered reform elsewhere. Perhaps railways were, at the start, viewed as an area of tort liability that could be hived off from the rest without difficulty. If this is correct, once the Damage Act (DA) came into operation in 1972, the view shifted and efforts were made to unify the effect of the different regimes both systematically (e.g. the calculation of damages) and where they overlapped (e.g. a car and train collision).

[53] See Saxén, *Adekvans och skada*, p. 151.

[54] J. Grotenfelt, 'Om ansvarighet för skada i följd av järnvägsdrift', *Tidskrift utgiven av Juridska Föreningen i Finland* (JFT) 1904, pp. 38–40.

The same kinds of processes and legal tools were used in Sweden. Legal change came through large-scale legislative reforms that proceeded from careful deliberation at committee stages. There was a keen awareness for comparative material, not just from other Scandinavian countries but also from, for instance, rail regulation in other civil law countries and England, as well as road regulation in North America. Judicial decisions did play a role in legal change, but they are often treated by commentators as signals of legislative deficiencies, rather than developers of the law itself.

One of the most characteristic features of the legal regime is the extensive involvement of insurance. The changes in tort law seem to rely very heavily on the support of the insurance industry. It would be fascinating to know the deals that went on between the reformers and that industry, and within the industry itself, but such deals tend to have a limited public aspect. The selective use of the recourse action is perhaps somewhat difficult to explain, other than as a feature of keeping the system simple and being felt to be socially or morally unacceptable in the Scandinavian context.

The model of socialised acceptance of risk is notable both for its breadth of factual triggers as for the number of states within Scandinavia that have accepted its rules. The concept of community is somewhat more expansive than in most of the rest of Europe.

2 Liability for personal injuries resulting from road traffic

2.a *Historical overview*

The first Swedish Act concerning traffic-accident law was introduced in 1906. Ten years later, in 1916, it was replaced by a new Act. The purpose of both these laws was to protect the victims of traffic accidents. In 1929, Sweden also passed a law on mandatory traffic insurance, obliging motor-vehicle owners to take out such insurance.

2.a.i The Act of 1906

With the Act of 1906, special legislation concerning traffic-accident liability was introduced for the first time in Sweden. General tort law rules, centred on fault, were replaced with a new regime. The Act also made the owner and the user liable for damage caused by the driver's fault. A condition for this vicarious liability, however, was that the damage had to have been caused to a person or property that was not being transported by the vehicle, or to a person who had been transported for payment.[55]

2.a.ii The Act of 1916

With the Act of 1916, the protection for victims was further strengthened. A liability built on presumption was adopted. The point of departure was the condition that the owner was strictly liable for damage caused by the vehicle in traffic to a person or property that was not being transported by the vehicle. This liability was not engaged if the vehicle had been taken without the owner's permission. It was also evaded if the owner could prove that the damage was caused neither by the defectiveness of the vehicle nor by the driver's fault. The driver bore the same presumption. He, too, could avoid liability: for him it was enough to prove that he had not caused the accident by fault. The legislator presumed that the damage was caused by the defectiveness of the vehicle or by the driver's fault until the contrary was proven.

2.a.iii The Act of 1929

For the victim, whether the liability to pay damages lay with the owner, user or driver depended on whether the person responsible could pay, either personally or through a voluntarily paid liability insurance. To cover the gaps this created, in 1929 an Act was adopted that charged the owner with a duty to have the vehicle insured.[56] This mandatory vehicle insurance not only covered the owner's liability, but also that of the driver and user. A right of direct action against the vehicle insurance was also granted. Through this Act, tort liability for traffic accidents changed its character. In reality, liability was transformed into a duty of the owners of motor vehicles to pay premiums to the insurer of the vehicle. The function of the Act of 1916 essentially became to accurately define the conditions of the right to claim compensation from the mandatory insurance, as well as the quantum of this indemnity.[57]

The Acts of 1916 and 1929 lasted until the 1 July 1976 (i.e. for sixty years). They were replaced by Trafikskadelagen no. 1410 ('Traffic Damage Act' – TDA). This Act, still in force, represents a milestone in Sweden, not only concerning the history of traffic-accident law but also the history of

[55] Cf. the 1974 SOU, no. 87, p. 55.

[56] Lagen den 10 maj 1929 om trafikförsäkring å motorfordon [Law on Traffic Insurance for Motor Vehicles] ('trafikförsäkringslagen').

[57] Cf. the 1957 SOU, no. 36, p. 32.

the whole law of torts.[58] It began the development through which no-fault insurance took hold and stimulated the growth of other similar systems.[59] Swedish tort law had already changed its character in 1972, when, for the first time ever, a new general Act on tort law was introduced: the DA.[60] The changes of this Act were immediately overtaken by the TDA, special legislation that can be said to have gone further. The new profile that Swedish tort law developed with the TDA has been retained ever since.

2.a.iv The Bill of 1938

In 1938, a bill was published, according to which the Act on Vehicle Insurance was to be changed in a sweeping way.[61] Vehicle insurance would have covered all kinds of personal injury or property damage due to traffic accidents. However, the insurance would never have compensated injuries to the driver or property damage caused by the motor vehicle.

Concerning the size of the compensation, different rules would have been applied, depending on whether a fault had been committed by the driver, owner or user. When there was fault, the insurance would have been based on general tort liability rules and principles, meaning full indemnity. Liability based on a presumption of fault would have be abolished, but contributory fault would have reduced the compensation received. Personal liability for the driver, owner or user would only have been accepted when it was proven that a fault had been committed by one of these persons.

[58] See also J. Hellner, 'Entwicklungslinien im schwedischen Haftpflichtrecht' in H. Baumann, H. Schirmer and R. Schmidt (eds.) *Festschrift fur Karl Sieg* (Karlsruhe: Verlag Versicherungswirtschaft, 1976), pp. 155–69; ibid., 'Haftungsersetzung durch Versicherungsschutz in Schweden' in J. G. Fleming, J. Hellner and E.von Hippel *Haftungsersetzung durch Versicherungsschutz* (Frankfurt am Main: Metzner, 1980), pp. 24–39.

[59] The most prominent of these systems is patient insurance. See J. Hellner, 'Sweden', in E. Deutsch and H.-L. Schreiber (eds.), *Medical Responsibility in Western Europe: Research Study of the European Science Foundation* (Berlin: Springer, 1985), pp. 683–728. Previously voluntary, the system today is found in Patientskadelag (1996:799; 'Patient Injury Act'). Another example is the still-voluntary drug insurance scheme. See B. W. Dufwa, 'Product Liability Legislation: General Problems and Techniques: The Swedish Experience' in IEFR, *Pharmaceutical Medicine – the Future* (Brussels: IFFR, 1978), pp. 144ff. and, with the same content in Portuguese: 'Legislacao da responsabilidade relative a produtos farmaceuticos: A experiencia Sueca', *Revista da procuradoria-geral do estado* 11(30) (1981), at 11–18. The spreading to other fields was also inspired by ideas developed by the American author Jeffrey O'Connell, particularly concerning 'elective no-fault insurance' (see below, note 69).

[60] 1972 Skadeståndslagen, no. 207. The Act came into force on 1 July 1972.

[61] See the 1998 SOU, no. 27.

If no fault could be shown, insurance compensation ought, according to the Bill, to have been paid in connection with the rules regarding work accidents. In these situations, a personal liability to pay compensation was excluded, but mitigation because of contributory negligence could take place. The calculation of the compensation would have been according to special rules in these situations, essentially built on patterns. In principle, no indemnity would have been granted for pain and suffering. For the insurer, maximum amounts were settled.[62]

Problems in a special field of the law might have difficulties in attracting interest. Even though traffic accidents are common and represent the greater part of all accidents, dealing with them still depends on politics and on other problems and circumstances dominating society. This dependence was fatal for the 1938 Bill. No great forces had set off the reform work. There had long been a tradition in the Nordic countries (Sweden, Norway, Finland, Denmark and Iceland) of collaborating in the field of legislation. However, this time such collaboration was missing. Norway, Finland and Denmark were at war, while Sweden remained neutral. In such a situation, a reform of this special character had no chance of survival. The Bill gathered dust.

2.a.v Ivar Strahl

When legislative work began after the Second World War, the tradition of Nordic collaboration was revived. In 1946, representatives of the Ministers of Justice of Denmark, Norway and Sweden submitted a programme for reform. Regarding the reform work of tort law, attention was paid to certain issues that were deemed to be significant, and compensation for traffic accidents was considered to be particularly important.

The whole proposal concerning tort law was discussed at a meeting between the Ministers of Justice of the three countries in November 1946. The goal for the work became to reform the law of the countries at national levels, with the orientation being towards a Nordic Tort Law Act. There was agreement that this idea should be examined by experts from the Nordic countries. Firstly, however, a preparatory investigation had to be done. This was brought about by every country conducting their own investigations, all of which were published in 1950. These investigations afforded new perspectives on tort law. The most sensational inquiry became the one presented by the Swedish expert, Ivar Strahl, professor of

[62] See the summary of the Bill made in the 1974 SOU, no. 87, pp. 83–4.

criminal law.[63] Together with its author, it became world famous. Strahl's idea was that tort law, to a large extent, should be replaced by insurance, particularly when concerning personal injury.

All of the preparatory investigations were characterised by a comprehensive view and rationality. The experts agreed that a Nordic Tort Law Act could not be introduced immediately. They therefore recommended that the work should be driven by stages, and that the first priority should be to initiate partial reforms in fields where the need for reform was most important. The three inquiries were discussed at the Nordic lawyers' meeting in Stockholm in 1950. There was sympathy in favour of the proposals, but also criticism. Traditional tort law was defended, but not without a wish for changes, for instance stricter liability in some areas. Opinions were divided on the core question of a general Nordic tort law.

This orientation of the work was broadly followed. However, it is possible that the planning of the work was flawed. The orientation towards particular fields had the advantage that one could try out the ideas about the general principles regarding the future of tort law that had been presented.[64] However, due to the fact that every country was working in its own interest when considering the special questions that arose, instead of directly contributing to the great tort law issues, the work became stuck in national paths. A Nordic Traffic Accident Act has still not been realised, and it is not easy to find anyone who believes that it ever will be. In the end, however, tort law legislation in the Nordic countries have grown very close to each other. This is particularly the case between Swedish and Finnish law, but also between Sweden and Norway.

2.a.vi The Bill of 1957

The first steps in the actual reform work towards a Nordic Damage Act were orientated towards traffic accidents. The experts highlighted the

[63] See the 1950 SOU, no. 16. See also I. Strahl, 'Tort Liability and Insurance', *Scandinavian Studies in Law* (1959), at 199. See also H. Ussing (who was the Danish investigator), 'The Scandinavian Law of Torts: Impact of Insurance on Tort Law' *American Journal of Comparative Law* (1952) 359. The ideas of Strahl influenced A. A. Ehrenzweig. See A. A. Ehrenzweig, *'Full Aid' Insurance for the Traffic Victim* (Berkeley and Los Angeles: University of California Press, 1954) and his article 'Assurance Oblige: A Comparative Study', 15 *Law and Contemporary Problems* 15 (1950), at 445. The development is also described in B. W. Dufwa, 'Responsabilité du fait des produits en droit suédois', *Revue internationale de droit comparé* (1977), at 525, 526–30; ibid., 'Liability in Tort and Liability Insurance: Sweden' in G. Wagner (ed.), *Tort Law and Liability Insurance* (Vienna: Springer 2005), pp. 147–72 with further references.

[64] Cf. the 1957 SOU, no. 36, p. 22.

mischief to be dealt with in the national work regarding these accidents. Tort law issues were to be considered against the background of the development of insurance. The experts intended that, as soon as the work regarding traffic accents was finished, a general Damage Act should be taken up.

A committee with the task of creating rules on traffic-accident compensation was established in Sweden in 1952. Its chairman became Ivar Strahl. After some time, a secretary was nominated, who later came to be a famous expert in tort law and who, as a member of the Supreme Court, was appointed as chairman of committees in the field of tort law: Erland Conradi. One could say that he shouldered the ideas of Strahl and brought them further into the future, since Strahl himself had more or less left the scene. Conradi continued his work until the early 1980s.

The committee published the results of its work in 1957. In this Bill, the outlines of a new modern traffic-accident law were elaborated. According to the main rule, compensation should be paid out from the mandatory vehicle insurance. This rule should apply irrespective of the fault of the driver; whether the damage was caused by the defectiveness of the vehicle or not should have no influence on the liability of the insurer. Liability built on presumption should be abolished, to be replaced with strict liability for the insurer. Two exemptions, however, were given. Firstly, if other motor vehicles were damaged, or if persons in them suffered injuries or if property in them was damaged, compensation should be paid out only if it was proven that the driver's fault or defectiveness of the vehicle had been the cause of the accident. Evidently, this rule concerned collisions. Secondly, corresponding limits of the liability should apply when there has been a collision with a stationary motor vehicle.

Rules proposed by the Committee on Contributory Negligence became more advantageous to the victim than the general rules of tort law. Strahl, as well as another member of the Committee, was, however, not satisfied with the Bill on this point. The rules made reservations. Instead, they argued that compensation for personal injury should be paid out without any possibility of mitigation, except for very grave contributory fault.

The committee proposed dispensing with the rules laid down in the Traffic Accident Insurance Act regarding maximum compensation for personal injury. Full compensation should be set according to the general tort law rules. Strahl made a reservation on this point too. He did not want income over a certain amount to be taken into account. Regarding property damage, the Committee restricted the compensation from traffic insurance to a certain sum.

The strict liability in traffic insurance did not mean that personal liability was completely abolished. The owner and the driver should be liable, but only according to the fault rule. Liability should, in principle, only apply in collision cases and, even then, when it was shown that fault or defectiveness had caused the damage. When there was fault or defectiveness on both sides after a collision, liability should be apportioned with regard to the fault committed on both sides. To the extent that the damage was higher than the insurance amount, liability was limited to intentional or reckless behaviour.

An owner injured while he was a passenger in his own vehicle was on an equal footing with other passengers in the vehicle concerning the right to compensation from the vehicle insurance. Compensation from the insurance to an injured driver was, however, not paid out. Damage to the vehicle or to property being transported in the vehicle was also not compensated. On the other hand, there was a right to compensation concerning damaged hand luggage.

Alongside the Swedish investigation work, the same activity was being undertaken in Denmark, Norway and Finland. Consultations between the committees took place. The proposals published in these other countries were essentially in accordance with the Swedish proposal.[65]

The Swedish Bill was met positively. Most supported the idea that strict liability should be adopted. There was, however, some criticism. Many bodies to which submissions were circulated wanted not only the owner but also the driver to be covered by the vehicle insurance. Most responses wanted to keep the rules concerning contributory negligence regarding personal injury. The need for prevention was stressed. Others agreed with Strahl that no mitigation at all should take place. Personal injury was serious, and the consequences of the present rules were not in reasonable proportion to the negligence of the victim. The complex debate concerning the matter of insurance liability versus personal liability resulted in a complete lack of continuity with the previous regime. Therefore the possibility of using previous experience was reduced.[66]

One key objection against the Bill addressed the attempt to reform but one part of a web of liability. Some argued that it was unsuitable to introduce such an important principle in a limited field before there was accordance about how the general tort law should be performed. This objection turned out to be fateful. It contributed strongly to the fact that the proposal was not directly legislated. The Bill lay dormant for many

[65] Cf. the 1957 SOU, no. 36, pp. 162–85, note 9. [66] Cf. the 1974 SOU, no. 87, pp. 85–6.

years while awaiting new general rules on damages for personal injury. Not until Sweden introduced a new DA in 1972 (later reformed)[67] did the Bill from 1957 bear fruit.

2.b The Act of 1975

2.b.i The legislation at work

The new Bill was published in 1974.[68] The initiative of the investigation had been taken by the insurance industry, which had paid attention to no-fault insurance, developed in the United States and Canada. There, the principle that the driver's fault was a condition for the victim's right to compensation had been dropped. In the terms of reference given to the new committee, it was suggested that foreign legislation in the field should be studied, especially no-fault principles founded on Acts that were in force or being prepared in the United States and Canada. The restricted time that was at their disposal, however, made it impossible for the committee to make visits for the purposes of study, or to conduct interviews with representatives of the states about how the systems had been functioning in practice. It all became a question of desk studies regarding the actual laws and selected parts of the rich literature concerning different types of no-fault systems that had been published in, above all, the United States but also in Europe.[69] The committee worked extremely fast and published a bill, which quickly resulted in legislation. On 15 December 1975, the new TDA was promulgated. It came into force on 1 July 1976, exactly four years after the DA.[70]

The chairman of the committee was Ulf K. Nordenson, at that time the State Secretary of the Department of Justice, later a Supreme Court judge. Nordenson was very familiar with tort law. He had worked from the beginning with the general reform of tort law, and continued to do

[67] Lag 1975:404 om ändring i skadeståndslagen. The Act came into force on 1 January 1976.

[68] See the 1974 SOU, no. 87.

[69] Ibid., p. 36. Special interest was paid to the remarkable reform plan of J. F. Keeton and J. O'Connell, *Basic Protection for the Traffic Victim* (Boston, MA: Little, Brown and Company 1965).

[70] Comments in French on the Act are given by B. W. Dufwa, 'Assurance no-fault dans le cadre des règles de la responsabilité civile', *Les Cahiers de droit* (Numéro spécial) 39 (1998), at 655–76; J. Hellner, 'La nouvelle loi suédoise sur l'assurance automobile obligatoire', *Revue Générale des Assurances Terrestres* (1977), at 153. See also M. Le Roy and H. Margeat, 'La réparation des dommages causés par un véhicule à moteur: l'exemple suédois', *Gazette du Palais*, (1976), at 473ff.

so up until 1972, when the DA was passed. While preparing the law on nuclear-accident liability, resulting in the Nuclear Liability Act of 1968,[71] Nordenson became a strong advocate for the idea of channelling liability.[72] Through him, this idea was adopted more generally in tort law by the DA, an Act that can be said to be built on the idea of channelling. By using the same weapon in the work with the TDA, he could easily slip into and realise the concept of no-fault liability.

2.b.ii The Traffic Damage Act

The most important parts of the construction and content of the TDA can be summarised in the following way. Strict liability is imposed regarding personal injury. Such liability is also prescribed for property damage that has not occurred in connection with a collision with other motor vehicles. Property damage due to collisions is regulated by the fault principle. The obligation to pay compensation for all these three categories of damage is placed on the vehicle insurance.

The TDA (article 1) concerns mandatory traffic insurance for motor vehicles and compensation from this insurance for damage resulting from traffic accidents. The Act is not applicable to the following:

- a motor vehicle intended to be driven by pedestrians
- a motor vehicle used exclusively within competition fields in an enclosure
- motorised tools.

The notion of 'damage resulting from traffic accidents' has been used in older legislation, and this judicial application undoubtedly gives some guidelines when applying the new Act. The transmission from personal liability built on fault to quasi-strict liability placed on vehicle insurance has possibly resulted in a change of the legal position, so that the notion has become a somewhat more extended field of application than before. It has been stressed that the question of whether damage has resulted from a traffic accident is clearly a technical matter that has to be decided without regard to the role that the driver of the vehicle or other persons have played in the course of events. The fact that the vehicle was being used for criminal activity has, for instance, no importance in this context.[73]

[71] See 1968 Atomansvarighetslag, no. 45.

[72] See B. W. Dufwa, 'Channelling in Tort Law', in B. Nyström, A. Westregård and H. Vogel (eds.), *Liber Amicorum Reinhold Fahlbeck* (Lund: Juristforlaget, 2005), pp. 91–109.

[73] See U. K. Nordenson, *Trafikskadeersättning. Kommentar till trafikskadelagstiftningen* (Stockholm: LiberFörlag, 1977), p. 87.

2.b.iii Two alternatives

The final choice was between the personal tort liability of the owner, user or driver, backed up by the mandatory vehicle insurance, and an independent insurance system. The former raised a problem. Compensation to the owner, user and driver could not always be paid out from the insurance. The simplest case is that the driver, alone in the vehicle, drives off the road and collides with a tree. In such a case, the legislator wanted damages to be paid. But damages could not be paid out by the insurer, since no one can be liable against himself, according to tort liability rules. In such a situation, an independent insurance system was the answer. One could have retained the construction with personal liability, completed with special rules built on mandatory accident insurance, but then the rule system would have been too complicated.

2.b.iv The transmission of liability

An independent insurance system simply means that the liability to pay compensation is placed directly on the mandatory vehicle insurance. The biggest and most evident change within the new legislation therefore became the transmission of liability to this insurance, whereby immediate contact with the tort law rules was loosened, albeit, in reality, to a limited extent (see below).

Legislation of such magnitude may have been motivated by the belief that there were 'certain deficiencies' in the old law.[74] This explanation, however, is not enough. It is possible to point to at least three important causes of the reform.

The most important reason for the reform can be said to have been the protection of the driver. Before the Act of 1975, he or she was protected by the driver's seat insurance, as well as by the state seat insurance for employees of the state, but these two insurances had the character of accident insurance, meaning that compensation was only paid out to a limited extent. The Act strengthened the protection of the driver dramatically. To be able to make this change, the legislator was forced to totally reconstruct traffic-accident liability, meaning that the strict liability for personal injury that was introduced (see below) was placed on the mandatory insurance, which was made so expansive that it also covered the driver.

Another explanation has to do with the rules of contributory negligence. Before the Act, such contribution could have resulted in mitigation to a comparatively great extent. After the Act, the possibility of mitigation

[74] By the then Minister of Justice. See NJA II 1975, p. 65.

was limited, particularly regarding personal injury. This was in conformity with the reform of general tort law from 1976.

The third explanation lies in the criticism against the fault rule. Because of this rule, the victim had been forced to make extensive, time-wasting and cost-demanding investigations concerning the fault issue. On the whole, the legal system in this field was complicated and difficult to apply.[75] By introducing strict liability to a great extent, this criticism was avoided in the traffic-accident field.

2.b.v The character of mandatory vehicle insurance

Mandatory vehicle insurance is a form of liability insurance. Thus, it does not cover damage to the insured person's vehicle or property transported therein. To protect himself, the owner of the vehicle might sign a voluntary motor-vehicle insurance. There are many kinds of such insurance. Bodywork insurance covers different types of damage to a vehicle as a result of the owner's or someone else's driving or of external circumstances, for instance a tree falling because of a storm. There is also fire, plate glass and theft insurance. Voluntary insurance might be combined with mandatory insurance. Property transported in the vehicle for commercial purposes might be covered by goods insurance. Damage to private property transported in the vehicle is likely covered by a householder's comprehensive policy.

In the legislation work, it was envisaged letting the mandatory vehicle insurance pay for damage to both the vehicle and the property carried therein. As for damage to the vehicle, it was found that such extended traffic insurance would incur higher costs and thereby also premiums. Mandatory insurance cover of this kind did not have the same importance as cover for personal injury, where social concerns dominated the picture. As for damage to conveyed property, this could not really be put on an equal footing with damage to the vehicle, since the property could belong to someone other than the owner. It was, however, said that it appeared natural from the risk-spreading point of view to protect third parties from the risk of incurring losses of this kind and, instead, let them fall on the collective of motor-vehicle owners. This idea did not seem to be sound in commercial transportation, or where damage to property in vehicles owned by private persons was covered by the householder's comprehensive insurance, which also covered the losses of third parties. Therefore,

[75] This criticism against the fault rule was explicitly and in detail developed in the *travaux préparatoires* of the DA. See Kungl Majt's proposition: 1972 no. 5 , pp. 78ff.

no measures were taken to realise the idea of extending mandatory traffic insurance to cover damage to conveyed property owned by third parties.[76]

Damage to clothes and other personal belongings of persons carrying them in the vehicle was already, to a certain extent, covered by the voluntary undertakings of the vehicle insurers prior to the TDA. The committee had proposed that this kind of property damage should be compensated by the driver's own vehicle insurance; this suggestion relied on the hope that the insurance industry would continue,[77] which it did.

As for personal injury, mandatory vehicle insurance is also liability insurance. Yet the insurance has another character as for personal injury caused by the insurance taker (the owner) himself, and this is so regardless of whether he or she is a driver or a passenger. In this regard, the insurance is also a personal insurance.

Mandatory vehicle insurance, accordingly, has a double character on the whole. It is an indemnity insurance, a liability insurance, but also, in a special sense (e.g. for personal injury caused to the owner), a personal insurance. This double character became the necessary result of the decision to shift liability to the mandatory vehicle insurance. That an insurance policy comprises both indemnity insurance and personal insurance is, of course, nothing strange for insurance contract law.

2.b.vi A complete Act

The TDA does not only consist of rules concerning the liability to pay compensation; the Act also has administrative rules that are more extensive than the liability rules. This means that the legislator did not, as did the Economic and Social Committee in discussions about the fifth motor-insurance directive, find a contradiction between these two kinds of rules. That Committee had prohibited a directive with administrative rules from also having liability rules.[78]

The liability rules of the Act are of two types: one only concerns the liability of the vehicle insurance (articles 10–12 TDA); the other only covers pure tort law (articles 18–19 TDA). Compensation according to the former type is by the TDA and is called 'trafikskadeersättning' (literally meaning 'compensation for traffic damage'), as well as just 'traffic compensation'. What is paid out according to the latter type of rules is called 'skadestånd' by the TDA, which is the same as damages.

[76] Ibid., pp. 87–9. [77] Ibid.

[78] See B. W. Dufwa, 'Insurance in a European Tort Law Perspective', in Mauro Bussani (ed.), *East and West in the European Tort Law Perspective: Acts from a Colloquium in Trieste, Italy, 23–24 April 2004* (Bern: Staempfli Verlag, 2006), pp. 1–13.

2.c *Traffic-accident compensation*

In spite of the sharp distinctions that the TDA makes between traffic-accident compensation and damages in the construction of the rules, the insurer's liability is essentially based on tort law rules and principles. This can be seen in the terminology: strict liability and liability based on fault are typical tort law notions. As regards the rest of the insurer's liability (i.e. causation), general tort law supplies the answers. The clearest connection between the liability of the insurer and tort law is to be seen in the size of the compensation. The TDA refers directly (article 9) to the articles concerning the size of damages in the DA (chapter 5, article 3). 'General tort law principles' are supposed to be applied when the insurance has to decide on traffic-accident compensation.[79] In the *travaux préparatoires* of the TDA it was said that the difference between such compensation and damages 'essentially' was 'of a purely formal nature' and the continuing importance of tort law for the vehicle insurance was also underlined.[80] In a country where tort law had been out in the cold for many years, this revival of tort law was surprising. But it was a reality. Tort law was brought back to life, but in the frame of a new compensation system. In Swedish discussions, it has been said that tort law, in this way, became the 'cement' with which the new system was built. This technique has been used and continues to be used in other liability fields,[81] such as work injuries, patient insurance, drug insurance and product liability.

2.c.i Damages

The pure tort law rules of the TDA retain the victim's ability to claim damages from persons who, according to the general tort law, might be personally liable. This is so even though the victim might receive compensation from vehicle insurance. This means that the DA or some special legislation is applicable, in principle; the insurance regime is not exclusive. In this way, the fault principle comes into the picture. The victim is able to sue the driver, the owner or someone else (i.e. a mechanic), alleging that his fault caused the accident. Nothing prevents a court from approving such an action if the victim succeeds in proving the conditions for fault liability. But such an action is extremely rare, if it has, indeed, ever taken place. Normally, the vehicle insurance is preferable, not only because the liability of the insurance is strict, but also because insurance on the whole

[79] Lagrådet (Council on Legislation); see ibid., p. 66. [80] Ibid., p. 67.

[81] Cf. note 59, above.

is a safer target from an economic point of view. Put simply, proving negligence means increased costs.

This economic reality supports the purpose of the Act. The Act seeks to secure compensation for traffic accidents by insurance: it would be curious if the victim, by using personal liability, could ignore the legislative allocation of the burden of compensation and instead place it on a tortfeasor. The legislator has therefore built in reverse coverage for this. The tortfeasor, who has been obliged to pay damages because of his fault, has gained the right to recover from the vehicle insurance what he has paid to the victim. He or she has been granted a right to recourse against the vehicle insurance (article 19). The result is that if a tort action is brought against the tortfeasor, the tortfeasor can pass on the burden of payment to the insurance system; that system is the destination of all claims, no matter what route they take.

But even though this recourse action is recognised, there are still extra and needless troubles for the tortfeasor, who has been obliged to pay damages. Why, then, permit such claims for damages? Prohibition was also discussed during the legislation work. Several circumstances were, however, said to count against such an obstacle for the victim. Particularly when the damage was caused by someone with whom the victim had a contractual relationship, it was considered to be both natural and practical that he or she, not the vehicle insurance, should choose the contract partner. A total ban was also said to be in conflict with international agreements concerning the transportation of goods by road or rail. To permit damages in contractual relationships only was no way out of the problem, since considerable problems would then appear regarding where to draw the line between contract cases and other cases. Nor was an action for damages in non-contractual relationships a more practical alternative. The possibility for the victim to claim damages was therefore finally permitted.[82]

In the DA, which had come into force two years before the real work with the TDA began, many rules had been developed regarding channelling liability. Channelling is a way of saving costs by concentrating liability on one subject, instead of spreading it to many tortfeasors. One way of doing this is to find ingenious ways of handling tort law. But the most important and effective manner is to do it by using insurance. The DA gives examples of complete legal channelling, where the victim has no choice in whom to pursue.[83] One of the articles of the DA directly concerns

[82] See Regeringens proposition: 1975/76, no. 15, p. 83.

[83] See, generally, Dufwa, 'Channelling in Tort Law'.

traffic-accident compensation. Chapter 3 of the DA deals with the liability of employers for damage caused by their employees in the course of their employment. It also covers the liability of the state, municipalities and rural districts for damage caused in connection with their exercise of public authority. The rules prescribe that the employer is liable if the employee has caused the damage intentionally or negligently. Normally, this would imply liability for the employer of a driver who has caused damage in a traffic accident in this way. The Swedish legislator, however, found that if and to the extent that compensation from mandatory traffic insurance could be paid out according to the TDA, the provisions of chapter 3 should not apply (chapter 3, article 8). A channelling thus takes place. The only condition is that traffic compensation really can be paid out, which is not always the case. The way of formulating this rule, being an exception from the rules of chapter 3, also excludes recourse actions from the vehicle insurance against the employer. Such recourse action was considered to make the whole system too complicated. Since chapter 3 only concerns vicarious liability, it does not prevent the victim or the traffic insurance from claiming compensation from an employer who himself is guilty of fault, because then the fault rule, prescribed in chapter 2, article 1, applies.[84] The victim is bound by chapter 3, article 8, and therefore has no choice but to bring an action against the employer. As has been seen, the TDA gives examples of another type of channelling that takes place, as the TDA works with two alternatives: insurance compensation or damages according to tort liability. This is what has been called 'economic' channelling. Although the victim has the freedom of choice, traffic insurance will ultimately bear the liability.

There are four particular points of the TDA to discuss, centred on the nature of the harms compensated for, and how compensation is achieved. These are: personal injury, property damage, contributory negligence and recourse action.

2.c.ii Personal injury

The TDA makes a fundamental distinction between personal injury and property damage. The principle for compensating personal injury is simple. Everyone who has been injured by a motor vehicle as a result of a traffic accident is entitled to compensation. Drivers, passengers, pedestrians and cyclists are covered, but also persons who had nothing to do with the accident (i.e. the man sitting on the park bench or the woman drinking

[84] See Nordenson, *Trafikskadeersättning*, 565–75.

tea in her garden). The context of the driving is of no importance: a driver acting against the law (an 'illegal driver') might also be covered if he sustains a personal injury. The thief who, chased by the police, drives into a tree and is injured is consequently entitled to insurance compensation.[85] The traffic insurance works here as social insurance. All victims are compensated. But there is, however, a difference. While social insurance never asks how the injury was caused, the victim of a traffic accident must prove that the injury was caused by a motor vehicle while in traffic.

The TDA makes a distinction between injuries caused to drivers and passengers on the one hand, and those caused to persons outside the vehicle on the other. The former category is always referred to the traffic insurance of the 'own' vehicle to recover insurance compensation. It is thus not possible to claim compensation from the traffic insurance of a colliding vehicle. Victims outside the vehicle can claim compensation from the insurer of the vehicle that caused the injury.

As far as drivers and passengers are concerned, this system mirrors an often-stressed function of no-fault insurance. To as large an extent as possible, traffic insurance has a 'direct' character. As insurance compensation is built on strict liability, there is no real need for drivers and passengers to also claim such compensation from the insurer of the colliding vehicle. Therefore, when there is a collision with another car, injuries caused to the driver and the passengers must always be compensated by the traffic insurance covering the vehicle in which they were travelling. It is prohibited by law to claim for traffic compensation from the insurance of the other vehicle. The advantages with this system are conspicuous. Firstly, simplification regarding the insurance regulation arises. Furthermore, the idea of channelling is facilitated.[86]

At the same time, it must be underlined that channelling only appears in the eyes of the victim. Insurance compensation in collision cases is not always finally borne by the insurer paying compensation to the victim. Recourse actions between insurers are permitted according to the TDA, and hence the whole problem of apportionment of the compensation is only moved forwards and transferred to the insurers themselves.

[85] Cf. the 1980 SOU, no. 37, p. 41, where illegal driving is also considered to be a crime that must be punished in the same way as car theft in this context.

[86] See Dufwa, 'Channelling in Tort Law'. The legislator envisaged letting the effect of channelling be extended to cover injury caused to the owner and the user when they were outside their own vehicle. Such a solution was, however, considered to raise technical complications for the legislator, so it was abandoned. Owners and users outside the vehicle therefore had the possibility to claim for compensation from the 'other' insurer. See Regeringens proposition: 1975/76, no. 15, p. 40.

However, this system is not completely closed and complete. If drivers and passengers have suffered personal injury in a collision with another motor vehicle, it is conceivable that they could be entitled to compensation from the insurance of the other vehicle. This is what happens if they can prove fault or some kind of defect in the other vehicle (article 22 TDA).

2.c.iii Property damage

Special rules are applied when property damage to a vehicle or its load has been caused by a collision with another motor vehicle. Collision is understood to mean not only cases where vehicles have been in physical contact with each other; the rules are also applicable if a vehicle has been driven in such a way that the driver of another vehicle has been forced off the road and has collided with a tree. A condition for the application of the rules is that both vehicles have to have been in traffic. This is not the case when one vehicle runs into a parked vehicle. The latter is, however, considered to be in traffic if it is evidently so badly parked that it is a danger to traffic.

According to the TDA, property damage is compensated by the traffic insurance of the other vehicle if the damage has been caused by fault in connection with the driving of this other vehicle or by a defectiveness of this vehicle. Fault covers all activity in the vehicle (i.e. not only by the driver, but also by the passengers); the driver might have been pushed, had his vision blocked or been disturbed in some other way.[87] For the traffic insurance of the other driver to be tapped, an application of the fault rule is needed, strengthened with a strict liability for defectiveness. One might ask whether the judgement of what constitutes fault is the same with traffic insurance as it is according to the general rules of tort law. This question was touched upon in the early discussion of the Act. The Minister meant that the liability of traffic insurance was more severe than elsewhere; subjective circumstances, for instance sickness, that were considered in tort law had no place in traffic insurance. The Council on Legislation[88] argued that this judgement ought to be handled uniformly in different contexts; otherwise, this should be made explicit in the Act.[89] The Minister explained what he meant by saying, that with traffic insurance, one did not need to investigate more closely who in the vehicle had caused the faulty driving. Considering this, there was less reason to consider different subjective circumstances. The whole issue was delivered to the courts.[90]

[87] Cf. NJA II 1975, pp. 91–2. [88] In Swedish: Lagrådet.
[89] See NJA II 1975, p. 94. [90] Ibid.

Before the TDA came into force and when liability was based on the fault principle, the owner, user and driver in collision cases presumptively had liability for damage to the other vehicle or property conveyed therein. They all had a duty to prove that they themselves had not acted intentionally or negligently in this context. If they could not show this, tort liability was imposed. The principles applied in these cases were complicated, and the system was often criticised, not least because of the peculiar and (for the man in the street) inconceivable results that could emerge in relation to criminal liability. A judgment could express the following: 'It has not been proven that the driver acted negligently. The prosecutor's action for penalty is therefore dismissed. However, the driver has not proven that he did not drive the car negligently. The action for liability regarding the damage to the other car must therefore be approved.' The liability of presumption was severe. In reality, it functioned as a strict liability, since the result was nearly always liability. It was said to be a kind of hybrid, with little correspondence in tort law.

To abandon liability of presumption in favour of fault liability and strict liability for defectiveness might seem to have meant a change for the worse for the owner suffering property damage. While the burden of proof previously lay with the other side in collision cases, it was suddenly placed on the victim. It might seem as if this change was difficult to reconcile with the other improvements in favour of the victim. If anything, it seems as if a neater way of working would have been to impose strict liability on the traffic insurance of the owner's own vehicle. This possibility was, however, rejected. The justification was that the owners of the vehicles were 'on an equal footing with themselves', and hence such a severe liability was considered to go too far. Since the presumption of liability was no longer suitable, the victim only had fault liability at his disposal. It was also said that such liability could only work to the disadvantage of the victim. Reference was made to an investigation that the committee had requested, according to which, (in insurance regulation work) in no fewer than about 90 per cent of all collision cases, fault by the driver of one of the vehicles had been proven.[91]

If property outside the vehicles is also damaged in a collision, the rules regarding collisions do not apply. Instead, the rules on single cases apply.

Outside collision cases, there is strict liability of the traffic insurance for property damage regarding the vehicle itself and property transported with the vehicle. If cycles, garage doors, fences, dogs and other things are

[91] NJA II 1975, pp. 90–1.

damaged by a vehicle in traffic, the victim has a right to compensation from the traffic insurance of the vehicle, irrespective of fault. Defending this change, various arguments were given in the *travaux préparatoires*. In particular, claim regulation became simplified. The same principles applied as when the victim at the same time was injured. Also, the transmission from a liability where fault was presumed to a strict liability should neither result in some more clear increase of costs for the traffic insurance.[92]

The parallel between compensation for personal injury and strict liability is, however, only one side of the coin. The situation for the victim in a single case is not as advantageous as when he has sustained personal injury. With contributory negligence taken into accont, the rules are more severe for the victim than those applied when he suffers personal injury. Furthermore, some victims are completely excluded from traffic compensation. As for property damage caused to the insured himself, by his own vehicle, compensation is only paid out if the vehicle was used unlawfully. Consequently, the owner of the vehicle cannot have compensation from his own insurance if he happens to run over his own bicycle when backing out of his garage. On the other hand, he will be compensated if it is a vehicle thief who has caused this damage. The same rules apply to the detriment of the driver or the user; they cannot damage their own property and then be compensated by the traffic insurance. In the same category as the owner, user and driver is the person who, knowing that the vehicle is being used unlawfully, becomes a passenger in it or has property transported in it (article 11, paragraph 2 TDA).

Damage to one's own vehicle or to property transported in it that occurs when the vehicle is in traffic cannot be compensated by the insurance covering that vehicle itself. Such damage can be covered by voluntary motorvehicle insurance above and beyond the compulsory set. Furthermore, there is always the possibility to claim damages by applying tort law rules. If, for instance, the vehicle has been driven by someone other than the owner, the latter might be able to turn to the driver and claim for damages, asserting that the driver caused the damage negligently. In the same way, the owner might recover damages from the repair shop if he thinks that the repairs have caused the damage. The DA applies, and normally the victim has to prove fault.

What about property damage to means of transportation other than motor vehicles? This topic was discussed during the legislation work.

[92] NJA II 1975, p. 95.

According to one opinion, such a case ought to be regulated according to the rules for collision cases. There were reasons for saying that when two equally valuable risks meet, they should be apportioned between themselves in such a way that they do not burden only one of them. Suppose that a car collides with a tram and that the tram is damaged. To be compensated by the traffic insurance of the car, fault or defectiveness ought to be proven against the car; if not, damages should be borne by the tram. This way of treating such a case was the one applied in Finland and Norway. The representative of the Minister of Justice, however, argued that collision rules should not be applied. Special regulation was not necessary concerning damage to ships or aircraft or to property transported therein. Damage of this kind was rare, and for the pool of traffic-insured drivers it was of little significance if this damage was compensated by the traffic insurance on the basis of strict liability. The same applied to collisions between motor vehicles and trams. The situation was different, however, concerning collisions between motor vehicles and trains; they were more frequent and had a greater economic impact. However, since reform was underway regarding the liability of the railways, it was necessary to wait until this was finalised.[93] When this happened in 1985, the rules of the TDA were changed. The collision rules then applied to both parties (article 11, paragraph 3). The single-case rules concerning ships and aircraft were not touched by these new rules; trams, however, came to fall under the same rules as trains, and were transferred to the collision rules.

2.d *Contributory negligence*

2.d.i Personal injury

The TDA unified the rules on contributory negligence regarding personal injury with the DA: damages could only be reduced if the victim had acted intentionally or with gross negligence.

A special provision was added to these general tort law rules, aimed only at traffic accidents. This provision implied that, even if there was neither intention nor gross negligence on the part of the victim, a reduction in damages might still be realised if the driver had driven the vehicle while under the influence of alcohol. However, there was a condition for this mitigation. The driver must have been guilty of 'simple negligence' (article 12, paragraph 1). Most, though not all, typical driving cases can

[93] NJA II 1975, pp. 97–8.

be considered to have this level of fault.[94] This rule was initiated late in the legislation work by the temperance movement of parliament. Experts found it improper in this context, since it broke dramatically with the main idea of the newly reformed DA: to put personal injury in a class by itself, where the most important goal was compensation.

After much discussion over the years, it is today considered that more importance ought to be attached to the problem of driving motor vehicles while under the influence of alcohol. So the Swedish legislator is planning to intervene and change the rules. The possibility to always be able to mitigate compensation when the driver has committed a crime of this kind was envisaged but rejected, since it was too big a deviation from accepted principles of compensation; in some cases, it could also lead to too severe a result. The latest proposal to be circulated implies that the negligence of the intoxicated driver, when he or his property is damaged, should be presumed. The insurance compensation shall therefore be mitigated if the driver cannot prove that he has not been negligent.[95]

If personal injury has caused death, compensation can only be reduced if the deceased intentionally contributed to the death. This rule was also a general tort law rule, introduced in the DA (article 12, paragraph 1). It evidently concerns suicide. In a traffic accident case in 1981, the Supreme Court applied the provision in a very generous way in favour or the survivors who claimed for compensation from the traffic insurance. The Court found, unanimously, that full compensation should be paid out.

The circumstances were as follows. A man who was desperately in love with a woman and who was driving his car with her at his side proposed that they should die together. Refusing the proposal, the woman tried to remonstrate with him, but in vain. On a main road he drove the car at maximum speed and said: 'Now we are going to die.' He then rammed the car into a parapet. A few minutes later, he died in her arms. His wife and their son claimed compensation. The insurer finally agreed to pay 75 per cent of the amount payable had it been an accident, but this was, as stated above, not accepted by the courts.

In the *travaux préparatoires*, it was said that the main rule was supposed to be full compensation. In the judgment of the Court of Appeal, affirmed by the Supreme Court, it was underlined that the way in which the suicide had been committed was not dictated by any intention to give the survivors financial security for the future. It was also said that the survivors did not live in such economic conditions that it could seem

[94] NJA II 1975, p. 109. [95] See Ds 2006, no. 12, pp. 97–132.

offensive with full compensation. In the doctrine, it was assumed that a social-insurance view lay behind this jurisprudence. It is doubtful that the judgment is still valid.

The size of the mitigation should correspond to what is reasonable regarding the contribution that has taken place on both sides, as well as all other circumstance (article 12, paragraph 3 TDA).

2.d.ii Property damage

Traffic compensation because of property damage can be mitigated if the victim has contributed to the damage. The rules of general tort law apply. Thus, mitigation can also take place in cases of 'simple' negligence on the part of the victim (article 12, paragraph 2 TDA).

The rules applied regarding the size of the reduction are the same as those applied to personal injury. A judgement according to reasonableness takes place; the contribution to the damage on both sides and other circumstances are considered (article 12, paragraph 2 TDA).

Since it could be inconvenient to apply different rules for the personal injury and the property damage from the same incident, some kind of merger of rules was discussed during the legislation work. Mitigation would then, in principle, never take place when the victim was only guilty of 'simple' negligence, and the application of the rules would be simplified. The idea was, however, rejected. In the same accident, different rules should apply to the victims concerning the damaged property; if the vehicle causes damage to many different items of property belonging to different owners, only the one who has suffered personal injury would be favoured, not the other victims.

2.d.iii Collision damage

It is true that if a driver (A) runs into another motor vehicle (the collision case) and is successful in proving fault or defectiveness of the other vehicle, he is entitled to compensation from the insurer of the other vehicle. But A must accept mitigation of the compensation from the other side if his opponent succeeds in proving that he, A, drove the vehicle in a careless way. When the question of fault is decided, it is not only the driving of the vehicle that is examined. The driver is identified with the owner, the user, the passenger and the owner of the transported property. As for the user, it does not matter whether he has driven the vehicle with or without permission.[96] This means that if fault of one of these persons has contributed

[96] DS 2006, no. 12, p. 104.

to the damage, the others are burdened with this fault, implying that each one might have his right to insurance compensation reduced. All the persons are thus regarded as a unity in this context.[97]

The proportions of the mitigation are decided after weighing the extent of the fault and the defectiveness that has contributed to the damage. If one side is considerably more at fault than the other, the result might be that no insurance compensation is paid out at all.[98]

Suppose that a driver happens to drive into and damage a bicycle. The traffic insurer of the motor vehicle has strict liability for the damage (see above). But if the victim is guilty of fault, the compensation must, according to general tort law, be mitigated. In the *travaux préparatoires* of the TDA, it was stipulated that the principles regarding contributory strict liability that were in force before the Act should continue to apply. This means that the mitigation operation should be orientated towards two questions: the degree of fault on the victim's side and the extent to which the parties can be presumed to have influenced the size of the damage.[99]

2.d.iv Recourse action

If the injury or damage for which insurance compensation has been paid out has been caused by intention or gross negligence by someone other than the insured person, the insurer gains a right of subrogation from victim to pursue damages from the tortfeasor. The same applies if the injury or the damage has been caused by the negligence of a driver who was guilty of road rage (article 20 DA). But outside these two cases, where liability is based on fault, there is no right to recourse when the tortfeasor has acted negligently. Consequently, there is, for example, no possibility of a recourse action against the bodies responsible for the upkeep of roads if they, without intention or gross negligence, failed in their responsibilities. This restraint of the right to recourse is general and is profoundly based on the Swedish tradition, according to the principle *generalia specialibus non derogant*.

As for those who, besides the traffic insurance, are strictly liable for the damage resulting from a traffic accident, the main rule is that a recourse action by the traffic insurance is not permitted. There are, however, two exceptions to this rule. Recourse is approved against anyone who, again, besides the traffic insurer, is liable according to the Product

[97] 'If there is fault or defectiveness regarding the vehicle, mitigation of the traffic compensation evidently must take place.'

[98] Ibid. [99] See Ibid.

Liability Act (article 20, paragraph 2 TDA) or who represents a railway or a tramway (article 20, paragraph 3 TDA).

2.e *Concluding remarks*

The rules on compensation for damage caused by the motor vehicle have developed slowly, but with decisive steps. Before the Act of 1906 came into force, the fault rule applied. The new Act introduced vicarious liability, according to which the owner and the user were responsible for damage caused by the driver's fault. The Act of 1916 went further and, to the detriment of the owner, prescribed a strict liability that was, however, a liability of presumption that could be avoided if he or she was successful in proving that the damage was caused neither by the fault of the driver nor by the defectiveness of the vehicle. The driver had the same liability, but could avoid it by proving that he had not been guilty of fault. In 1929, mandatory traffic insurance was introduced by the legislator.

Inspired by this insurance, a reform was proposed in 1938, according to which this insurance should cover all kinds of personal injury and property damage caused by traffic accidents. However, the proposal was never realised; it remained dormant in the Department of Justice. There are several reasons for this. One is that the chances for success of a reform proposal in a special and limited law field are greater when the change is built on ideas that have been expressed in general law. Another reason might have been the threatening clouds that came over the world at this time; the Second World War had broken out. Only a collection of strength, encouraged by the whole society, could probably have saved the proposal. Such a collection of strength could have taken place within the Nordic collaboration in law. But this collaboration was also threatened. Denmark, Norway and Finland were all victims of the war, but Sweden stood apart from it.

After the war, the common Nordic legislation work began and a Nordic Tort Law Act was discussed. Ivar Strahl became the protagonist, the idea being that the whole tort law should be reformed with the help of insurance. In this connection, one of the first topics that was discussed was compensation for the victims of traffic accidents. Strahl became the chairman of a committee that in 1957 proposed a new compensation system concerning these accidents, based on the idea of insurance. But this proposal could not be realised immediately. The context was changed as larger reforms were proposed. This work was not ready until 1972. But then the ideas of Strahl in his Bill could be performed in quite another situation.

The TDA came into force in 1976. It is still in force and has, on the whole, been a great success. Some lawyers feared that it would be too complicated.[100] But the misgivings turned out to be unjustified. Five features of the Act are prominent. The first one is the tremendous importance of mandatory traffic insurance in this context. Mainly it is the insurance that has taken over servicing of liability. By this means, the legislator has succeeded in its aim of protecting the driver as well as the victim. The second feature is that the liability of the insurance is built on tort law principles. Liability is strict in its most important issues (personal injury and property damage in single cases), but also on tort (property damage in collision cases). The third feature is the channelling with which the Act, in many respects has been built up and which has been particularly important to escape the problems of fault liability, a liability which, in principle, is not denied as an alternative to traffic compensation. This way of working has facilitated the fourth feature: the closeness to the ideas presented in the United States and Canada about no-fault liability. The fifth feature of the Act is the strong support it has received from general tort law. One might even ask whether the sweeping change that characterised the Act would ever have been possible without this harmonisation with general tort law.

[100] Cf. B. W. Dufwa, 'Vår komplicerade trafikskaderätt och framtiden', *Svensk Juristtidning* (1979) at 401–90.

APPENDIX: CODE PROVISIONS

The texts provided in this appendix provide the main provisions of national codes dealing with delict that were applied in relation to rail and road traffic, together with the major legislation on road traffic.

1 French Civil Code (1804)

Delict

1382 Any human act whatsoever which causes damage to another obliges him by whose fault it occurred to make reparation.

1383 Each one is liable for the damage which he causes not only by his own act but also by his negligence or imprudence.

1384

[para. 1] He is liable not only for the damage which he caused by his own act, but also for that which is caused by the act of persons for whom he is responsible, or by things which he has in his keeping.

[para. 2][1] However, he who possesses by whatever right all or part of a building or of personal property in which a fire occurs is liable vis-à-vis third persons for damage caused by such fire only if it is proved that it should be attributed to his fault or to the fault of persons for whom he is responsible.

[para. 3][2] This provision does not apply to relations between owners and tenants which remain regulated by Articles 1733 and 1734 of the Civil Code.

[para. 4][3] The father and mother, to the extent that they exercise the right of custody, are jointly liable for damage caused by their minor children living with them.

[para. 5] Masters and principals (are liable) for damage caused by their domestics and employees in the functions for which they have been employed.

[para. 6] Teachers and artisans (are liable) for damage caused by their pupils and apprentices during the time when they are under their surveillance.

[1] Text resulting from the law of 7 November 1922. [2] Ibid.

[3] Text resulting from law n°s 70–459 of 4 January 1970.

[para. 7][4] The above liability arises unless the father and mother and the artisans prove that they could not prevent the act which gave rise to such liability.

[para. 8] As to teachers, the faults, imprudence or negligence alleged against them as having caused the damaging act must be proven according to ordinary law by the plaintiff in the suit.

1385 The owner of an animal or he who avails himself of it while it is being put to his use is liable for the damage which the animal causes, whether the animal was in his keeping or whether it had strayed or escaped.

1386 The owner of a building is liable for damage caused by its ruin, when this occurred through want of maintenance or by a construction defect.

Road Traffic Law of 5 July 1985

1 The dispositions of the present chapter apply to the victims of traffic accidents in which a motor vehicle or its trailer is involved, even if the victims are being carried pursuant to a contract; they do not apply to trains or trams which run on their own tracks.

2 Neither *force majeure* nor the act of a third party provides the driver or custodian of a motor vehicle with any defence against victims, including drivers.

3 (1) Victims other than drivers of motor vehicles are indemnified for the harm resulting from personal injury regardless of their own fault, unless it was inexcusable and constituted the sole cause of the damage.

(2) If such victims are less than sixteen or more than seventy years old or, whatever their age, have been held to be permanently disabled or incapacitated to at least eighty per cent, they are entitled in all cases to full damages for their personal injuries.

(3) However, no damages are due in such cases if the victim deliberately incurred the harm suffered.

4 The fault of the driver of a motor vehicle can limit or exclude his claim for damages.

5 Fault on the part of the victim can limit or exclude the damages he may claim for damage to property, save that the rules relating to personal injury apply if the items damaged are medically prescribed.

6 Claims by third parties are subject to the limitations and exclusions which affect the claim of the primary victim of a traffic accident.

[4] Text resulting from the law of 5 April 1937.

2 German Civil Code (1900)

Delict

§ 823 (1) A person who wilfully or negligently injures the life, body, health, freedom, property, or other right of another contrary to law is bound to compensate him for any damage arising therefrom.

(2) The same obligation attaches to a person who infringes a statutory provision intended for the protection of others. If according to the purview of the statute infringement is possible even without fault, the duty to make compensation arises only if some fault can be imputed to the wrongdoer.

§ 826 A person who wilfully causes damage to another in a manner *contra bonos mores* is bound to compensate the other for the damage.

§ 828 (1) A person who has not completed his seventh year of age is not responsible for any damage which he does to another.

(2) A person who has completed his seventh but not his tenth year is not responsible for the harm which he inflicts on another in an accident with a motor vehicle, a railway or a hover rail. This does not apply if he has caused the injury deliberately.

(3) A person who has not yet competed his eighteenth year is, in so far as his responsibility is not excluded under paragraphs 1 or 2, not responsible for the harm which he inflicts on another if, on the commission of the action causing the harm, he does not have the necessary intelligence to realise his responsibility.

§ 831 (1) A person who employs another to do any work is bound to compensate for damage which the other unlawfully causes to a third party in the performance of his work. The duty to compensate does not arise if the employer has exercised ordinary care in the choice of the employee, and, where he has to supply appliances or implements or to superintend the work, has also exercised ordinary care as regards such supply or superintendence, or if the damage would have arisen notwithstanding the exercise of such care.

(2) The same responsibility attaches to a person who takes over the charge of any of the affairs specified in paragraph 1, sentence 2, by contract with the employer.

§ 839 (1) If an official wilfully or negligently commits a breach of official duty incumbent upon him towards a third party, he shall compensate the third party for any damage arising therefrom. If only negligence is imputable to the official, he may be held liable only if the injured party is unable to obtain compensation elsewhere.

(2) If an official violates his official duty by a decision in a legal issue, he is only responsible for the harm arising from this if the violation of duty consists of a criminal act. This provision has no application to a refusal or delay which is contrary to duty in exercise of the office.

(3) The duty to compensate does not arise if the victim has intentionally or negligently refrained from averting the harm by the use of a legal remedy.

§ 847 [REPEALED IN 2002; see now § 253(2)] In the case of injury to body or health, or in the case of deprivation of liberty, the injured party may also demand an equitable compensation in money for damage which is not a pecuniary loss.

Property

§ 903 (1) In so far as the law or the rights of third parties do not conflict with this, the owner of a thing can deal with the thing at his discretion and can exclude others from any interference with it …

§ 906 (1) The owner of land cannot forbid the introduction of gases, steam, smells, smoke, soot, heat, noise, vibrations and similar things coming from the land of others in so far as these do not interfere with his use of his land or interfere only to a negligible extent. A negligible interference typically occurs where the limits or targets established by statute or regulation are not exceeded by the interferences laid down and assessed by these provisions. The same applies to standards in general administrative provisions that have been promulgated under article 48 of the Federal Environmental Impact Protection Act and represent the state of art.

(2) The same applies to the extent that a material interference is caused by a use of another plot of land that is usual in that location and cannot be prevented by measures that are economically reasonable for users of this kind. Where an owner is obliged under these provisions to tolerate an interference, he may require the user of the other land to pay compensation, if the interference impairs a use or revenue of the former's land that is usual in that location beyond a degree that the owner can be expected to tolerate …

§ 907 (1) The owner of a plot of land may require that no facilities are created or maintained on a neighbour's plot of land where it can be predicted with certainty that their existence or use will have an impermissible effect on the owner's land. Where an installation satisfies the provisions of the law of the *Land* concerning the distance from the boundary or other protective measures, then the removal of an installation may only be required if the impermissible interference actually occurs.

(2) Trees and bushes are not facilities within the meaning of these provisions.

§ 1004 (1) Where ownership is interfered with through the removal or deprivation of property, the owner can request that the interfering person remove the interference. Where further interferences are anticipated, then the owner can demand a prohibitory injunction.

(2) Such claims are excluded where the owner is bound to tolerate the interference.

Road Traffic Law of 19 December 1952 on Road Traffic

§ 7 (1) If in the course of the operation of a motor vehicle a person is killed, the body or the health of a person is injured or an object is damaged, the custodian of the motor vehicle is obliged to compensate the injured party for the damage resulting from it.

(2) The duty to compensate is excluded if the accident was caused by an unavoidable event which is not due to a defect in the construction of a vehicle or to the failure of its mechanism.

An event is deemed to be unavoidable in particular if it is due to the conduct of the injured party or of a third party who is not an employee or an animal and if both the custodian and the driver of the vehicle have applied that care which is required in the light of the circumstances.

§ 9 If the injured party contributed to the damage by his negligence, § 254 Bürgerliches Gesetzbuch applies with the proviso that if an object was damaged, negligence on the part of the person exercising factual control over the object is treated as equivalent to negligence on the part of the injured party.

§ 17 (1) If damage is caused by several motor vehicles and if the custodians of the vehicles involved are bound by law to pay compensation to a third party, the liability to pay compensation of the custodians of the vehicles and the extent of the compensation to be paid as between themselves depends upon the circumstances, especially according to whether the damage has been caused predominantly by one or the other of the parties. The same applies to the liability of one of the custodians of the vehicles if the damage was caused to another custodian of a vehicle involved in the accident.

§ 18 (1) In the circumstances covered by § 7(1), the driver of the motor vehicle is also liable to pay compensation in accordance with the provisions of §§ 8 to 15. No liability exists if the damage was not caused by the blameworthy conduct of the driver.

3 The Netherlands

Civil Code (ordinary delict provisions)

6:74 Any failure to perform an undertaking obliges the debtor to compensate the damage suffered by the creditor, unless the failure cannot be attributed to the debtor.

6:99 Where the damage may have resulted from two or more events for each of which a different person is liable, and where it has been determined that the damage has arisen from at least one of these events, the obligation to repair the damage rests upon each of these persons, unless he proves that the damage is not the result of the event for which he himself is liable.

6:101 When the damage is partly caused by an occurrence that can be imputed to the injured party, the obligation to pay compensation is reduced by apportioning the damage between the injured party and the liable party in proportion to the degree in which the occurrences that can be imputed to the parties have contributed to the damage, provided that account is taken of the disparity in the seriousness of the respective faults, or other circumstances of the case, to decide whether fairness demands that an alternative apportionment or full recovery takes place or that the obligation to pay lapses.

6:106 (1) For damage which is not property damage, the victim has the right to compensation fixed according to fairness:

a. where the person responsible had the objective of bringing about such damage;
b. where the victim has suffered physical injury, his honour or good name is harmed or he is affected in any other way in his person; or
c. where the damage relates to the memory of a deceased person and the claim is brought by a spouse who is not separated, a registered partner, or a blood relative to the second degree, that person may take the place of the deceased if, were he still alive, the deceased would have had a right to compensation for injury to his honour or good name.

(2) The right to compensation set out in the previous paragraph is not capable of being transmitted by way of seizure unless an agreement is established or a claim is made in law. The transfer is complete under the general title when the person has informed the other party responsible for making compensation.

6:162 A person who commits an unlawful act towards another, which can be imputed to him, must repair the damage, which the other person suffers as a consequence thereof.

Except where there is a ground of justification, the following acts are deemed to be unlawful: the violation of a right, an act or omission violating a statutory duty or a rule of unwritten law pertaining to proper social conduct.

An unlawful act can be imputed to its author if it results from his fault or from a cause for which he is answerable according to law or common opinion.

6:163 No duty to compensate arises whenever the violated norm does not protect against the damage that the victim has suffered.

6:168 (1) The judge may reject a claim to forbid unlawful conduct on the ground that it should be tolerated by reason of pressing social interests. The victim retains his right to compensation under the relevant title [of this Code] …

(3) Where an order for compensation or for conserving a situation is not complied with, then the judge may, if necessary, forbid the conduct.

6:169 A person who exercises parental authority or guardianship over a child of under fourteen years of age is liable for damage done to another by such conduct of that child *which must be considered as an act*, where this act, but for the child's age, could be imputed to him as an unlawful act.

Civil Code: Book 8: contracts of domestic public carriage of persons[5]

Definition of carriage

8:102 (1) Carriage of persons only includes the period during which the passenger is on board the means of transportation, is embarking or is disembarking.

Liability for death and personal injury

8:105 (1) The carrier is liable for damage caused by the death of, or bodily injury to, the passenger as a consequence of an accident which has occurred in connection with and during the carriage.

(2) By derogation from the first paragraph, the carrier is not liable to the extent that the accident has been caused by a fact which a prudent carrier has not been able to avoid, and to the extent that such carrier has not been able to prevent the consequences thereof.

(3) Physical or mental disabilities of the driver of the vehicle, as well as defects in or malfunctioning of the means of transportation or the material which he uses for the transport are considered facts which a prudent carrier has been able to avoid and the consequences of which such a carrier has been able to prevent. Material does not include another means of transportation on board of which the means of transportation finds itself.

(4) In applying the second paragraph, the conduct of a third person is taken into consideration only if the carrier is not answerable for any other fact which has also contributed to the accident.

[5] Translation: P.P.C. Haanappel and E. Mackaay, *New Netherlands Civil Code. Book 8 Means of Traffic and Transport* (The Hague and London: Kluwer Law International, 1995).

Liability for the loss of goods

8:106 (1) The carrier is liable for damage caused by total or partial loss of, or damage to, hand baggage, a vehicle or vessel accepted as baggage for carriage and the things on board thereof, to the extent that this loss or damage has arisen during the carriage and has been caused:

a. by an accident to the passenger and for which the carrier is answerable; or
b. by a fact which a prudent carrier has been able to avoid and the consequences of which such a carrier has been able to prevent.

8:109 (1) The liability of the carrier can be wholly or partially eliminated if he proves that the fault or negligence of the passenger has caused the damage or has contributed thereto.

Limitation of the amount

8:110 (1) The liability of the carrier referred to in this section is limited to an amount or amounts to be determined by, or pursuant to, regulation.

8:111 (1) The carrier may not invoke any limitation of his liability to the extent that the damage has arisen from his own act or omission, done either with the intent to cause that damage or recklessly and with the knowledge that that damage would probably result therefrom.
(2) Any stipulation derogating from this article is null.

Contractual conditions always apply

8:116 Where the carrier, his co-contracting party, the passenger or a servant of one of them is sued extra-contractually, articles [8:]361 to [8:]366 inclusive and 1081 apply *mutatis mutandis*.

8:364 (1) Where a ship owner, a charterer of a vessel or a carrier by vessel is sued extra-contractually with respect to the death of, or bodily injury to, a person, or with respect to damage to a thing by a person who is not party to a contract of operation, the former is liable to the latter no further than he would be pursuant to the contract …
(4) Where the person or thing was board the vessel otherwise than pursuant to a contract, a contract of carriage is deemed to be a contract referred to in paragraph 1.

8:365 Where an action, as referred to in articles [8:]362 to [8:]364 inclusive, is instituted extra-contractually against a servant of a party to a contract of operation, and where that party, in order to rebut its liability for the conduct of the servant, can derive a defence against the plaintiff from the contract governing its liability pursuant to those articles, the servant may also invoke this defence, as if he were a party to the contract himself.

Prescription

8:1751 (1) An action against the carrier with respect to bodily injury suffered by a passenger is prescribed by the lapse of three years; this period commences with the beginning of the day following the one on which the incident or accident happened to the passenger.

(2) An action against the carrier with respect to the death of a passenger is prescribed by the lapse of three years; this period commences with the beginning of the day following the day of death of the passenger, but this period does not run for longer than five years commencing with the beginning of the day following the one on which the incident or accident happened to the passenger.

Road Traffic Law

Article 185 WVW provides:[6]

1. If a motor vehicle which is being driven on a road is involved in a traffic accident which causes damage to persons or goods not carried by that motor vehicle, except for the limitation following in paragraph 3 below, the owner of the motor vehicle, or – if there is a keeper of the motor vehicle – the keeper is obliged to compensate that loss, unless it is plausible that the accident is due to *force majeure*, even where it is caused by someone for whom the owner or keeper is not liable.
2. The owner or keeper, who does not drive the motor vehicle himself, is liable for the conduct of the person whom he causes or allows to drive the motor vehicle.
3. [This provision was abolished in 2005. It contained a limitation of the compensation for property loss to the value of the motor vehicle at the moment of the accident, with a minimum of €250.]
4. Paragraphs 1–3 do not apply to damage caused by a motor vehicle to unleashed animals, to another moving motor vehicle or to persons or goods which are being transported by the motor vehicle.
5. This article leaves unimpaired the liability following from other statutory provisions.

4 Spanish Civil Code (1889)

Property

7.2[7] The law does not protect the abuse of rights or the antisocial use of them. All action or omission that, by the intention of its author, by its object or by the

[6] Translation: W. H. van Boom, in U. Magnus and M. Martín-Casals (eds.), *Unification of Tort Law: Contributory Negligence* (The Hague, London and New York, NY: Kluwer Law International, 2004), p. 129.

[7] As inserted by the Decree of 31 May 1974.

circumstances in which it is done, would exceed the normal limits of a right, with nuisance to another individual, will give rise to compensation or to the necessary administrative or judicial measures to prevent the abuse from continuing.

590 No one may build sewers, aqueducts, ovens, forges, chimneys, stables, stores for corrosive materials, steam-powered machinery or installations which, of themselves or by their outputs, are dangerous or noxious, near to a communal well or a neighbour's well without following the distances prescribed by regulations and local custom and without taking any protective measures necessary for the work, as also laid down by regulations. Where there is no regulation, the builder shall take all precautions which are deemed necessary, according to the established opinion of experts, to prevent any damage to neighbouring tenements or buildings.

Delict

1902 The person who by action or omission causes damage to another by fault or negligence is obliged to repair the damage caused.

1903 The obligation imposed in the preceding article applies not only for a person's own acts or omissions, but also for those persons for whom a person is responsible.

The father and the mother are responsible for the harm caused by their minor children who are living with them.

Tutors are liable for the harm caused by minors or incapacitated persons under their authority and living with them.

Employers or directors of an establishment or firm are liable for the harm caused by their employees in the performance of tasks that are entrusted to them or of their functions.

The State is liable under this head for the acts of its special agents, but not when the harm has been caused by a civil servant entrusted with practical administration, for which case the preceding paragraph applies.

Masters and directors of arts and trades are liable in respect of the harm caused by their pupils or apprentices, as long as they remain under their control.

The liability under this article ceases when the persons mentioned prove that they have shown the diligence of the good father of the family to avoid the harm.

1905 The possessor of an animal or a person who makes use of one is liable for the harm that it causes, even where it has strayed or escaped. This liability only ceases when he proves that the harm resulted from a fortuitous event or from the fault of the person who suffered the harm.

1906 The owner of a building is liable for the harm caused to neighbouring property when he has not taken the necessary steps to prevent them increasing …

1907 The owner of a building is liable for the damage resulting from its total or partial ruin if this was caused by the failure to make necessary repairs.

1908 The owner of objects is also liable for harm caused:

1. By the explosion of machines that had not been kept with due care and by the burning of explosive substances that were not stored in safe and suitable place.
2. By excessive smoke that is injurious to persons or property.
3. By the falling of trees located on thoroughfares, when this is not caused by *force majeure.*
4. By emanations from sewers or deposits of toxic matter, built without the precautions appropriate to the place in which they were.

INDEX

For EU product safety concerns, contact us at Calle de José Abascal, 56–1°,
28003 Madrid, Spain or eugpsr@cambridge.org.

www.ingramcontent.com/pod-product-compliance
Lightning Source LLC
LaVergne TN
LVHW052303200926
848481LV00002B/446
9781107475755